SOCIAL POLICY AND THE BODY

Also by Kathryn Ellis

SQUARING THE CIRCLE: User and Carer Participation in Needs Assessment

ACCESS TO ASSESSMENT: Perspectives of Practitioners, Disabled People and Carers (*with A. Davis and K. Rummery*)

Also by Hartley Dean

DEPENDENCY CULTURE: The Explosion of a Myth (*with P. Taylor-Gooby*)

WELFARE, LAW AND CITIZENSHIP

POVERTY, RICHES AND SOCIAL CITIZENSHIP (*with M. Melrose*)

Social Policy and the Body

Transitions in Corporeal Discourse

Edited by

Kathryn Ellis
Senior Lecturer in Social Policy
University of Luton

and

Hartley Dean
Professor of Social Policy
University of Luton

Consultant Editor: Jo Campling

First published in Great Britain 2000 by
MACMILLAN PRESS LTD
Houndmills, Basingstoke, Hampshire RG21 6XS and London
Companies and representatives throughout the world

A catalogue record for this book is available from the British Library.

ISBN 0–333–71384–2 hardcover
ISBN 0–333–71385–0 paperback

First published in the United States of America 2000 by
ST. MARTIN'S PRESS, INC.,
Scholarly and Reference Division,
175 Fifth Avenue, New York, N.Y. 10010

ISBN 0–312–22058–8

Library of Congress Cataloging-in-Publication Data
Social policy and the body : transitions in corporeal discourse /
edited by Kathryn Ellis and Hartley Dean.
p.   cm.
Includes bibliographical references and index.
ISBN 0–312–22058–8 (cloth)
1. Body, Human—Social aspects.   2. Social policy.   3. Welfare
state.   I. Ellis, Kathryn.   II. Dean, Hartley, 1949–   .
HM110.S62   1999
361.6'1—dc21   98–49905
                                                          CIP

This book is printed on paper suitable for recycling and made from fully managed and sustained forest sources.

10   9   8   7   6   5   4   3   2   1
09   08   07   06   05   04   03   02   01   00

Printed and bound in Great Britain by
Antony Rowe Ltd, Chippenham, Wiltshire

Dedication

The editors wish to dedicate this volume to one of its contributors, Noel Parry, who very sadly died on 14 October 1998. He will be greatly missed, not least by his beloved wife, co-researcher and author, José.

Contents

Acknowledgements

The editors are indebted to a number of people. When first we conceived the project to which this book gives expression, we sought the views of the social policy academic community on the Internet, using the Social Policy Association's 'social-policy mailbase', and we are grateful to all those colleagues who responded so supportively: we hope you will not be disappointed by the eventual outcome! Secondly, we are especially grateful to Jo Campling, our consultant editor, for the faith she placed in the book, for her encouragement and helpful advice. Thirdly, we should acknowledge the support and stimulation provided by a number of colleagues at the University of Luton who, though they have not contributed chapters to the book, played an important role in developing our thinking. In particular, Tony Fitzpatrick read and commented constructively on early drafts of certain chapters. Most of all, however, we should like as editors to thank our fellow contributors: the book has been very much a collaborative effort and has involved a considerable amount of valuable discussion and debate between the authors.

The end result, we believe, is a collection that is greater than the sum of its individual parts. We are conscious nonetheless that there is a great deal more to be written on the subject of social policy and the body. Working on our own chapters and with the other contributors, we became aware that this book could do little more than scratch the surface of an array of fantastically rich and complex issues. Limitations of space have meant that it has not been possible to accommodate every change that has been suggested to us or to develop every argument in the manner we might ideally have wished. In places, therefore, we decided to retain certain clearly arbitrary and prolegemenary elements in order that they might assist the central purpose of the book, which is to stimulate debate. In so doing, of course, we must ourselves accept responsibility for some of the book's inevitable deficiencies.

Post-script*

Among the contributors included in this volume is one from the Parrys. It is an unusual piece to find in a collection such as this because it reminds us of the important contribution of humanitarism in the social and legal reforms introduced in early-nineteenth-century Britain. This strand has been screened from view with the rise of the humanistic perspective, which gives prominence to humans as the primary concern of welfare policy and legislation. The humanitarian movement, one of the leading intellectuals of which was Jeremy Bentham, sought to diminish or abolish cruelty and foster compassion: its attitude towards the 'suffering' body included the treatment of animals amongst its concerns. In view of his own particular convictions, it is a fitting tribute to Noel Parry – a distinguished sociologist of great originality and imagination – that in his last piece of work, written with his partner, José, he should so inimitably challenge the orthodoxy of anthropocentrism in social policy and the 'insuperable line', as Bentham called it, between humans and non-humans.

Kathryn Ellis and Hartley Dean,
University of Luton

Editors' note: To avoid unnecessary duplication we have presented the references as one list at the end of the volume.

Notes on contributors

Alison Assiter is Professor of Feminist Philosophy and Dean of the Faculty of Economics and Social Science at the University of the West of England. Her recent publications include *Enlightened Women: Modernist feminism in a post-modern age* (1996).

Fiona Brooks is a Principal Research Fellow in the Institute for Health Services Research at the University of Luton.

Hartley Dean is Professor of Social Policy at the University of Luton. His recent publications include *Dependency Culture: The explosion of a myth* (with P. Taylor-Gooby, 1992), *Welfare, Law and Citizenship* (1996) and *Poverty, Riches and Social Citizenship* (with M. Melrose, 1998).

Kathryn Ellis is Senior Lecturer in Social Policy at the University of Luton. Her recent publications include *Squaring the Circle: User and carer participation in needs assessment* (1993) and *Access to Assessment: Perspectives of practitioners, disabled people and carers* (with A. Davis and K. Rummery, 1997).

Helen Lomax is a Research Fellow in the Institute for Health Services Research at the University of Luton.

Martin Mitchell is a Research Fellow in the Institute for Health Services Research at the University of Luton.

John Paley is Assistant Director of the Institute for Health Services Research at the University of Luton. He has published a number of journal articles on the philosophy of professional practice.

José Parry is Senior Lecturer in Sociology at the University of Luton. She has published a number of articles on animal rights.

Noel Parry was Visiting Professor at the University of Luton until his death in October 1998. He taught at several universities in Britain and the United States and was the author of several books and articles on the professions, and empirical studies of work and leisure.

Gurch Randhawa is a Lecturer in Epidemiology at the University of Luton. He has published a number of journal articles on the subject of organ donation.

Introduction: Towards an Embodied Account of Welfare

Hartley Dean

> For the representatives of state welfare in direct contact with the subjects for whose well-being they are concerned, observation of bodies is a crucial skill; 'the gaze' is both a literal description of social practices and a metaphor for the monitoring and surveillance of subjects undertaken by the state apparatus. (Leonard 1997: 43)

> [O]nly bodies suffer. Only by a studied concentration on the body can we bear adequate witness to this suffering. Only an ethics or a social science which witnesses suffering is worthy of our energies and attention. (Franks 1991: 96)

Social policy is both a substantive process and a field of social scientific enquiry. The above epigraphs are intended to illustrate the critical sense in which the body is central to social policy in each of its meanings.

There is a trite and obvious sense in which social policy and processes of social welfare have always been focused on bodies: on bodily potential, bodily functions and bodily needs. However, one of the key themes of this book relates to the extent to which the 'gaze' of professionals and administrators has a problematic as well as a benignly self-evident aspect. Health-care professionals, teachers and social workers each fasten their specialized 'gaze' upon the bodies of their patients, students or clients; they are concerned with the capacity of such bodies to produce, consume and be orderly; their skills are directed to ensuring the fitness of such bodies for labour, leisure and social interaction. Additionally, administrators and managers may fasten the users or 'customers' of welfare benefits and services with an ostensibly less intimate kind of 'gaze', but it is a gaze which precisely locates the bodies of their subjects in time and place; which determines the 'needs' and therefore the visibility of such bodies.

Nonetheless, social policy as an academic subject area or discipline has devoted relatively little attention to the body and its theoretical significance. This book seeks to make a modest contribution towards a more embodied account of welfare. In so doing it will present a variety of critical stances by which we might question the 'scientific' orthodoxies of social policy. Analyses which start with the body and its capacity to suffer and to struggle pose a very particular set of challenges both to the expertise of professionals and the rationality of administrators.

This book will firstly elaborate a narrative account of the transitions in corporeal discourse which have been associated with the rise of the welfare state; it will then focus upon the disciplinary practices which have evolved as the modern welfare state has developed and transformed; and it will finally turn to some of the welfare struggles of the current era.

THE BODY, THE STATE AND MODERNITY

Bodily order and political anatomy

The explicit premise on which Bryan Turner has constructed his sociological theory of the body is that of the 'Neo-Hobbesian problem of the order' (1996: 107). Social order depends, he argues, upon the reproduction and regulation of human populations in time and space, and the forms of internal restraint and external representation which are applied to the bodies of individuals. These are the material factors which every social system must seek to address, much as Hobbes – the seventeenth-century English philosopher – had sought to apply principles from the geometry of inanimate bodies and the principles of motion to the animated rational bodies of men in society. Hobbes, in fact, had been specifically concerned with the role of the state in relation to the individual. His contention had been that human beings are primarily self-interested, pleasure-seeking, pain-avoiding individuals and that, in a state of nature, social life would amount to a war of all against all. Civilized society, therefore, required a compromise by which individual sovereignty would be surrendered to a powerful state machine or *Leviathan* (1651) which should, in return, protect and guarantee the liberty of the citizen (or more particularly, for Hobbes, the male property-owning individual) against the predations of others.

Hobbes is important because his materialist liberal thinking articulates the essential relationship between the individual and the state that was cemented by processes of legal reform which were begun in England in the seventeenth century. In particular, the Petition of Right of 1628 had sought more generally to extend the liberties originally conceded by the Crown to the nobility in the Magna Carta of 1215. Central to the Petition of Right was a demand that the writ of *habeas corpus* should be established as a right of every subject, a right which was finally enshrined in the Habeas Corpus Act of 1679 (Perry 1964). The concept of *habeas corpus* was seminal to the development of modern law throughout the Anglo-Saxon world and its significance lies in the protection it purports to afford against imprisonment, banishment or destruction of the body without due process of law. *Habeas corpus* was a challenge to the divine right by which feudal kings could dispose of their subjects at will. Whereas ancient and feudal states wielded the power of life and death over the individual, the modern state affords constitutional recognition to the integrity of individual bodies and the separateness of the embodied subject from the machinery of state.

Foucault (1977) has graphically illustrated the extent to which sovereignty in the pre-modern age was equated with spectacle and display. The power of the sovereign was legitimated by means of public violence and gruesome forms of punishment exercised upon the bodies of those that had threatened or offended the sovereign. Power was signalled through ostentation in bodily appearance or performance, and the conspicuous might of the sovereign and his attendants. In the modern age liberal democracy purports to have dispersed sovereignty amongst its individual subjects, but beneath this fiction, according to Foucault, new forms of administrative state power arose; new disciplinary techniques by which individual bodies may be ordered and controlled; new processes of discreet and continuous state intervention.

The right to a writ of *habeas corpus* did not in fact extinguish the power of the state but legitimated the basis for interventions which, while respecting the body, were calculated to bear upon the soul of the subject. This new mode of intervention was epitomized in the nineteenth century concept of the panoptican reformatory, in which duly sentenced miscreants were not physically harmed but isolated under conditions of unremitting surveillance. Foucault's contention had been that, in essence, the panoptican 'gaze' which was brought to bear upon the body of the convicted felon exemplified the disciplinary mechanisms by which human bodies were ordered both within the factory system and in the workhouses, schools and hospitals which prefigured the institutions of the capitalist welfare state:

The growth of a capitalist economy gave rise to the specific modality of disciplinary power whose general formulas, techniques and submitting forces and bodies, in short 'political anatomy', could be operated in the most diverse political regimes, apparatuses and institutions. (Foucault 1977: 221)

Commodification of the body

This insight provides a starting point for an analysis of the transitions in corporeal discourses of welfare that have occurred within the twentieth century. To that insight, however, it is necessary, we believe, to add another. Marx had contended that what constituted capitalism was not a modality of disciplinary power, but the ascendancy of the commodity form. When the products of human labour are traded as commodities they assume values related not to their utility, but to the amount of human labour which they embody. Simultaneously, labour-power itself is reduced to a commodity to be bought and sold like any other, and labourers become alienated from the products of their labour. So it is that workers are alienated from their very humanity and 'a definite social relation between men [sic] ... assumes ... the fantastic form of a relationship between things' (1887: 72). What Marx described as 'commodity fetishism' involved the commodification of social life and of the body as a source of labour-power.

In practice, labour-power cannot be separated from the body of its owner (Polanyi 1944) and recent commentators have argued that welfare state capitalism depended upon a degree of 'de-commodification' (for example, Esping-Andersen 1990). In order to make labour-power optimally efficient and ready for sale as a commodity, it may be necessary to provide non-commodified welfare benefits and services directed to the bodies in which labour-power is vested. To the extent that labour-power is very much a gendered commodity and that readiness for paid labour presupposes and obscures the role of unpaid domestic labour, it must be remembered that processes of commodification and de-commodification are accompanied by processes of 'familialization' and 'defamilialization' (McLaughlin and Glendinning 1994; Dean and Thompson 1996). Nonetheless, we should accept that the original form of the modern welfare state emerged because 'a supportive network of non-commodified institutions is necessary for an economic system that utilizes labour power as if it were a commodity' (Offe 1984: 263).

A narrative of transition

The history of the welfare state in the twentieth century can therefore be understood both as a process of the perpetual refinement of the disciplinary gaze (Leonard 1997, and cf. Dean 1991) and as a narrative concerning the changing status of the body as a commodity within capitalist relations of production, distribution and exchange.

The first phase of that history occurred between the late nineteenth century and the beginning of the twentieth, when Britain was pre-occupied with its competitive position as an economic and military imperial power (e.g. Thane 1982). Bodies and the families in which they were nurtured were a productive resource to be harnessed by the machinery of state to the needs of industry and the demands of war. The focus was upon the ascetic ordering and surveillance of the normal productive body and the containment of abnormal bodies.

Nineteenth-century public health legislation had been concerned to provide sanitation and a municipal infrastructure so as to minimize the spread of contagious disease. Factory legislation prevented industrialists from engaging in counterproductive over-exploitation of labour-power. Elementary state education was introduced so as to ensure both 'industrial prosperity ... and the safe working of our constitutional system' (Forster 1870). The workhouse regime instituted under the Victorian Poor Law became progressively more discriminating as conditional classes of 'out-relief' were developed (prefiguring modern social assistance), the 'boarding out' of children was permitted (prefiguring modern forms of fostering and child protection), and the status of workhouse infirmaries and their inhabitants was adapted (prefiguring the development of municipal hospitals and old people's homes).

The onset of the twentieth century witnessed new forms of selective incarceration (for example, for persons adjudged mentally defective), but also new forms of compulsion for ordinary workers, as they were required to join social insurance schemes. In fact the twentieth century gave birth to an entirely new kind of disciplinary gaze which may be identified with the emergence of the dispensary (Armstrong 1983). In addition to dispensaries, health visiting services and school health inspections were introduced so as to monitor the nurturance of future generations. In its precoccupation with physical efficiency the incipient welfare state was beginning to reach out and regulate not only individual bodies, but the social spaces which are occupied or lie between those bodies; to locate and mitigate the dangers which might emerge within such spaces.

The second phase of the historical narrative we seek to outline, therefore, entailed a development from narrow concerns with physical efficiency to broader concerns with social efficiency. This phase was most fully expressed between the second world war and the 1970s, during the highpoint of modern capitalism. Continuous capitalist development required, not only 'ascetic production', but also 'hedonistic consumption' (Turner 1996: 115). This was the age of mass production and mass consumption, of full employment and Keynesian economics: it was the 'golden age' of welfare states (Esping-Andersen 1996) when de-commodified provision for the body – 'from cradle to grave' – was both the proof and a guarantee of national prosperity. In the post-colonial era, the body of the Western subject had become not only a source of labour-power but, importantly, the site of domestic consumption. The pragmatic collectivism of state welfare continued firmly to locate the body of the individual within discourses of family and nation (Williams 1989), but body, family and nation were constituted as components of economic demand, or consumption. The commodified body can be appropriated, not only through the exploitation of its labour-power, but also, as Frank points out, in the very process of consumption: 'Consumption is a willingness to be appropriated. The consumer thinks he or she appropriates the commodity, while it appropriates its consumer' (1991: 94).

The post-war welfare state developed a range of universal services and regulatory provisions for the normal subject or citizen, and a more specialized array of services for those adjudged abnormal. The National Health Service, National Insurance and state education provided the bedrock of the welfare state and the mechanisms by which citizens might share the ordinary hazards of modern life, while special welfare services provided for the needs of the poor and disadvantaged. Though monolithic 'total institutions' (Goffman 1968) tended to dominate the welfare state, new professional and political discourses began to emerge which favoured more 'holistic' approaches to human need, a more community-oriented approach to service provision (Hadley and Hatch 1981), and the 'decarceration' of the abnormal (Scull 1977). The impetus to social efficiency began to project the gaze of the welfare expert ever deeper into the social fabric and, in the process, began to transform that gaze.

The third phase of our narrative, therefore, is the current phase; the era of global capitalism or post-modernity. It is widely supposed that the golden age of the Keynesian welfare state is past. The globalization of capital, the international mobility of labour and the development of information technology now require that nation-states compete with each other for shares of transnational investment and trade in goods and services. The new political orthodoxy embraces what Jessop (1994) has characterized as the 'Schumpeterian workfare state', which responds to global competitive pressure, retrenches welfare provision and emphasizes supply-side management. Mass production has given way to specialized production and niche marketing. The mass domestic market has given way to the global market. As labour markets in consequence become ever more polarized, bodies as sources of labour-power become highly differentiated according to the skills possessed by their owners. As society becomes ever more unequal, bodies as sites of consumption become highly differentiated according to the purchasing power of their owners.

It has been argued that we now inhabit a 'risk society' (Beck 1992) in which the function of the welfare state is merely to manage the risks to which we are individually subject (Giddens 1994) and not, as Titmuss (1963) had argued, to provide collectively for states of dependency. Individuals are to be enjoined or assisted to make independent provision wherever possible; to be more responsible for the health, fitness and well-being of their own bodies. The state is concerned less with the provision of care than with the management of provision (Taylor-Gooby and Lawson 1993); the rights of the dependent client are increasingly overshadowed by the obligations of the independent customer (Roche 1992). What is at stake is not so much the anatomical body with internally generated needs, as what Fox (1994) has termed 'a body without organs'; a body that is constituted as a political surface on which expert and managerial discourses are inscribed.

Another way of understanding this transition is in terms of what Offe has called 'administrative recommodification' (1984: 125). The crisis occasioned for welfare states in the face of the globalization of the capitalist economy is attributed by Offe to the paralysis of the commodity form as tendencies towards commodification and decommodification come into conflict. The remedy foretold by Offe was that Western governments would use their administrative power to sustain the commodity form, for example by promoting regulated forms of market competition and investing in the supply side of the economy (education, training, research and development, transport and communications). The administratively recommodified body is at one and the same time an independent consumer of regulated services and an object for selective investment to enhance its productivity.

This narrative of transition is further explored and developed from a distinctively feminist perspective, by Kathryn Ellis in Chapter 1.

NEW DISCIPLINARY PRACTICES

The administratively recommodified body, therefore, is the site of a new set of disciplinary interventions and circumstances. This book will argue that it is the object of a new managerial gaze; it is the subject of new modes of compulsion; it has resulted in a peculiar inversion of classical liberal dualism; and it is constituted by a particular recombination of discursive and moral repertoires.

In Chapter 2, Kathryn Ellis will demonstrate that, while the dispensary and the psycho-social gaze represented a refinement of the clinical/panoptic gaze and extended the range of expert intervention beyond the physical boundaries of state institutions, the new managerial gaze, exemplified by the transition in the 1990s to 'community care', entails a certain displacement of professional expertise. However, this has not of itself lessened the disciplinary constraints to which disabled and frail elderly people may be subject. Where social workers had hitherto assessed need with a view to integrating frail or disabled bodies into the social body, now care managers assess risk with a view to connecting consumers with the market. The new emphasis on consumer sovereignty and the promotion of independence are not empowering; the provision of bodily care 'in the community' results in new modes of physical segregation and surveillance; the mixed economy of care results in a dehumanizing recommodification of the body and its needs.

The current era has witnessed not only a realignment of the processes by which welfare professionals engage with 'impaired' bodies but a fundamental change in assumptions about the basis of the relationship between the state and the embodied individual in general. Le Grand (1997) has characterized (or caricatured) the relationship which existed in the post-war era as that between the altruistic 'knights' of the welfare state and the passive 'pawns' of the general population. However, the acceptance within political and popular discourse of the critiques of public choice economists means that the providers and the recipients of welfare provision are now to be regarded as neither knights nor pawns, but as self-interested 'knaves': welfare providers seek power for their own advantage, while welfare recipients seek ways to maximize the benefits they personally receive while minimizing or avoiding the necessity to make any contribution towards the services received by others. The welfare state must contend, in other words, with a Hobbesian social firmament of animated rational bodies in resolutely independent motion. Le Grand's solution to the problem of achieving social order is that the welfare state should adopt a 'robust' strategy which will appeal 'to both the knight and the knave' (1997: 165).

In Chapter 3 Gurch Randhawa will draw on current debates about the legal basis of human organ donation to illustrate the direction in which such 'robust strategies' might take us. The voluntaristic basis on which blood and organ donation arrangements had been constructed in the days of the post-war welfare state is under severe pressure. The favoured and logical strategy that is on offer is one which appeals in a sense to both the knight and the knave, since it guarantees the right to donate while ensuring that the body organs of all but those who specifically opt-out would be compulsorily available for donation. In place of a system based on notions of regulated social reciprocity, we may have to accept a system based on the management of individual obligation. We have argued that the transition from feudal absolutism entailed or resulted in a certain commodification of the body. Nonetheless, the modern welfare state entailed a degree of decommodification, not least to the extent that it restored what Titmuss (1973) famously called 'the gift relationship': the opportunity for people unilaterally to give, not only through compulsory taxation, but through voluntary donations of blood or even bodily organs to anonymous strangers. What we may soon see in Britain is *re*commodification: in place of the positive right to give may come a negative right which may be waived. What this signals is a potentially different way of addressing proprietorship and rights in relation to the body.

In Chapter 4 Alison Assiter not only reminds us that modern understandings of the body have their origins in classical liberal dualism, but will argue that feminist epistemologists and critics of policy reform have tended to reinforce or recast rather than challenge dualist assumptions. The essence of Cartesian dualism lay not only in the idea that body and mind are distinct and separable entities, but that mind is, as it were, the active ingredient of the self: it is mind that constitutes the active subject, while nature – including the body – is the passive object. Equally central to classical liberalism is the notion of property as an alienable good; an object in which an individual can have rights and may be entitled to give away, to trade or to sell. To the extent that dualism acknowledged the body as alien to the self, liberalism has accommodated the possibility that the body can be a commodity. This is the sense in which, from a Marxist perspective, the capitalist process of commodification (which classical liberalism essentially facilitated) is not only exploitative of human labour, but inherently dehumanizing.

The modern welfare state is characteristically understood as an attempt to ameliorate the 'dis-welfares' of the commodification process. One of the classic revelations of the failure of the welfare state in Britain was the 1980 Black Report (see Townsend *et al.* 1988), the findings of an officially commissioned Working Group on Inequalities in Health. The report demonstrated that, in spite of the welfare state, mortality rates are steeply and inversely related to social class and there is an enduring material relationship between poverty and ill-health. The recommendations of the report, which sought to redress underlying social inequalities, were ignored by the government. The government's eventual response was a strategy which sought to address the *Health of the Nation* (DH 1992a) by a set of targets addressed, not to the social conditions which determine health outcomes, but to those improvements in health which are primarily achievable by changes in individual behaviour. It was a strategy which chimed both with post-modern preoccupations with personal health, self-image and individual lifestyle on the one hand, and with moral authoritarian concerns for the regulation of individual behaviour on the other. It is a strategy which is also consistent with communitarian preoccupations with individual responsibility and an economistic reinterpetation of the body as both a potential personal asset and an ultimate liability. This approach to health promotion is far more than a reversion to puritanical ideals of bodily self-discipline; it represents a new synthesis which, though clearly founded in Cartesian dualism, now keeps the body in view and counsels actively against either neglect or abuse of the body. The recommodified body is a capital resource to be guarded and invested in. To the extent that frailty will ultimately threaten the alienability of the body as a commodity, health is promoted as a matter of personal commitment: the active self is immanent in the body, without which the mind can exert no influence and will realise no value.

However, in seeking to characterize the ways in which for the purposes of welfare provision the body has been discursively reassigned and administratively recommodified, we do not wish to suggest that the techniques which are brought to bear within changing welfare regimes represent a single or coherent disciplinary strategy, nor that there is any single or entirely ascendant corporeal discourse. Conceptions of welfare, like conceptions of the body itself, are both historically and culturally specific. In Chapter 5 I will seek to classify the variety of moral repertoires upon which both political and popular discourse tend to draw and, from this, to trace the different kinds of bodily metaphor which equate with different kinds of welfare regime. Recent changes to the British welfare state suggest that policy is founded upon a complex mixture of metaphors and moral/discursive repertoires (see also Dean with Melrose 1998). The political consensus represented by the New Labour government is one which draws most strongly, we would suggest, on economic-individualism and conservative-communitarianism: it implies a view of the body that is on the one hand mechanistically instrumental, but which fears on the other the vulnerability and corruptability of the body. Nonetheless, beneath the surface, within political debate and popular discourse, other corporeal discourses survive. Some are deeply morally authoritarian and revile the body, while others are redolent of an earlier (albeit ambiguous) social democratic consensus which had sought to integrate the body as an organic whole: discourses which emerge continually in opposition or contradiction to more dominant discourses. What is more, such a taxonomy does not capture every kind of discourse or opposition. The body is not only the object of discipline; it is also the site of resistance (Foucault 1981) and of alternative discourses and struggles against the disciplinary power of the administrative state.

NEW WELFARE STRUGGLES

In characteristically eliptical but evocative style, Foucault has argued that the very existence of power relationships depends

> on a multiplicity of points of resistance: these play the role of adversary, target, support, or handle in power relations. .... Resistances .... are inscribed in [relations of power] as an irreducible opposite. Hence they too are distributed in irregular fashion: the points, knots, or focuses of resistance are spread over time and space at varying densities, at times mobilizing groups or individuals in a

definitive way, inflaming certain points of the body, certain moments of life, certain types of behaviour. .... [I]t is doubtless the strategic codification of these points of resistance that makes a revolution possible, somewhat similar to the way in which the state relies on the institutional integration of power relationships. (1981: 95–96)

We seek in this book to provide examples of such 'points of resistance'; of alternative practices and alternative accounts which challenge the orthodox and the dominant.

In Chapter 6 John Paley will draw upon a critique of 'new' nursing to suggest that the claims made for radical and 'holistic' alternatives to the health and social care practices of the past are largely a sham. At the same time, the medical profession is retreating ever further from forms of practice that might respond to the embodied individual. It is at present only in the realm of alternative therapies that effective challenges are being made to the orthodoxies of Cartesian dualism or in which body and mind can be embraced within a single sphere of meaning and expertise. What this hints at is far more than the potential for alternative therapies, but the possibility of an alternative politics of expertise. In a similar vein, in Chapter 7 Fiona Brooks and Helen Lomax will argue that such innovations as the natural childbirth model have not effectively challenged the orthodoxies of the medical establishment and the traditional ways in which midwives have discounted the embodied experiences of women in labour. There is scope, nonetheless, for an alternative discourse and alternative practices and for connections to be forged between situated knowledge and professional practice.

The 'disembodying' approaches of established medical and welfare professionals and the no less problematic orthodoxy of the new rationalistic managerialism have all been called into question by the critiques of the feminist, disability, and gay and lesbian movements. In Chapter 8, Martin Michell will provide an account of just one specific struggle through which the gay community has sought to challenge the rationalistic discourse of health promotion professionals. While rationalistic discourses constituted gay men's behaviour as problematic, the gay community itself has mobilized to raise awareness of HIV/AIDS in ways which take account of the ontological basis of human behaviour and which give credence to the embodied experience of gay men.

Finally, in Chapter 9 José and Noel Parry will provide a rather different and controversial perspective upon the inherent tension between human technologies and scientific 'wisdom' on the one hand, and natural processes and ontological well-being on the other. The scientific welfare state, they argue, is fundamentally anthropocentric in its origins and the humanistic impetus which informed it incorporated contradictory moral assumptions in relation to human welfare and the bodily suffering of animals. As the concerns of the modern welfare state have unravelled into processes of managerial control and identity politics, one of the contested arenas relates to the humanitarian cause of animal welfare. The moral controversies raised by that cause must be numbered amongst those which would have to be addressed by any fully embodied account of welfare.

LOOKING FORWARD

In social policy as a substantive process, therefore, the body tends to be or to have become an abstract object; the surface upon which the expert and managerial gaze is brought to focus; a fetishised commodity or quasi-commodity. In social policy as a critical academic subject, however, the possibility which will be mooted throughout this book is that the body can also be and ought to become the suffering subject; the source of alternative discourses of welfare; the site of material experience. The ascendancy of social constructionism has meant that most social theory has focused on the body as a receptor, rather than as a generator of social meanings (Shilling 1993). Though the body is in one sense 'shaped, constrained and even invented by society' (*ibid*: 70), any emancipatory approach to social policy must begin to look at the ways in which the body can assert itself as the subject of welfare discourse.

One theorist who has endeavoured to combine a social constructionist analysis of the body with a normative or ethical stance is Arthur Frank. Frank has constructed an analytical typology of the body which distinguishes the disciplined/regimented body of the monastic order, the dominating/forceful body of the army at war, the mirroring/consuming body of the department store, and – his 'culminating type' – the communicative/recognizing body which, he suggests, may be observed through such processes as 'shared narratives, dance, caring for the young, the old, and the ill, and communal ritual' (1991: 54). The communicative body, he insists, 'is less a reality than a praxis'; it is 'an ideal, illusive to descriptions' (*ibid*: 79 and 89). We interpret his vision as something quite close to what Habermas (1987) may have had in mind when he sought to define the 'ideal speech situation'. It is also a notion which, if it were translated into a normative political project, would speak to such concepts as 'associative democracy' (Hirst 1994) or 'dialogic democracy' (Giddens 1994). The communicative body, as we understand it, is the authentic creator and not the constituted object of social welfare.

In opposition to Turner, Frank contends:

> *there is no 'social order' problem*. .... Bodies certainly have problems among other bodies, but the point is to hold onto the fundamental embodiment of those problems rather than allowing the problems to be abstracted from the needs, pains and desires of bodies. .... When bodies encounter each other, there is a problem of aligning individual contingencies and coping with new mutual contingencies which arise in the interaction. .... I .... think of those problems as those of communication. Not the social 'ordering' of bodies, but individual bodies 'coming to terms' with each other is the foundational topic. (1991: 91)

It is from this premiss that we may argue that bodies, though clearly different from one another, are equal: they are equal in their mutual interdependency and equal in their vulnerability to exploitation. In practice, experiences of dependency and exploitation vary substantially, depending on such social constructions as are placed on bodily difference (e.g. 'gender', 'sexuality', 'race', 'age', 'disability'). Fundamentally, however, our capacity as embodied beings to suffer is a materially levelling feature of our existence; a feature born not of the rhetorical *egalité* of political discourse, nor of the fetishised 'equity' of economic discourse, but of prosaic and potentially painful reality.

Titmuss (1973) has argued that the post-war welfare state provided a rational basis for the kind of altruistic commitment to the care of neighbours and strangers which in an earlier era had depended on myth and custom. The individual and mutual contingencies of bodies in interaction could be aligned and accommodated on the basis of state-mediated reciprocity. Mutual recognition between bodies was brokered by the expert and the administrator. Whether or not the altruistic welfare state was anything more than a modern myth, it is clear that its survival is now in question (Page 1997). The managerial state (Clarke and Newman 1997) of the current era, as we have seen, eschews notions of altruism and reverts on either principled or pragmatic grounds to an essentially neo-Hobbesian paradigm in which social order is a question of reconciling competing self-interests; in which the body is understood in fetishised terms as an asset or a burden; in which welfare is a matter of managing bodies.

An embodied account of welfare, we would argue, furnishes a critique of both the altruistic welfare state and the managerial state. Both in their way deny the primacy of the embodied welfare subject that is capable of negotiating her or his dependency, of resisting exploitation, of interpreting competing moral discourses, and of generating new meanings from shared bodily experiences.

1 Welfare and Bodily Order: Theorizing Transitions in Corporeal Discourse

Kathryn Ellis

This chapter will use the fourfold taxonomy of bodily order developed by Bryan Turner (1996) as a framework for discussing the corporeal discourses of welfare with which this book is concerned. The first section outlines Turner's approach and its relevance to social policy analysis. Subsequent sections deal in turn with each of the three discourses already outlined by Hartley Dean in the Introduction to this volume, namely 'physical efficiency', 'social efficiency' and 'the independent body', and link them to the shifts in welfare capitalism with which they are associated.

Turner's taxonomy addresses the question of social order, which depends, he suggests, on governments successfully accomplishing four tasks – the reproduction and restraint of bodies over time and their regulation and representation in space. Taking Hobbes as his starting point, Turner argues that the stability of social systems depends on ensuring the continuity of bodies over time and controlling a multitude of unregulated bodies in space. He elaborates this two-dimensional model by adding the distinction made by Foucault (1981) between the regulation of populations and the disciplining of the singular body and that made by Featherstone (1991) between the interior and exterior of the body. Turner seeks to demonstrate that a system of patriarchal and gerontocratic controls over fertility, reinforced by an ascetic ordering of the interior of the body through the restraint of sexual desire, has traditionally ensured the orderly reproduction of populations over time. From the late eighteenth century onwards, the regulation of bodies in space has been accomplished by means of a panoptic system of disciplines, bolstered by the ordering of the exterior of the body through a regularization of methods of self-presentation.

In his taxonomy, Turner argues that the maintenance of bodily order also depends on governments regularizing production of the means of existence with the management of reproduction and corresponding mode of desire varying according to the economic mode of production. To preserve the stability of inheritance through male heirs, feudal property relations depended on a patriarchal ordering of women's sexuality amongst the ruling landowning class. When family capitalism played a major role in industrial economies, patriarchal controls similarly maintained the unity of the bourgeois family and the dominant distribution of property. Industrial capitalism also depended on the ascetic ordering of the labouring body and the relegation of sexual desire to the patriarchal household. With the restructuring of the social order around corporate ownership rather than the family, however, the traditional relationship between property, sexuality and the body disappeared. Post-industrial capitalism, moreover, is driven by hedonistic consumption and the stimulation of desire which still requires a household as a unit of consumption but not necessarily of the nuclear family type.

Feminist analyses of welfare emerging in the 1970s and early 1980s similarly pointed to the social relations of class and gender underlying the capitalist order (McIntosh, 1996). Women's unpaid labour in home and family was central to the main function of welfare under industrial capitalism, identified by Gough (1979) as the reproduction of labour-power on the one hand and the maintenance and control of the non-working population on the other. Welfare systems assumed a patriarchal division of labour in the family and reinforced women's economic dependency on the 'family wage' earned by the male breadwinner. Under late capitalism, however, economic restructuring and the withdrawal of the social wage have led to contradictory policies which seek both to encourage women's paid employment and bolster the traditional sexual division of labour. Moreover, despite the transformation in patterns of paid work and family life, women's vulnerability in both domains is still centrally related to a lack of control over their own sexuality and fertility (Mayo and Weir, 1993: 47).

According to Gough (1979), welfare also aids accumulation and legitimation in pursuit of capitalism's major objective of social reproduction. These functions can be linked, in turn, to the tasks of regulating and representing bodies in space outlined in Turner's taxonomy. To ensure the accumulation of property in line with dominant class interests, governments must produce politically stable bodies. Interventions in poverty, disease and squalor have been made in the name of human welfare yet have been central to the regulation of bodies in urban space. In his taxonomy, Turner argues that the task of representation – or the production of socially harmonious bodies – has been managed by commodification since the spread of mass consumerism blurred the external marks of social esteem which formerly denoted individuals' position in the social hierarchy. In late capitalism, there is a new emphasis on the surface appearance of the body and its reshaping in accordance with the culturally valued norms of youth, beauty and athleticism. The new asceticism to which this has given rise has been harnessed to contemporary governmental concerns with promoting welfare as a matter of self-reliance, hard work and bodily care on the part of the individual.

Thus the maintenance of bodily order can be linked to transitions in welfare capitalism. As outlined in the introductory chapter, the editors have chosen to express these in terms of three corporeal discourses. We argue that a discourse of 'physical efficiency' dominated welfare during the period of industrial capitalism, particularly after the 1880s. The period of managed capitalism after 1945 was associated with a discourse of 'social efficiency' until the post-industrial period of 'disorganized capitalism' (Lash and Urry, 1987) ushered in the discourse of the 'independent body' from the mid-1970s onwards.

Whilst persuaded of the illuminative potential of Turner's taxonomy for mapping the development of British welfare systems, we have nevertheless sought to avoid the trap of functional determinism to which critics of his model draw attention (Frank, 1991; Shilling, 1993). As Turner himself points out, discourses are neither unified in their content nor uniform in their effects but offer oppositional spaces for strategic action (1996: 173). The mechanisms of resistance to power operate through human agency and consciousness to develop bodies in different directions which, reflexively, affect discourse. This chapter therefore also sketches in some of the ways in which the particular constructions of social policy and the body characterizing each period have both shaped and been shaped by welfare struggles and protest.

PHYSICAL EFFICIENCY

Before discussing the emergence of the first transitional phase in welfare capitalism in the last decades of the nineteenth century, it is necessary to explore the antecedents of the bodily discourse of 'physical efficiency' in the preceding phase of industrial capitalism.

The productive economy was separated from the family under early industrial capitalism, reconstituting the existing relations of patriarchy on which security of reproduction had rested. Working-class women were increasingly excluded from industrial work and assigned to the domestic sphere in line with the bourgeois model of the family. Predicated on assumptions of the 'family wage' earned by the male breadwinner, the Factory Acts of 1844 onwards, together with the gradual expansion of state education, began to exclude both women and children from the economy (Walby, 1986). The Victorian Poor Law reinforced women's marginal position in the workforce by forcing those without breadwinner partners either into low-paid 'women's work' or into dependency on a liable male relative (Williams, 1989).

Turner (1996) points out that regulating the means of reproduction in the new capitalist order also depended on an ascetic ordering of the interior of the body. Amongst the ascending bourgeoisie, the restraint of sexual desire served the requirements for capital accumulation and conservation. Whilst deferred consumption promoted investment, delayed sexual gratification helped secure the dominant system of property distribution. For the working population, though, it was the reproduction of labour rather than the inheritance of property which required regulation. Under early industrial capitalism, Malthusian population controls in the form of celibacy and delayed marriage functioned both to secure a surplus and integrate the workforce into a bourgeois moral order of restraint, sobriety and hard work. With the growth of factory production, however, the ascetic ordering of the labouring body was increasingly accomplished through the autonomizing of work and the relegation of desire to the private domain and women's bodies.

Bodily order further depends on regulating bodies in space and, from the end of the eighteenth century, the concentration of bodies in cities attendant on demographic growth and the rise of capitalism posed a threat to political order. Foucault (1981) illustrates how the anatomo-politics of the human body combined with the bio-politics of the population to allow governments in a detraditionalizing society far greater control over individuals in urban spaces.

Anatomo-politics can be traced to the emergence of rational science at the end of the eighteenth century, particularly medical science. As a medical bipolarity of normal and pathological became the mode in which humanity in general was thought about (Foucault, 1973), a normal/abnormal dichotomy was established on the site of the body which came to divide man from animal, male from female, national from foreign, sane from mad, healthy from ill, able-bodied from disabled. Naturalized as a biological given, normality came to represent the legitimate basis of order in a humanist world (Branson and Miller, 1989).

Foucault (1973; 1977) examines the institutionalization of binarism through a system of panoptic disciplines which became integral to the spatial ordering of abnormal groups. He traces the shift in criminal punishment from the public spectacle of sovereign power to incarceration in prison under the continuous surveillance of the Panopticon. Panoptic power was extended by the medical gaze beyond the judicial domain into a new institutional order of clinics, hospitals and asylums. As the abnormal came under the scrutiny and control of the emergent human sciences, individual bodies were differentiated, compared and ranked against a multiplicity of norms of conduct.

Panopticism articulated with the rise of industrial capitalism and the consolidating nation-state. Because the normal was closely associated with productive work and a particular outlook on life, namely industriousness (Giddens, 1994), state regulation of the unproductive was required both to deter pauperism and to avert the risk of civil unrest associated with poverty and unemployment. The New Poor Law was connected to older laws of settlement which empowered the host parish to send individuals and families back to their place of origin to claim outdoor relief. That this power of removal particularly affected Irish immigrants (Williams, 1989) highlights its function in regulating the movements of foreign bodies within the spaces of the nation-state.

Oliver (1990) points out that effective discipline of those unwilling to work depended on separating out those unable to work. The norm of 'able-bodiedness', which derived from the identification of a certain group of people as unable to perform the standardized functions demanded of the body in factory work, provided the means for distinguishing the two groups. The New Poor Law identified the able-bodied as requiring punishment in the workhouse whilst those classified as 'sick', 'insane', 'defective', 'aged and infirm' were deemed deserving of humanitarian treatment and confined to increasingly specialized institutions.

The task of regulating bodies in space was closely entwined with the reproduction of bodies over time. The normalizing practices of law, medicine and religion assigned rationality exclusively to men, affirming their rightful ownership of public spaces. Women, by contrast, embodied desire and private emotion, their mental and physical inferiority to men making them unsuitable for the rigours of the public life (Ehrenreich and English, 1978). Thus medical knowledge, for example, suggested women were governed by their sexuality and reproductive functions and only able to lead healthy lives if they were sexually engaged with a man in a marriage centred around reproduction (Shilling, 1993).

Bio-power shifted the disciplinary gaze from abnormal groups to the population as a whole (Hewitt, 1991). With the emergence of statistical science in the early nineteenth century, the abnormal came to define the limits of, and reinforce, normality in relation to the entire population (Davis, 1995). Thus epidemiology compared the body of the patient not just with other patients but with the healthy, shifting attention from disease in separate individuals to the health of the whole population (Armstrong, 1983). The scope of the carceral state expanded in line with the requirement of industrial capitalism to secure the health, welfare and productivity of the totality of bodies, and attempts were made in the latter part of the century to sanitize the living conditions of the general population through improvements in sanitation and water supply, urban planning and housing. Unlike punishment under sovereign power, bio-power was not simply repressive but productive, concerned with life rather than death (Shilling, 1993).

From the 1880s, state intervention was directed more decisively at the promotion of physical efficiency amongst labouring bodies. Williams (1989) discusses the domination of bio-politics by a discourse of social imperialism which linked the health, prosperity and security of Nation and Empire to national efficiency. Measures were taken to secure the physical fitness of the Nation on which military strength and heavy industrial production depended. Compensating the working classes for the worst excesses of free market capitalism also promised to stave off the threat of political unrest posed by organized labour.

National efficiency further depended on national integration and the management of abnormal groups. The body had to be fit in order to fit into the Nation (Davis, 1995), and threats to imperial and economic power were posed by an increase in urban poverty and illegitimacy coupled with medical problems such as venereal disease, tuberculosis, malnutrition and infant mortality. Sanitary laws of health were promulgated to subject infectious bodies to forcible hygiene with the working classes and those of foreign nationalities particularly signalled out for attention as agents of disease (Lupton, 1994). Enforcement of the Contagious Diseases Acts addressed the task of simultaneously ordering women's bodies through time and in space by attempting to contain the spread of venereal disease through controls on female sexuality.

By the beginning of the twentieth century, however, Armstrong (1983) suggests that preventive concerns had been incorporated into public health. Emerging out of the tuberculosis dispensaries established in the early part of the twentieth century to provide diagnostic, screening, health education and treatment services, the Dispensary gaze relocated the origins of illness in the social domain rather than the physical domain of the body: 'The new gaze … . identified disease in the spaces between people, in the interstices of relationships, in the social body itself' (Armstrong 1983: 8).

As tuberculosis, venereal diseases and other public health hazards were now known to be directly spread between people, the institutional forms of the Dispensary – the tuberculosis dispensary, the venereal disease clinic, the school medical service inspection clinic, the child welfare clinic – brought the whole community under constant surveillance in order to identify the healthy who were nevertheless at risk from increasingly preventable health dangers. By mapping and regulating patients' contacts and relationships within a particular geographical area, Armstrong suggests that the Dispensary became an instrument for locating risk which transformed the physical space between bodies into a social space traversed by power.

Within that community, Donzelot (1980) demonstrates how the family became the target of welfare reforms aimed at enhancing physical efficiency as well as policing unhygenic behaviours. Hitherto relatively free of carceral discipline, the family management of child care, physical exercise, food preparation, inoculation, vaccination and domestic hygiene came under the scrutiny of a 'tutelary complex' of welfare professionals. Investing mothers with new skills and powers, and a new moral authority as guardians of the imperial race, undermined private patriarchy (Williams, 1989). At the same time, the patriarchal sovereignty of the state was bolstered by welfare interventions which increasingly regulated motherhood, supervised women's domestic lives and reinforced their economic dependency on men.

Underlying the bio-politics of reproduction were assumptions about the perfectibility of the human body and the body of the population. Social Darwinism offered a legitimating theory for the 'civilizing mission' abroad and bourgeois supremacy at home; and the science of eugenics provided the means for their perpetuation (Barnes, 1991). Unlike the 'ideal' of the spiritual world, Davis points out that the normal was integral to rather than outside of human society (1995: 29). Indeed, the norm of the average worker on which a calculation of labour was based became the ideal of Victorian society. Eugenicist campaigns sought to prevent the reproduction of those deviating from the desired physical and moral average – recidivists, vagrants, the sick, the insane, the illegitimate, the mentally or physically defective, the alcoholic, the work-shy. The bio-politics of reproduction and regulation intertwined in the 1913 Mental Deficiency Act which conflated disability with depravity in the formulation 'defective class' (Davis, 1995: 37). On the basis of statistical proofs of intelligence and ability, the defective were segregated in 'colonies' to remove the danger they represented to the progress of British capitalism, the British family and the British imperial race (Williams, 1989).

Thus the development of welfare during the nineteenth and early twentieth century served to reproduce bodies over time and regulate them in space in line with dominant class interests. The threat of socialism was averted as a new social commitment was forged out of social imperialism which made social rights to work, education and welfare dependent on the prosperity of Nation and Empire. A limited form of citizenship addressed the concerns of individual capitalists to promote the health, reliability and discipline of their own workers without diverting resources from capital accumulation or breaching the limits of state action. The costs of social reproduction were further contained by confirming the Family as the primary source of welfare and shoring up family savings and assistance as a buffer against pauperism (O'Neill, 1985: 88).

Women were denied the full rights of welfare citizenship, along with 'aliens' and the morally undeserving (Williams, 1989), in order to underline their role in reproducing, socializing and servicing bodies. However, their economic dependency and political powerlessness did not go unchallenged with feminist struggles throughout this period for property rights, access to higher education and the professions, the vote, equal pay for working-class women, divorce law reform and support for women's family responsibilities. Women also sought control over their own bodies, in the fight for birth control and the repeal of the Contagious Diseases Acts. Such corporeal struggles were at the centre of Women's Liberation Movement campaigns from the 1960s onwards, a phase of welfare shaped by the discourse of 'social efficiency'.

SOCIAL EFFICIENCY

In Britain, the second transitional phase in welfare capitalism is marked by the creation of the 'welfare state', a term employed after 1951 to cover legislation implementing the Beveridge Report together with housing, transport and fiscal policy promoting work-based forms of welfare (Whiteside, 1996). Although a humanitarian discourse framed popular thinking about the welfare state, Armstrong (1983) links this burgeoning apparatus to a reconceptualization of the spatial relationship between bodies in medical science which changed and intensified the regulatory functions of welfare.

Armstrong maintains that the welfare state, comprehensive health care and the later invention of community care were simply manifestations of a new and pervasive gaze which identified hazards in the spaces between bodies. Rather than categorizing bodies as normal or abnormal against an external referent, the survey uncovered the continuity between them. During the inter-war years, Armstrong argues, survey technology was fused with the disciplinary practices of the Dispensary in the new discipline of 'social medicine'. Emphasizing the social context of illness, Armstrong suggests that social medicine gained ground during the Second World War when the state was concerned with managing risk in a community under threat. Together with the medico-social survey, social medicine extended the Dispensary gaze to the whole population satisfying the need to know and make visible bodily hazards.

In the mass society to develop in the inter-war years, the identification of the space between bodies as 'social' made possible a politics of the social (Armstrong, 1983: 40). Rational disciplines of the population revealed as predictable and manageable hazards once conceived as part of nature. Further, notions of risk as opposed to fate implied an ethics as they suggested that economic and social life not only could but should be humanely controlled (Giddens, 1994). The mass regulation of bodies and populations in wartime created an integrated community in which the politics of mutuality and common kinship could flourish.

This was a politics of risk-sharing, which Giddens (1994) identifies as the inspiration behind the welfare state. National efficiency depended on national unity which, in the 1940s, was based less on an appeal to Empire than to British justice and fairness – the welfare state was the 'civilizing mission' brought home again (Williams, 1989). Implementation of the Beveridge Plan promised social justice by compensating the working class for the 'diswelfares' of capitalism (Titmuss, 1974). In particular, a system of social security would redistribute risks, especially those not subsumed in the wage-labour relationship, in order to protect individuals from the insecurity of the labour market (Giddens, 1994). The apparatus of welfare was no longer directed at locating risks to the physical efficiency of individual bodies within the social body but at sharing risks in order to ensure the efficiency of the social body itself.

The prior determinant of national efficiency was central planning of the economic order which, as Giddens (1994) points out, articulated with the socialist goal of greater equality in the post-war Labour administration. Keynesian demand management would overcome the hazards of an unstable market economy and sustain the continuous factory production and mass consumption on which the Fordist economic order was based. Economic efficiency was also the basis for political consensus, the means by which the interests of centrally organized capital and labour could be reconciled and the prosperity and full employment promised by the Beveridge Plan delivered.

Once again, however, the post-war welfare settlement expressed a limited form of white male egalitarianism (Williams, 1989) which accentuated the shift from private to public patriarchy. The goal was full employment for men but economic dependency for women, or white women at least. The costs of social reproduction would be minimized by encouraging women to act as unpaid welfare workers in home and community and low-paid workers in the welfare state. The politics of gender and 'race' shaped policies around contraception. In the light of the concern expressed in the Beveridge Report that wives and mothers play their part in ensuring the continuance of the British race by replenishing the national stock, free access to birth control was not made available until 1967 (Lewis, 1992a: 93). Meanwhile the fertility of women recruited from the Black Commonwealth as full-time workers during the post-war economic boom was restricted by eugenicist medical practices, such as over-prescription of dangerous injectible contraceptive drugs (Bryan, Dadzie and Scafe, 1985).

Institutionalized patriarchy was bolstered by the internal ordering of the body. Giddens (1994) suggests that the male breadwinner was guided by the ethos of productivism which privileged industry as the bearer of moral meaning. The productive body was thus protected from the disruptions of desire and harnessed to the imperatives of mass production, set in train during the early twentieth century by the development of Taylorism and scientific management. Giddens also points out the extent to which productivism was locked into gendered lifestyle patterns and habits with the 1940s welfare reforms refocusing desire on home and family after the disruptions of war. Social security legislation, social work, health and education services were infused with an ideology of familism which positioned women as housewives and mothers rather than as paid workers, a position reinforced over the 1950s and 1960s by the popularization of John Bowlby's theory of 'maternal deprivation' (Pascall, 1997).

Social efficiency also depended on assimilating the newly-arrived immigrants from the Black Commonwealth whose presence posed a moral and cultural threat to the integrity of the Nation. Williams (1989) argues that the British state remained ambivalent about meeting the social costs of its new citizens who were seen primarily as units of disposable labour. When their labour was no longer required, progressively tighter immigration controls were imposed and their rights of settlement reduced. Black people were seen to represent a threat to the 'British way of life' whose presence required containment or hygienic measures, such as those prompted by the smallpox scare in the Pakistani community in Bradford in the 1960s (Williams, 1989).

Given fuller expression in post-war social reforms were the twin concepts to which bio-politics had given birth – needs and rights (Hewitt, 1991). By guaranteeing the satisfaction of basic human needs, the welfare state would free the whole population from the social evils associated with a capitalist economy. The concept of welfare citizen-ship tied the redistribution of risks to the principle of universality with entitlements to income maintenance, health care, education, housing, personal care built into legislation to afford all citizens protection against 'states of dependency' (Titmuss, 1963). Yet social efficiency also depended on selectivity, mirroring the dual conceptualization of the body in medical science outlined by Armstrong (1983). Although bodies were placed along a continuum in the medico-social survey, the incorporation of a clinical gaze distinguished bodies in terms of a normal/abnormal dichotomy and not merely by the spaces between them. Generalizations about the population were therefore accom-panied by countervailing processes of individuation which identified people as separate and different.

Welfare reforms similarly allowed for both comprehensive cover against normal social risks and the regulation of abnormal populations and individuals. The philosophy of active citizenship underpinning the Beveridge Report (Oliver, 1996) represented full employment as not only a right but an obligation. Disciplinary controls were built into the social security system to ensure that those outside the labour market were treated less favourably than the thrifty, hard-working citizens whom the national insurance scheme was designed to reward. After 1951, Conservative governments further shifted the universalist social policies promoted by the 1945 Labour government towards the more selective targeting of social expenditure on those most in need (Whiteside, 1996).

Securing social efficiency was also tied to a Fabian belief in a functional society in which professionals, both managers and workers, would provide expert services for those in need (Perkin, 1996). Categories, classification systems and forms of knowledge created around the concepts of dependency and social need (Hewitt, 1991) provided the basis for the expert identification and measurement of social problems, the allocation of resources to needy groups and the assessment of outcomes (Sanderson, 1996). The individual assessment of need was elaborated as a professional tool both for diagnosing and treating special needs and for restricting access to benefits and services to the genuinely needy. The pliability of the body was further extended by the incorporation into social medicine of an expanded medical gaze which played over the mind of the patient and reconstituted the body as a subject rather than an object (Armstrong, 1983). The expertise of the welfare professional more generally came to consist in seeing the client as an individual or a 'whole person'.

From the 1960s there was a burgeoning of self-help and user organizations pressing for welfare rights and the recognition of special needs. However, their campaigns tended to reinforce rather than challenge the regulation of bodies by a centrally controlled system of bureaucratically run and professionally administered welfare. Health movements and pressure groups resisted professional, particularly medical, domination by campaigning for greater access to knowledge. Paradoxically, though, the demand for knowledge as the basis for achieving greater control over the body supports the mind/body dualism on which the medical model and the regulation of bodies ultimately rests (Morgan and Scott, 1993). The search after self-knowledge reinforced the perceived need of professionals to acquire communication skills in order to deal with clients as minded subjects. This, in turn, tended further towards self-regulation and compliance with expert interventions.

THE INDEPENDENT BODY

From the 1970s onwards there was a transformation in the economic, social and cultural landscapes of advanced capitalist societies which heralded the third phase of welfare capitalism with which this book is concerned and the emergence of the corporeal discourse of the 'independent body'.

From the mid-1970s, economic restructuring undermined national control over the conditions of welfare. Faced with global competition, capitalist enterprise developed a strategy of 'flexible specialization' to respond to rapidly shifting markets (Piore and Sabel, 1984). Coupled with the search for greater productivity of capital and labour, this led to the development of 'lean production systems' in which production was decentralized to a casualized workforce at the periphery operating under the control of a managerial elite at the core (Sayer and Walker, 1992). As male unemployment grew in line with the decline of manufacturing industry, the flexibilization of the labour market and the increased importance of service industries pulled more women into paid work. Combined with the increasing complexity and diversity of family relationships, these changes disrupted the traditional patterns of paid work and family life on which post-war welfare settlements were founded.

As the predictability of the life course in post-industrial societies was disrupted, so the nature of the regulatory task performed by welfare states also changed. As Giddens points out, it became less feasible to offer social protection for individuals against the external risks of birth, sickness, old age, death through social insurance schemes or to provide 'precautionary aftercare' for dependent groups (1994: 182). Further, the manufactured risks of global capitalism, such as pollution and environmental degradation, are less predictable – and therefore less controllable – than external risks, particularly with the erosion of national sovereignty (Beck, 1992).

In Britain the demands of post-industrial capital for release from restrictive employment practices and the fiscal burden of welfare were addressed by the incoming Conservative government in 1979. The Keynes–Beveridge welfare state was presented as the major cause of national economic decline, responsible for interfering with free market forces, stifling enterprise and acting as a drain on the productive economy. Economic liberalism enmeshed with public choice theory in 'New Right' critiques of inefficient and paternalistic welfare bureaucracies consuming an ever-increasing level of resources yet operating in the interests of the producers rather than the consumers of welfare. So far as the new Conservative administration was concerned, state intervention should be limited to protecting the freedom of the market which alone could secure individual freedom, entrepreneurial activity and the efficient distribution of resources.

The spread of mass consumption had also wrought a transformation in cultural life in the post-war period. Giddens (1990) locates the consumption ethic at the centre of the increasing reflexivity which, he maintains, characterizes the contemporary period of 'high modernity'. On the one hand, the demise of the traditional class culture and consciousness of industrial capitalism has left individuals to establish and maintain values to make sense of their everyday life. On the other, the growth of the service sector, shorter working days and early retirement has combined with consumerism to promote a lifestyle in which individuals are encouraged to find personal salvation and meaning through consumption (Lasch, 1980).

The privatization strategy underlying Thatcherite welfare reforms in the early 1980s articulated with changes in cultural life. According to Carter and Rayner (1996), popular experiences of low quality public services were crucial in preparing the way for radical, free market solutions. The rhetoric of low taxation also resonated with what Featherstone terms the calculating hedonism of consumer culture (1991: 187). As only the subjective preferences of self-interested individuals had any validity, people had to be free to pursue their own maximum good in the marketplace. Centring around the prestige value of goods rather than the part they play in biological or material reproduction (O'Neill, 1985: 97), consumerism arguably makes it harder for individuals to commit to state-controlled welfare systems as the optimum way of meeting human needs or as the basis of social progress. At the same time, reflexively, privatization further threatened the cultural basis of welfare by eroding the social spaces surrounding the individual. Based on an economy of altruism rather than exchange relations, Fabianist welfare systems had had at their centre the reciprocal gift. As the better off were encouraged to take out commercial cover against the contingencies of sickness and old age, formerly collectivized risks were personalized and recommodified. The sense of social obligation for shared risk on which the Beveridge welfare state depended was thereby further undermined.

If the disciplinary power of the post-war welfare state rested on the autonomous realm of the 'social' (Armstrong, 1983), this interplay between welfare and consumerism suggests that its regulatory role in

the late twentieth century may have been eroded by the commodification of the social spaces between bodies and the emergence
of a multiplicity of independent bodies. Yet Williams (1989) suggests
that the familiar regulatory principles of Work, Family and Nation
were merely reworked within New Right welfare discourse during the
1980s, albeit in ways which justified the supremacy of the market, less
state intervention and the maintenance of inequalities.

To take Work first, Turner (1991; 1996) points out that late capitalism has produced competing demands for a calculating hedonism at
the point of consumption and asceticism in the workplace. On the one
hand, contemporary forms of capital accumulation are no longer
entirely dependent on ascetic modes of desire. Generating consumption depends on stimulating rather than suppressing desire which, in
turn, threatens the work ethic and traditional norms of thrift, sobriety
and restraint. On the other hand, the demand for increased productivity depends on improving the efficiency of the workforce
through neo-Taylorist methods of production and a new ascetic
disciplining of the body.

The competing demands of late capitalism were reflected in New
Right policy discourse. Despite the promotion of a consumer spending spree, a discourse of active citizenship re-emphasized the traditional virtues of voluntary work, thrift and self-help; and the better
off were encouraged to behave prudently by taking out personal protection against life-course contingencies. As welfare dependency
represented a disincentive to work and take responsibility for individual and family welfare, those excluded from the labour force had to be
persuaded to obey the work ethic. Trends in social security legislation
in the 1980s therefore represented attempts to reassert its role in disciplining the workforce and encouraging the acceptance of low-paid
work (Williams, 1989; Dean 1991). Moreover, by giving the better off
the ability to pay for their own welfare, the state was only required to
intervene to meet 'real' need. The principle of selectivity was privileged over that of universality and welfare benefits and services were
increasingly closely targeted.

In terms of Family, the bio-politics of reproduction were shaped by
contradictory attempts on the part of Conservative administrations to
reduce welfare dependency by shoring up traditional gender and
family systems and respond to new patterns of employment. Women's
increased participation in paid work began to be acknowledged and
encouraged in the 1990s through state subsidy of the costs of child
care, particularly in respect of lone parents. Yet support was minimal

and the national insurance system, together with policies around community care, continued to ignore the high numbers of women entering the labour market (Pascall, 1997).

Women's position in the labour market and family is linked to the control they exercise over their sexuality and fertility, and this was subject to a series of challenges over the 1980s and 1990s. The reproductive capacities of the body had been separated from the economic and political order of the post-war period by a combination of political struggle, changes in legislation, and medical technology. In the 1960s and 1970s, the Women's Liberation Movement had achieved some success in securing greater control for women over their bodies and their own sexuality through improved access to abortion and contraception. Subsequently, heterosexuality was further transformed by new reproductive technologies which effectively abolished social fatherhood by separating reproduction from the corporeal relations on which heterosexuality is based (Shilling, 1993; Turner, 1995).

However, the patriarchal family form was vigorously defended over the 1980s as the moral right attempted, on the one hand, to limit women's access to abortion and, on the other, to restrict the access of single women and lesbians to artificial insemination by donor. The 1990 Child Support Act represented an attempt to shift financial responsibility for children onto the father as the pathologization of the single mother, a persistent theme in social policy, fused with drives to reduce the burden of dependency in New Right discourse. When the dangers of sexual freedom were linked to the appearance of HIV/AIDS in the early 1980s, defence of the patriarchal family form was also mobilized through advocacy of a return to the traditional values of monogamy and marital fidelity in health and sex education. Section 28 of the 1988 Local Government Act outlawed the promotion by local authorities of the 'pretend family form' constituted by same-sex relationships.

Williams (1989) suggests that the new disciplinary state is concerned with the control of the depraved rather than the care of the deprived. Policies forged in the name of moral and economic regeneration were directed at gay men and lesbians, social security fraudsters, disruptive pupils, young offenders and immigrants. The depraved were defined not only in terms of a failure to conform to the norms of work and family, or to the rule of law, but to the cultural norms of Nation. Nationalism was entwined with racism in the assertion of a dominant British culture, in education for example, and in law and order campaigns directed at black youth and asylum-seekers.

The cultural contradictions of late capitalism also centre on the body in ways which have been incorporated into welfare policy as a means of tackling the twin pressures of economic downturn and a rapidly ageing population. Not only has consumer culture sexualized desires, wants and pleasures and transformed the body into their principal vehicle, but bodily qualities are no longer perceived to be ascribed by nature. Thus cosmetics, fashion, diet and sports industries foster the illusion that the exchange value of the body can be enhanced by reshaping it in line with idealized images of youth, fitness and beauty (Giddens, 1992; Shilling, 1993; Falk, 1994). The body is subjected to 'bodily maintenance' regimes (Featherstone, 1991: 182) by a new asceticism which, paradoxically, is intended to create rather than restrain desire.

Corporeal cleavages have opened up with the transformation of bodies into a form of 'physical capital' which is convertible into other types of capital – economic, social, cultural. As the exterior of the body becomes increasingly involved in the formation of social inequalities and oppressions (Bourdieu, 1984; Shilling, 1991), social relations are no longer determined simply by differential access to key resources. To the extent that normality and social acceptability rest on an appearance of youth, beauty and athleticism, ageing, sick and disabled bodies have been transformed into a source of anxiety in contemporary culture (Lupton, 1994). Bodies which stubbornly refuse to conform to dominant cultural norms, offering neither pleasure nor labour, are therefore liable to exclusion. Conversely, the social and economic success of the new middle classes is linked to their privileged access to the means of maintaining their bodies in line with desirable bodily attributes and to their adoption of those interpersonal skills – forcefulness, magneticism, sociability – which enable them to perform effectively in competitive social spaces (Featherstone, 1991).

The appearance of the outer body is linked in consumer culture to the maintenance of the inner body in ways which have remoralized health and reinforced the exclusion of imperfect bodies (Featherstone, 1991). Sickness, impairment and ageing threaten the body beautiful and must be combated by healthy living. Because the new asceticism makes health dependent on intentional acts, such as dieting or exercise, the healthy body has come to signify worthiness as a person, evidencing foresight, self-control, hard work and personal responsibility (Lupton, 1994). Similarly, the welfare discourse of the independent body has encouraged individuals to be future-oriented and take personal responsibility for their health by taking care of their body.

Featherstone (1991) points out that public health discourse in the 1980s began to incorporate the category 'self-inflicted illness'. The moral deviants who voluntarily burdened the state by abusing their bodies evidenced a new form of depravity. Health education campaigns urged the good citizen to avoid the dangers of hypertension, heart disease and cancer by spelling out the benefits of preventive medical regimens, such as giving up smoking, jogging, dieting, resting and avoiding stress.

Risk management is therefore still the central regulatory task of welfare, but the emphasis has shifted from sharing the risks of dependency to protecting the state from dependency – or preventing states of dependency from ever arising. From the mid-1980s onwards, British welfare systems were restructured in line with the new demands of risk management. A strategy of privatization was replaced by the contracting out of housing, health and personal care services to the private and voluntary sectors. According to the rhetoric of the new mixed economy of welfare, competition would drive down costs as well as make public services more responsive to the 'consumer'. Yet market flexibility was at odds with the demands of fiscal probity. Thus deregulation and fragmentation at the periphery were accompanied by a centralization of powers at the core. The consumer lacked any direct purchasing power in the quasi-markets to emerge in health, education and community care and tight central control over budgets and the design of services was retained.

Management was central to the new modes of controlling dependency and risk on which the regulation of bodies in space now depended. Perkin argues that, in post-industrial society, human capital in the form of managerial expertize has replaced the dominance of landlords in pre-industrial society and of capitalists in industrial society:

> Professional managers of corporations and government stand at the apex of new society controlling its economy, administering its policies and increasingly distributing the income and arranging its social relations. (1996: 6)

Private sector managers achieved a pivotal position in lean production systems, identified as the means by which organizations could be made to function more efficiently and effectively. Pollitt (1990) explains how economic power was translated into political power as managers demanded the 'right to manage', a claim strengthened in Britain by recession, the weakening of trade union power and the loss of political consensus around the welfare state. As social progress was seen to depend on the increased productivity which managers uniquely could deliver, managerialism became an ideology prescribing management as a cure for economic and social problems.

As Pollitt (1990) points out, managers were accorded a similarly strategic role in the restructuring of British welfare systems over the 1980s and 1990s, charged with transforming the public sector into dynamic and effective organizations able to deliver 'value for money' services on a competitive basis. Newman and Clarke (1994) describe the interplay of the two styles of management involved in restructuring. Both neo-Taylorism and 'new managerialism' stressed greater productivity and value for money but differed in the way these should be achieved. Taylorization of the new core/periphery workforces was designed to drive down labour and 'production' costs by curtailing professional discretion and replacing the old 'bureau-professional' control systems with the managerial specification of duties, performance measurement, cost centres and consumer surveys. New managerialism stressed commitment rather than compliance, emphasizing the role of managerial performance in motivating workers to strive for quality for themselves. However, the imperative of fiscal discipline ensured the dominance of neo-Taylorism in restructuring, supported by the widespread use of new technology.

The managerialization of welfare has also reconstituted the body of the service user as an object rather than a subject. With increasing selectivity and the erosion of the social body, tests of eligibility for a range of benefits and services are narrowly based on bodily functioning. Whereas the relative needs of social actors were visible to the professional gaze, it is the absolute needs of independent bodies which are visible to the managerial gaze (see Ellis, Chapter 2 in this volume). Those who accomplish eligibility experience what Dominelli terms a 'cafeteria approach' to welfare (1996: 159). In the case of community care, for example, 'packages of care' are shaped not by the individual preferences of the consumer but by standardized measures of economy, efficiency and effectiveness. Just as Fordist theories have been used in McDonald's food production to regularize patterns of consumption (Ritzer, 1993), the search for greater cost-efficiency has also led to standardization at the point of welfare consumption. Once bodily needs have been satisfied, the state then withdraws.

Welfare systems are increasingly centred on the regulation of risky bodies in cyberspace rather than needy bodies in social spaces. Just as computerization has provided 'invisible monitoring systems' to ensure the compliance of workers to budgetary disciplines and performance measures (Newman and Clarke, 1994: 20), so information technology has facilitated myriad calculations of risk in terms of the actual or potential cost of dependency to the public purse (Henman, 1997). Service outcomes such as school meals, packages of care or hospital treatment are based on measures of cost-efficiency which are only indirectly related to bodily needs. The new orthodoxy of evidence-based medicine, for example, is designed to ensure that interventions are based on statistical calculations of the efficacy of selected treatments (see Paley, Chapter 6 in this volume). The welfare client is becoming a virtual service user, a construction of the tools designed to measure his or her existence.

CONCLUSION

Although the nature of the four tasks of bodily order outlined by Turner has changed in line with key transitions in capitalism and political struggle, welfare systems remain centrally involved in reproducing, restraining, representing and regulating bodies through time and space. Yet those tasks have become increasingly contradictory under advanced capitalism.

Despite women's increased participation in employment and the diversification of family forms, patriarchal welfare systems still shape the reproduction of bodies over time as residualization is linked to an assumed continuity in women's unpaid domestic and caring labour. With the election of a New Labour government in Britain in May 1997, Family has been linked to Community as parental responsibility is spelt out for supervizing homework, preventing truancy, controlling disruptive children and remoralizing troublesome local spaces.

Despite the breakdown of traditional patterns of employment and the spread of consumerism, welfare discourse still resonates with the productivist norms of industrial capitalism. New Labour's interest in reviving the savings model provided by the mutual aid organizations of the late nineteenth and early twentieth century gives this emphasis on the work ethic, thrift and self-reliance a new twist. Work is represented by New Labour as the route out of welfare dependency for groups with a traditionally marginal relationship to the labour market, such as young people, lone parents and disabled people. Incentives to engage in paid work, including the subsidization of child care, are designed to draw women with a low-earning or no breadwinner partner into employment. With the predicted burgeoning of the child-care industry, the reproduction of bodies seems increasingly set to consist in freeing up one group of women to enter low-paid employment by leaving their children in the care of other groups of low-paid workers, including women, young people and 'low-achievers'.

The ethos of bodily restraint to derive, paradoxically, from the commodification of the body has been incorporated into a new public health emphasizing personal responsibility for health, fitness and longevity. Yet the body has been transformed by both consumer culture and political struggle into a source of self- and social identity, emerging as a point of resistance to new welfare regimes. Morgan and Scott (1993) point to the barriers health educators faced in trying to get rationalistic messages about self-preservation and 'safer sex' across in campaigns designed to prevent the spread of HIV/AIDS. The body is constituted in consumer culture as a present source of pleasure rather than a future site of disease. Moreover, the sexual identity of gay men has been constructed as a political identity since the 1970s which, in turn, transformed free engagement in a diverse range of same-sex practices into a political act which the gay community sought to defend against the normative incursions of health educationalists (see also Mitchell, Chapter 8 in this volume).

By relocating disability in social barriers rather than bodily impairment, the disability movement has also politicized corporeal identity in ways which challenge new modes of risk management. Moves to decriminalize euthanasia have been interpreted as a hostile act against people with impairments, linked to the withdrawal of social support and the management of dependency (see Crow, 1996). Whilst health care generally tends to be seen as benevolent, and preventive health checks articulate with individual anxieties about the corporeality of the body and concerns to preserve health, fitness and youth, Turner points to their regulatory function in identifying risky bodies and reducing the fiscal drain of curative medicine (1995: 227). The disability movement has similarly named the screening of the pregnant body to detect foetal defects as a contemporary form of eugenics directed at the elimination of defective, and potentially dependent, bodies.

The attempts of the disciplinary state to manage the risks of dependency are therefore subject to a number of constraints. Demand for health care is fuelled by rising expectations and technological advances in medicine, neither of which are easy for governments to control (Turner, 1996). In the case of organ transplantation, technology has outstripped the supply of organs, which is calling into question the reliance of the British donor system on voluntarism and an economy of altruism (see Randhawa, Chapter 3 in this volume). The withdrawal of the state from collectivized cover for the life-course risks of impairment and old age generates conflict between the sick and the healthy, the old and the young (Walker, 1996). The more the commercial sector is called on to substitute for formerly state-run insurance schemes, the more governments are obliged to intervene to ensure adequate coverage for individuals.

The discourse of the independent body may be further challenged by the intriguing mix of communitarianism and free market economics which go to make up the bio-politics of New Labour (see Dean, Chapter 5 in this volume). The new government has announced its intention to transform the National Health Service into a 'public health organization'. The goal of health promotion is still to reduce dependency on expensive curative medicine yet the emphasis of initiatives such as 'health action zones' and 'healthy living centres' is not simply on changing individual behaviours and life-styles but on regenerating the environments in which individuals live. The emergence of health-related community development may mean the Dispensary once again plays a part in regulating bodies within the social spaces of the community.

2 The Care of the Body

Kathryn Ellis

This chapter examines British community care policy and practice in the post-Second World War period in terms of a transition from the dominant corporeal discourse of 'social efficiency' to that of the 'independent body' from the mid-1970s onwards. When 'states of dependency' (Titmuss, 1963) were constituted as social risks, the psychic and social spaces to surround bodies under the Dispensary gaze were elaborated; and human subjects were entitled as citizens to have their care needs met outside the institution. Nevertheless, bodily dependency remained a fiscal problem for the welfare state, managed through disciplinary practices redolent of the old institutional order. With global economic crisis and the resurgence of neo-liberal economic orthodoxy, the 'burden' of care grew increasingly onerous and the 'social' was displaced by market and 'family'. Constituted by the discourse of the independent body, dependency in the new mixed economy of care was ever more tightly managed through a reworking of panoptic norms in neo-Taylorism and the banishment of old, sick and disabled bodies to the hinterland of institutional care.

'PROMOTIONAL WELFARE'

As discussed in the Introduction and in Chapter 1, the emergence of a social space around individual bodies can be linked to shifts in public health discourse in the late nineteenth and early twentieth century. With the development of community care policy after the Second World War, this space came to be identified as the 'community'. The roots of community care lie in the powers and responsibilities acquired by local health and welfare departments under the 1946 National Health Service Act and the 1948 National Assistance Act (NAA). In abolishing the Poor Law, the NAA confirmed the social spaces of the local community as the rightful place for older and disabled people.

Sainsbury (1995) suggests that Section 29 of the NAA, which empowered local authorities to 'make arrangements for promoting the welfare of disabled people', heralded a period of 'promotional welfare' for this group. A labour shortage meant that 'promotional welfare' was initially inflected towards disabled citizens fulfilling their obligation of productivity, and local authorities were required to use their powers to reinforce the national system of rehabilitation, training and employment services set up under the 1944 Disabled Persons (Employment) Act. Ascetic norms gave work a moral imperative beyond its contribution to national efficiency, however, and local authorities were also empowered under the NAA to provide sheltered workshops, hostels and homeworking schemes for those unable to participate in open employment.

In the Keynes–Beveridge welfare state, national efficiency was closely allied to social efficiency. As employment and training services provided under the 1944 Act were increasingly regarded as a national responsibility, the discourse of promotional welfare refocused on the social relationships of disabled people. A Ministry of Health Circular issued in 1951 extended local authority responsibility under the NAA for promoting the access of disabled people to cultural, religious, educational and leisure activities (cited in Sainsbury, 1995). Social isolation for disabled people was to be overcome by encouraging and enabling people to participate in social activities, organizing social centres and recreational facilities, and recruiting volunteers to help implement the Act.

The extent to which older people belonged within the social body in the early post-war years was more ambiguous. Their welfare was to be promoted by ending the 'warehousing' of individual bodies in the public assistance wards of the former workhouses for which the new National Health Service and local authorities had acquired responsibility. Under the NAA, local authorities were to provide homes not institutions; the retirement home, modelled on the small seaside hotel to which the genteel classes retired, would provide a more humane type of residential care, marked by greater privacy and qualitatively different relationships between staff and residents (Sainsbury, 1995).

MANAGING DEPENDENCY: RIGHTS AND NEEDS

The term 'community care' came into general use at the end of the 1950s and early 1960s when the depersonalizing regime of the institution

– one of the chief mechanisms of the Panopticon – was critiqued by new discourses around labelling, stigma and institutionalization (Armstrong, 1983). Over the 1960s, claims made by campaigning groups about the abuse of patients in geriatric, mental and mental handicap hospitals led to a number of public inquiries and widespread publicity.

The clinical gaze of the institution drew a dichotomous distinction between the normal and the abnormal by defining the normal in relation to an external referent. Normalization discourse identified people in mental hospitals as 'really normal' in line with the redefinition of 'normal' as the relative position of all bodies in a social space. With the advent of new drug therapies, those formerly incarcerated in institutions came to be seen as having not only the right but the means to live in their own homes, or in homelike situations, in the community. Where there had been two communities there was now one (Armstrong, 1983).

The status of older people as 'really normal' took longer to establish, illustrative of the extent to which community care has also been a vehicle for managing dependency. Levick (1992) suggests that the concept of 'substitutability' has helped to contain the costs of community care throughout the post-war period. After the war, health and local authorities had joint responsibility for the many elderly inhabitants of the 500 former workhouses (Lewis and Glennerster, 1996: 1). A policy of substituting costly hospital beds for local authority beds gave rise to boundary disputes between hospital boards and local authorities which were fought out in terms of normal/abnormal bodily distinctions. Thus a Ministry of Health circular issued in 1957 spelt out the nature and extent of local authority responsibility for people 'in need of care and attention' under the NAA in terms of the level of infirmity of body and mind, the extent to which individuals were bedfast, the temporary or permanent nature of the illness and so on (cited in Means, 1995).

The contraction in long-stay hospital beds was initially linked to an expansion in the responsibilities of local health and welfare departments for a range of provision: hostels, workshops, home help, laundry, meals-on-wheels, occupational therapy, social work, day centres and warden services. In the case of older people, though, expenditure restrictions meant that neither domiciliary care nor smaller residential homes in the community materialized until the 1960s (Lewis and Glennerster, 1996). Indeed, the legal power to provide a full range of domiciliary services to older people was initially withheld from local authorities out of fear that they would be improperly used as a substitute for 'family' care (Means, 1995). Despite the abolition of the Poor Law, the principle of the 'liable relative' survived in the practical support family members, particularly women, were expected to provide to elderly relatives (Finch, 1989).

Campaigns on behalf of patients 'wrongly' confined to mental hospitals in the early 1950s tied the bio-politics of community care to civil rights struggles. In the 1960s and early 1970s, the physical body became a site of struggle for disabled people seeking to challenge dominant medical theories about the origins of disability in individual bodily impairment. A study conducted at the invitation of residents of a Cheshire Home, as part of a wider campaign for the democratization of residential homes, argued that to commit disabled people to institutions was to define them as 'socially dead'. Institutions essentially functioned to help inmates 'make the transition from social death to physical death' (Miller and Gwynne, 1972: 89). This notion of 'social death' paved the way for the subsequent development of a 'social theory' of disability which relocated the barriers to full citizenship from the physical domain of the body to the social body.

Yet the early campaigning activity of what later became the disability movement centred around claims for a national disability income (Campbell and Oliver, 1996). These were readily accommodated within Fabianist welfare discourse as compensation for the undeserved 'personal tragedy' of bodily impairment. Here disability has such a traumatic physical and psychological effect on individuals that they are unable to secure a reasonable quality of life for themselves by their own efforts (Oliver, 1990). They are in need, and the satisfaction of need was not only a desirable but an attainable objective of a social democratic state. The discursive practices of 'objective necessity' (Hill and Bramley, 1986: 58), permitted the objective identification and measurement of need by politicians, planners, administrators and professionals alike.

The first disability survey conducted by the Office of Population Censuses and Surveys in 1971 was designed to assess the financial consequences of providing more services to disabled people and to clarify eligibility for the allocation of cash benefits (Sainsbury, 1995). Need was objectively measured as the social restrictions to arise out of loss or reduction of functional ability, traced ultimately to bodily impairment. Similarly reliant on the objective measurement of need, the 1970 Chronically Sick and Disabled Persons Act (CSDPA) strengthened the duty of local authorities under the NAA to compile registers of disabled people and gave them a new duty of estimating the number of people in need as a basis for service planning.

As 'chronic care' groups were displaced from the ambit of health care, their rights to 'social care' were protected at the statutory level, although Oliver argues that the services to be provided under Section 2 of the CSDPA amounted to little more than those prescribed by Section 29 of the NAA (Oliver, 1996). However, Salter (1994) points out that the 1946 National Health Services Act was the only aspect of the post-war welfare settlement to offer an absolute and unconditional social right universally applicable to the whole population. The right to care of the body free at the point of delivery was subsequently negated by the 1968 Health Services and Public Health Act and the 1970 Act under which charges for services were permitted.

As costly long-stay hospital care was replaced by the apparently cheaper option of community-based services, the problem of dependency was increasingly managed by substituting needs claims on the individual body for rights claims on the social body. At service delivery level, rights to social care were made contingent on the categorization of 'need' within Fabianist 'bureau-professional regimes': a combination of professional expertise and rational administration articulating with a policy framework set by elected politicians (Newman and Clarke, 1994). Although the CSDPA was heralded by some as a charter of rights, the task of managing dependency ensured that individuals' only entitlement was to an assessment of need (Oliver, 1996). Access to services therefore depended on satisfying a test of eligibility, based on an examination by welfare professionals of the bodily needs of individuals in a social space.

Community care therefore reflected the dual conceptualization of the body in medical knowledge as sharing universal features yet distinguishable as normal or abnormal. The CSDPA confirmed disabled people's rights to occupy ordinary social spaces by strengthening those clauses of the NAA promoting access to public places and by introducing parking concessions for disabled drivers and passengers (Sainsbury, 1995). At the same time, social efficiency was preserved by segregating the dysfunctional in 'special' day and residential services designed to compensate older and disabled people for loss of functional ability and reduce their social isolation. The 'anatomo-politics' of needs assessments helped contain the costs of dependency by selectively distributing social care according to tests of body and mind based on individualized and medicalized norms.

THE 'PSYCHO-SOCIAL' GAZE

In linking the individual to the social spaces of the community, it is perhaps the 'psycho-social' gaze of the social worker and the 'personal social services' which most clearly bear the imprint of the Dispensary.

Langan (1993) identifies 1970 as the 'high tide' of the social work profession. Following the recommendations of the Seebohm Report, the hitherto fragmented functions of local health and welfare departments were unified in social services departments. Reorganized around geography and function rather than client group (Lewis and Glennerster, 1996: 45), the Seebohm departments were designed to provide a 'single door' through which the local community could gain access to the personal social services. Administrative rationality would be bolstered by a new professional coherence, unified by a common training, workplace and client group (Aldridge, 1996: 179). Generic social work would dissolve the boundaries between professional and client group specialisms and offer a common response to individuals and families approaching the single door.

Welfare goods were distributed rationally in bureau-professional regimes in line with administrative categorizations of need but also flexibly according to the needs of the unique individual. Professional training in psychological theories and therapeutic methodology enabled social workers to build relationships with individual clients and uncover need (Aldridge, 1996; Dominelli, 1996). Where the clinical gaze created individual bodies by objectifying them, the psychosocial gaze of the social worker played over the body of the 'whole person'. Social work theory, which reflected the emergence of the body as a subject rather than an object, was described by Cheetham as:

> a dual and integrated focus on the inner and outer worlds, linking psychological and social perspectives, with the social worker acting as interpreter, broker and mediator between two worlds. (1993: 157)

The human subject was constituted within the psychic and social spaces opened up between people by community-based health and social care (Armstrong, 1983). Social services departments were to give expression to the social worker's role of promoting social cohesion by bringing about adaptive change in individuals, in their social relationships and in the social environment (Webb and Wistow, 1987).

The double mapping of locality and social relationships characteristic of the Dispensary (Armstrong, 1983) was reinforced in the early 1980s by the development of decentralized area or neighbourhood offices and 'patch' principles in social work practice (Gladstone, 1995). Yet confusion over the principle and practice of genericism in the post-Seebohm departments (Bamford, 1990) meant that specialisms organized around the anatomical body were perpetuated. Similarly the dominance of administrative over professional categorizations of need (Blaxter, 1976; Smith, 1980), and the use of categorizations as a means of restricting access to selective services, ensured that people assessed for community care continued to be measured against panoptic norms of abnormal physical and psychological functioning.

THE 'BURDEN' OF CARE

White Papers published by successive governments over the 1970s identified people requiring chronic care as priority groups to be protected against spending restrictions. Community-based provision was still regarded as a cheaper option than hospital care, particularly in view of the predicted rise in the numbers of older people requiring care in the future (Dalley, 1993).

The share of income allocated to the personal social services increased fivefold between 1955 and 1976 (Judge, 1978). The creation of a single door service in 1970 had the effect of dramatically increasing the number of clients (Lewis and Glennerster, 1996). However, the rapid rate of service expansion was short-lived. Global economic crisis in the mid-1970s led to the identification of a fiscal crisis in welfare, shifting the policy emphasis from priority groups, planning and targets for community care to expenditure restraint (Evandrou *et al.*, 1991). The 1976 DHSS Priorities for Health and Social Services was explicit about the requirement to identify priorities in expenditure and manage within existing budgets (Levick, 1992).

Spending restraints intensified the managerialization of the personal social services as concepts of economy, efficiency and effectiveness were imported into discussions about the professional function in social care (Audit Commission, 1985; 1986). The bombardment of referrals after the setting up of the Seebohm departments led to experiments with intake teams, team managers who monitored the flow of work and group allocation meetings (Dominelli, 1996; Lewis and Glennerster, 1996). Corporate management techniques and theories supportive of managerialist objectives, such as systems theory, time-limited contracts with clients and task-centred practice, were incorporated into social work theory (Cheetham, 1993; Dominelli, 1996).

A 'burden of care' discourse began to dominate the bio-politics of community care as fiscal crisis enmeshed with panics about the 'demographic timebomb' of an ageing population and declining fertility rates. Feminist theorists inspired a number of empirical studies of family care which pointed to the physical, emotional and financial costs of care. Older and disabled people came to be represented not only as a fiscal and demographic burden but also as a burden on family members, particularly women.

Constructed by the post-war welfare state as a bulwark against the hazards of a market economy, the social body came under attack from neo-liberal economic orthodoxy after 1979. Need for care no longer constituted a social risk as states of dependency were remoralized as personal, family and community responsibilities. The community was redefined as the source of care rather than the social and geographical spaces within which care took place. In an early statement of policy priorities for older people, *Growing Older*, the new Conservative administration identified the role of public authorities as sustaining and, where necessary, developing informal networks of family, friends and neighbours but never displacing them. 'Care in the community must increasingly mean care by the community' (DHSS, 1981: 3). The social body was no more than the 'natural' groupings of family and local community.

From the early 1980s, the Conservative government also signalled its intention to reposition social services departments as 'enablers' rather than direct providers of care. By promoting, funding and regulating other sectors of the 'mixed economy of care', statutory responsibility for meeting needs uncovered by assessment would be limited. Historic shortfalls in provision meant that central government spending on the personal social services over the 1980s, pegged as it was to demographic need, bore little resemblance to actual need (Baldock, 1994). Whilst local authority discretion over definitions of need was curtailed by charge- and expenditure-capping (Lawson, 1993), much of the 85 per cent revenue spending provided by central government over the 1980s related to financial rather than service-related targets.

As a focus on the 'burden' of care gave primacy to the position of the care-giver (Warnes, 1993), the informal 'carer' gained prominence in public policy documents (Twigg and Atkin, 1994). Carers were presented as undertaking heroic responsibility for heavily dependent and demanding people as if they were the essential cause of their problems (Croft, 1986). This in turn fuelled debates about the need to promote support for carers to maintain them in their caring roles (Means, 1995).

Supporting carers was a highly cost-effective strategy given that only a small outlay by social care agencies was required for extensive outputs (Twigg and Atkin, 1994). Upholding the rights of disabled people, in contrast, was a riskier proposition for cash-strapped local authorities. The 1986 Disabled Persons (Services, Representation and Consultation) Act, which included provisions designed to enhance disabled people's access to and involvement in the needs assessment process, was never fully implemented. The Conservative government argued that its planned reforms of community care superseded this legislation, promising as they did a new kind of right: consumer sovereignty.

THE NEW MIXED ECONOMY OF CARE

Following a number of critical reports published in the 1980s, Sir Roy Griffiths was charged by Margaret Thatcher with reviewing arrangements for community care (DHSS, 1989). Most of his subsequent recommendations were accepted and incorporated into the 1990 National Health Service and Community Care Act (NHSCCA).

Wistow *et al.* (1994) suggest two possible interpretations of the 'enabling authority' role identified in the early 1980s: that of 'competitive council' or 'community government'. It was the former which dominated the Griffiths Report and subsequent legislation. In the new mixed economy of care, social services departments would no longer directly provide services but purchase them under contract from local voluntary and private organizations. The Seebohm departments were to be reorganized according to the market-based logic of the purchaser/provider split, transforming geographical and social spaces into a quasi-market. Whereas a community government would work with local people to define and meet social need, the competitive council commodified need as purchasers were charged with commissioning services to meet need uncovered in population-level and individual assessments (Lewis and Glennerster, 1996: 144).

Competition was designed to expose and reduce costs, offering better value for money as well as enhancing the quality and choice of care (Langan and Clarke, 1994: 78). Consumer sovereignty reconstituted the citizen as an economic actor pursuing his or her preferences in the marketplace rather than making claims on the basis of citizenship entitlement. A turnstile was installed at the single door with the introduction of charging policies based on the expectation that people who could afford to do so would meet the 'economic cost' of community care services.

Given that only unintentional market outcomes can effect a just distribution of resources, economic liberalism delegitimizes the pursuit of social justice through central planning. Nevertheless, central government remained the ultimate principal in contracting arrangements for community care. As purchasers rather than providers, the power of local authorities was limited to specifying and awarding contracts (Clarke and Stewart, 1990: 5). Moreover, 85 per cent of the cash-limited Special Transitional Grant – established to enable local authorities to take over responsibility for the funding of care from the social security system – had to be spent in the independent sector. Central government also sought to regularize the performance of local authority agents in what Lewis and Glennerster describe as a determinedly top-down mode of implementation (1996: 18). Thus tight fiscal control was underlined by detailed guidance from the Audit Commission and Social Services Inspectorate (SSI) aimed at transforming bureau-professional regimes into competitive councils. Emphasizing efficiency, economy and effectiveness in resource use, official guidance formed a highly rationalistic blueprint against which action could be measured (Lewis and Glennerster, 1996: 18).

The regulatory hand of the manager was required to control market forces at the local level. Hadley and Clough suggest that the production of highly specific products demanded a focus within social services departments on the technical tasks of production and their co-ordination (1996: 12). Despite the promised 'flexibility', they argue that the logic of the purchaser/provider split, and the government's detailed emphasis on process and output, imposed a factory or industrial model on the production of care. According to the imperatives of McDonaldization (Ritzer, 1993), devolving the production of care to a plurality of organizations increased the need for control in order to standardize patterns of consumption.

Once the 'command and control' Seebohm bureaucracies had been dismantled, managerial control over the production of care would be maintained by developments in new technology. Devolved budgeting enabled the decentralization of purchasing decisions as close to the individual consumer of care as possible and provided the necessary flexibility to create customized 'packages of care'. Cumbersome bureaucratic controls over spending decisions would be replaced by computerized management and financial information systems (Lawson, 1993; Dominelli and Hoogvelt, 1996: 52).

The dominance of neo-Taylorist managerialism has been tempered to some extent by an emphasis on inputs. The spread of new public management orthodoxy over the 1980s and 1990s led to the promotion of an 'enterprise' culture throughout the public sector, according to which organizations had to demonstrate their worthiness of investment by taking on the style and identity of private sector concerns (Aldridge, 1996: 188). Local authority managers were not only charged with imposing prescribed systems of care but with bringing about cultural change in social services departments:

> Winning the hearts and minds of social services members and staff to a different role for social services is the key to success of community care (Audit Commission, 1992 cited in Langan and Clarke, 1994: 79)

MANAGING RISK

A stated aim of the NHSCCA was to replace established services with patterns of provision more closely geared to existing and future needs. In implementing new arrangements local authorities were therefore advised to separate the assessment of need from the commissioning of services (SSI, 1991a). Needs-based assessments, including information on unmet need recorded in individual assessments, would then guide purchasing decisions at authority-wide and front-line levels.

Yet services also had to be targeted on those most in need in order to give effect to what Lewis and Glennerster identify as the core policy objective of capping social security spending on residential care (1996: 8). Local authorities were to assess all people whose needs went 'beyond' health care, a definition set to become ever more inclusive. On the one hand, health authorities had responsibility for defining entitlement to 'continuous care' at a time when they were retreating back into acute hospital care (Means, 1995; Browne, 1996: 61; Twigg, 1997). On the other, nursing home care was redefined as social care under the new funding structure, giving local authorities responsibility for the financial support of people in the full range of institutional care (Henwood, 1992).

Pilot case management systems developed in Kent suggested that effective targeting depended on tight management of the interface between institutional and home-based care. Greater cost-efficiency required that people were supported in the least dependent settings which, in turn, meant that new arrangements for assessment and care management (as it became) had to achieve a degree of 'downward substitution' at the margin between settings (Challis, 1992).

The Audit Commission stated that 'the definition of "need" depends on priorities' (1992: 31); and local authorities were to prioritize the needs of the most 'dependent' who were also at risk of entering institutional care because of the lack of – or apparent fragility of – informal support. Despite the rhetoric of needs-based rather than service-led assessments, need was circularly defined by the Department of Health as 'ability to benefit from care' (DH, 1993: 6). Similarly, the SSI had made it clear that local authorities only had a duty to assess if they believed a person had need of the services they provided (DH, 1992b). The key objective of new arrangements according to the Audit Commission was to put the needs of users and carers at the centre, yet the way for local authorities to achieve this was to:

> introduce assessment procedures at the operational level, and set priorities at the strategic level which translate into eligibility criteria. (Audit Commission, 1993: 3)

In order to manage dependency, local authorities were effectively instructed to define need in terms of eligibility for services.

New definitions of need lacked the open-ended commitment of promotional welfare and the principles of participation and citizenship with which it was associated (Sainsbury, 1995: 192–3). The Audit Commission equated unmet need with shortfalls in service (1993: 4), whilst the injunction to record and feed information on unmet need into service planning was subverted in 1992 when the threat of judicial review led the SSI to warn social services departments that they had a legal obligation to provide services for which they had admitted a need (DH, 1992b).

Local authorities were advised that service criteria should 'allow through just enough people with needs exactly to use up their budget (or be prepared to adjust their budgets)' (Audit Commission, 1993: para. 15). Access to assessment and care management systems had therefore to be tightly managed and the Seebohm principle of universality was replaced by rigorous targeting. The SSI advised managers to distinguish between differing types and levels of assessment (1991a). Although a decision about eligible need was apparently to be taken only after a judgement about the type and level of assessment required had been made, to the extent that they related to a common set of service criteria, these processes were likely to be inseparable in practice.

New arrangements governing access to assessment were consistent with the overarching objective of keeping a check on the number of comprehensive assessments in relation to financial resources (Lewis and Glennerster, 1996: 148). Whilst disabled people retained the right to a comprehensive assessment conferred by previous legislation under new arrangements, a recent study suggests this is widely ignored in practice, particularly amongst generic teams dealing predominantly with older people. Further, the close prescription of eligible need in client information systems constitutes an inbuilt disincentive for staff to spend time on anyone deemed ineligible for the limited list of services provided or funded by the local authority (Davis *et al.*, 1997).

Formerly part of a welfare state designed to provide 'precautionary aftercare' for the life-cycle risks of old age, sickness and impairment (Giddens, 1994), social services departments now concentrate on managing the risk of people becoming dependent on state assistance. The preventive welfare systems to develop around risk management provide novel modes of surveillance, matching prospective service users against an abstract calculation of risk factors without any direct contact with the individual necessarily being made. In new systems of assessment for community care, front-line workers frequently consult with referral agents to determine eligibility against needs/risk matrices without the person concerned ever being aware they have had their 'needs' assessed. Inasmuch as a 'phone call to a referral agent can be logged as an initial assessment and added to the number of assessments completed then computerized systems of assessment and care management arguably offer incentives for such invisible calculations of the risk of dependency (Davis *et al.*, 1997).

MANAGERIALIZATION AND THE PSYCHO-SOCIAL GAZE

One of the early acts of the incoming Conservative government at the beginning of the 1980s was to charge the Barclay Committee with defining the 'role and tasks' of social workers (Barclay, 1982). The subsequent introduction of 'competences' into social work training enabled central government to specify the core skills required by professionals to do the jobs employers wanted them to do (Dominelli and Hoogvelt, 1996: 55). The functional analysis of social work as a set of competences articulated with case management, an approach whose origins Dominelli traces in the corporate management theories and techniques developed to manage the professional function in the post-Seebohm departments (1996: 156).

Hughes identifies new arrangements as an 'administrative' rather than professional model of community care in which assessment is designed primarily as a means of managing and justifying how resources are allocated (1995: 142). Constructed around the purchaser–provider split, new systems separated the function of assessment from the provision of services. A cornerstone of social work practice and the personal social services, assessment in the Seebohm departments was a holistic process incorporating both the initial stage of 'diagnosis' and the subsequent design of appropriate interventions to meet need (Hughes, 1995: 66). New systems, however, were designed less as a process of human interaction than as a linear sequence of interrelated decisions about eligibility for services.

A distinction between simple and comprehensive assessments had to be made at an early stage. Department of Health guidance rejected the classic professional defence of a full assessment as always necessary to 'probe beneath the presenting problem' on two counts:

> The professional argument that a more comprehensive assessment may be justified on the grounds that it may uncover other needs, loses weight in the context of departments struggling to meet even presenting needs. It is further diminished by the new emphasis on trusting the judgement of users and carers about their own needs. (DH, 1991: 45)

Only a minority of people would qualify for a comprehensive assessment, leaving social workers with less time for the long-term work of uncovering and responding to emotional needs (Cheetham, 1993: 167; Hadley and Clough, 1996: 185; Lewis and Glennerster, 1996: 139–40). The 'essence' of social work, according to Dominelli, is the establishment of a therapeutic relationship between professional and client so as to provide the individual with the wherewithal to change his or her lifestyle in more socially adaptive and purposeful directions (1996: 171). Whilst this casework model of social work was the subject of radical critiques in the 1970s, the competency-based approach is also antithetical to the principles of anti-oppressive practice subsequently incorporated into professional training (*ibid*). Social reality would no longer be known as structural inequality; and the role of the social worker was to articulate the consumer and the market, not the human actor and the 'social'.

Identified with the purchasing strand of newly restructured social services departments, care management led to the penetration of market forces into a hitherto sacrosanct professional arena: the 'client-worker relationship' (Dominelli, 1996: 141). Because the concern of the care manager centred on the product purchased from the contractor, the relationship between provider and receiver of care was no longer mediated through the purchaser but determined by it – a long way, as Dominelli points out, from Titmuss's 'gift relationship' (*ibid.*). Care management systems also undermined the role of the bureau-professional as advocate, promoting clients' interests whether the resources were available or not. The care manager had both to represent users' needs and ration resources directly. Indeed, one study suggests that even drawing attention to unmet need in the new order is seen as a hostile act (Hadley and Clough, 1996: 117).

As Cheetham points out, the denial of a distinct role for social work in new assessment and care management systems was underlined by the determined reference to an all-embracing 'practitioner' in official guidance (1993: 157). The requirement for greater transparency and consistency in decision-making placed a new premium on standardized practice (Lewis and Glennerster, 1996: 205). Fragmentation and specialization enabled the practitioner's work to be prescribed and routinized as a series of administrative tasks: collecting information for assessments in accordance with specified criteria, planning packages of care within a fixed budget, and co-ordinating services which would then be provided by others (Langan and Clarke, 1994: 80; Dominelli and Hoogvelt, 1996: 58–9; Lewis and Glennerster, 1996: 139–40). Computerized client information systems ensure compliance with new arrangements by making access to each stage of assessment and care management contingent on the completion of a separate screen and laying practitioners' actions open to managerial scrutiny (Davis *et al.*, 1997).

Aldridge argues that defending social work against charges of a disempowering professionalism has passed from being discredited to seeming irrelevant, as all claims to knowledge are now judged pragmatically in terms of their outputs rather than being privileged *a priori* (Aldridge, 1996: 178–9). The social work performance in the newly-

Taylorized regimes of community care is scripted and choreographed by managers and employers whose output measures displace truth claims based on professional expertise. Quality assurance mechanisms mean that the quality of relations between workers and users has become a bureaucratic measure under the control of managers rather than professionals (Dominelli and Hoogvelt, 1996: 57). A social worker commented in an article in Community Care that:

> A lot of information is taken on a question-and-answer basis before a relationship of trust is built up. But one may be left feeling what makes social workers different from the Department of Social Security officer or salesperson making out a hire purchase agreement. (Bounds and Hepburn, 1994)

Whereas the confessional relationship between professional and client demanded cognitive and interpersonal skills on the part of the social worker, the practitioner requires only technical skills. The key performer in the new mixed economy of care is the manager on whose communication and interactive skills depends the transformation of bureau-professional regimes into enterprise cultures.

The objective of targeting services on frail older people at risk of entering institutional care is consistent with what Hugman describes as the privileging of the instrumental over the interpersonal (Hugman, 1994: 245). Need is equated with the lowest level of intervention, largely in the form of practical services delivered by domiciliary and day care workers (Cheetham, 1993: 167; Hughes, 1995: 142). Older people approaching social services departments have long tended to be assessed only for specific services, such as practical aids, frequently by unqualified staff (Hughes, 1995: 67). Older people were often excluded from the psycho-social gaze on relationships and family dynamics and denied the interpersonal skills of the professional social worker. Typically perceived as less capable of change and development, intervention was generally short-term, and characterized by surveillance rather than direct work with older people and their families (Hughes and Mtezuka, 1992: 233). It is to an intensification of that surveillance that the last section now turns.

TARGETING THE PHYSICAL BODY

Doyal and Gough suggest all needs can ultimately be reduced to two basic ones: physical survival and personal autonomy (1991: 54).

According to *Caring for People*, community care should concentrate on people in greatest need and provide services which intervened no more than necessary to foster independence (DH, 1989, para 1.8–1.10). Independence carried the dual meaning of ability to pay for one's own care and self-care in respect of bodily functions, requiring both financial and functional assessments of need. Services to the dependent would be distributed according to an absolute concept of need, guaranteeing no more than a 'minimum quality of life' (SSI, 1991b).

Bodily independence forms both part of the test of eligibility and part of the service objective. The managerial gaze constitutes the body as an object whose eligibility for state assistance is tested against risk/needs matrices. Whereas the Dispensary sought out those at risk in the community by maintaining surveillance over the still healthy, the preventive role of domiciliary services has been eclipsed and housework, shopping and 'pop-in' services recommodified. The priority is personal care for the already vulnerable – the tasks of getting up and putting to bed, dressing and undressing, washing, feeding and toileting. The vulnerable body is scrutinized for signs of ill-health, poor mobility, inability to perform the tasks of daily living unaided and, if possible, helped back to independent functioning. This search for self-care skills renders psychic well-being invisible. During a home care assessment observed by the author, the assessor ticked the box 'can see with spectacles' after an older woman had just described how sad she was that failing sight meant she was no longer able to do oil painting, an activity that used to give her a lot of pleasure (Ellis, 1993).

Autonomy is no longer seen in terms of the pursuit of valued personal goals through collectivized forms of support. Services to support the 'personal development' of people with learning difficulties are threatened, as is the traditional role of the home help in encouraging, motivating and acting as confidante to frail older people (Hadley and Clough, 1996: 109, 116; Lewis and Glennerster, 1996: 121). As a member of a district purchasing team in Hadley and Clough's study said: 'We are here to preserve life, not to enhance it' (1996: 118).

The body is not a subject to be cared about but an object to be cared for. Only the discrete tasks of caring for the body, those which can be counted and costed, are visible in neo-Taylorist regimes: the number of meals delivered, baths given, sheets changed (Brown and Smith, 1993: 188). Tight scheduling of the performance of specified tasks means that staff lack the flexibility, time or incentive to deviate from their roles (Land, 1991: 16). Any emotional labour undertaken by the worker is hidden within the concrete tasks of caring for the body, slotted in as time permits (Baines, Evans and Neysmith, 1991: 282).

The 'industrialization' of care has replaced forms of human welfare based on the quality of relationships between people (Hadley and Clough, 1996). Quality is measured in terms such as the number of people processed by assessment and care management systems within a certain period of time, rather than by the quality of their experience (Dominelli, 1996: 172). Efficient time management means staff visiting the home to undertake assessments must turn down the offer of a cup of tea or look at the photo album. As the requirement for staff to elicit and record intimate details intensifies, so they feel they have less time to be 'human' with people (Ellis, 1993). Professional discretion is replaced by quality indicators against which the citizen-as-consumer can measure performance and, where necessary, seek redress through complaints procedures and the Citizen's Charter.

In transactions between care agency and household, the 'user' and 'carer' are treated as separate cost and assessment units, obscuring the interdependence of human relationships. The more reciprocity and inter-subjectivity are stripped out of caring, the more dependency is pathologized and the more visibly caring is about control. Service users' behaviour and functioning is scored on dependency ratings developed to calculate the cost of care in contracting arrangements in terms of the nature and intensity of the 'care-giver burden' (Warnes, 1993: 325–7). In home care systems, managerial surveillance over household arrangements is maintained in 'task sheets' specifying the division of labour between worker, user and carer. The informal arrangements which used to build up over time between home help and client are outlawed as unauthorized 'dependencies'. The dangerous link between dependency and resource use is also reflected in the informal judgements front-line workers make about the moral worthiness of actual or potential service users. The norms of self-sufficiency and able-bodiedness dictate that the needs claims of people who are inclined to 'give in', become 'lazy' or 'spoilt', or 'abuse' provision must be resisted (Ellis, 1993; Davis *et al.*, 1997).

According to Twigg's differing models of interaction between informal carer and service agency, carers tend to be treated as a free resource within managerialism, their availability for 'caring about' taken for granted as 'natural' (1989). Whereas the professional gaze used to surround bodies, identifying normality within the psychic and social spaces between bodies, social work assessments are now bounded by eligibility criteria, proformas and required entries into client information systems. Screened out is the mix of strain, anger, ambivalence, fear, anxiety, affection and reciprocity on which caring relationships are founded (Cheetham, 1993: 169–70). As Land explains:

> Tending doesn't include the moral obligation or time involved in caring, nor does it include the restrictions it imposes nor the fragmentation of the carer's time. (1991: 12)

A recent study suggests that the carer's own body must be vulnerable before she attracts support (Davis *et al.*, 1997). At the same time, contract governance means that the informal supply of bodily care is more closely specified and monitored in packages of care. As carers become increasingly 'professionalized' through training in lifting, giving injections, administering blood tests, changing dressings and catheters, so they move closer to the 'co-worker' model of interaction in Twigg's taxonomy.

Given that services were normally available either from home, in the case of day care, or at home in the case of domiciliary care, Higgins (1989) suggested that the real distinction in community care was not between residential and community-based services but between institutions and the home. Yet the latter distinction was always fuzzy. Although early resettlement plans for people from long-stay hospitals were based on principles of normalization and clients' rights, facilities such as telephones or showers were installed in people's own homes for the benefit of staff (Hadley and Clough, 1996: 108). In the case of people already living in the community, the targeting of services on the bodily care of those on the brink of entering institutional care has further blurred the distinction.

Twigg distinguishes the institution as the place where no boundary between the medical and the social exists; all aspects of life are rationalized as part of the condition or treatment (1997: 229). In new community care regimes, social need is relegated to the lower levels of hierarchies of need with social services departments providing only 'life and limb' protection. Access to services designed to prevent the risk of social isolation, such as day care, is restricted by charging whilst holidays and other social activities are abandoned (Sainsbury, 1995: 192–3). As the social spaces around and between bodies disappear, so the function of respite care, and increasingly day centres, is to care for the body. Providing baths in suitably-equipped day centres offers a cheap alternative to bathing individuals in their own homes or funding multiple aids and adaptations. The operation of a 'tea 'n' tub' service, reported in a recent study (Davis *et al.*, 1997), suggests that social interaction within the day centre now derives meaning from rituals associated with care of the physical body.

As service users are banished to the hinterland of institutional care by minimal 'packages of care', amounting to little more than the 'warehousing' of frail, older people in the community (Hughes and Mtezuka, 1992: 233), so the home itself has arguably been transformed into a scientifically managed space. Older, frail people are confined to living in a downstairs room, equipped with bed, commode and high-backed chair, whilst the upstairs regions of the house are closed off as uneconomic to clean. Cultural meanings are screened out by redesignating the cleaning of the domestic space and the body in the domestic space as 'hygienic cleaning' (Twigg, 1997). Personal possessions are open to outside scrutiny as familiar staff are replaced by a battery of workers, frequently working for different agencies. Because the home help was often assimilated into the frail older person's informal network as a family friend, intimate care could be negotiated within a continuous interpersonal relationship (Twigg, 1997: 215). Now bodily frailties and needs must be constantly rehearsed and the work of caring continually directed by users and carers. Those cared for are naked to the touch of strangers who invade the home to perform intimate bodily tasks in a manner and at times dictated by managerial schedule.

CONCLUSION

The development of community care in the post-war period is frequently represented as a break with the old institutional order of the Poor Law. Deviant populations were revealed as 'really normal', bearers of the right to live ordinary lives in the community. As 'social' risks, the proper remedy for life-course dependencies was compensation and an array of day and domiciliary services provided both preventive care for the still independent and precautionary aftercare for the dependent. Yet, as Twigg points out, the medical is not separate from but defines the 'social' (1997: 216). The management of dependency depended on maintaining a boundary between the normal and the abnormal, and care in the community merely extended the disciplinary gaze of the Panopticon beyond the walls of the institution. The fault was ultimately traceable to the individual, the impaired body or mind providing the basis for the calculation of liability for social restrictions or functional limitations. The special benefits and services set up to meet the 'needs' of impaired individuals or populations served to segregate recipients within rather than from the community.

Nevertheless, as an integral component of a normative discourse of social administration, need offered a rich conception of human experience capable of rendering control respectable as humane treatment (Squires, 1990: 111). Whilst administrative categorizations of need ensured a rational distribution of goods and services, the task of the professional was to respond to the needs of the unique individual. Professional status, suggests Hugman, relates to 'person-focused' rather than 'resource-based' objectives (1994: 245). Within the new mixed economy of care, the commodification of need obscures the whole person at the centre of a web of interpersonal and social relationships, whilst Taylorized assessment and care management systems operate to ensure the practitioner allocates resources according to administrative rather than professional imperatives. The task of the care manager is not to integrate the human subject into the community but to connect the consumer to the market.

Davis argues that the body is constructed within the social relations of disability through the modalities of function and appearance (1995: 11). When the economic and social order centred on industrial production, able-bodied norms excluded the disabled on the basis of functional incompetence. The discursive practices of promotional welfare briefly offered the possibility of transforming abnormal bodies into independent bodies. Ageing bodies, however, were irretrievably dependent. Unable to discharge the citizenship obligations of full employment, older people were consistently accorded the least favourable treatment throughout the post-war period.

The independent body valorized within neo-liberal economic orthodoxy is that of an economic rather than a social actor. With self-identity sought through consumption in the late twentieth century, the labouring body has been refashioned as the hedonistic body. Transformed into a fetishized commodity, the body is defined as much in terms of ability to consume as ability to produce. The sick, the disabled and the aged are excluded by norms of youth, beauty and athleticism as ablebodiedness is made synonymous with worthiness for consumption. The reworking of the body project within New Right welfare discourse reconstitutes impairment, poor health and age as self-inflicted dependencies. Good health belongs to good citizens who avoid states of dependency by maintaining their bodies and personally insuring themselves against the risk of becoming dependent on the state. Deservingness also belongs to the informal carer who tends the dependent body in the stead of or on behalf of the state.

Sickness and old age have been reconstituted as natural curses which separate the individual from the world of the active and must be cared for in isolation as if they were shameful (Giddens, 1994). Whereas the Victorian workhouse was the visible symbol of the consequences of wilful neglect of the duty to work and improvident living, new regimes of health and social care warn the young and the fit of the dangers of neglecting bodily maintenance or of failing to insure themselves against sickness and infirmity. The body is revealed once again as an object rather than a subject, the reciprocal gift replaced by the marketized and managerialized transactions of the new mixed economy of care. Only the bodily needs of the most vulnerable are visible to the managerial gaze, the aged and infirm once again banished from the community and reinstitutionalized within the home. The exchange goods of the quasi-market are those of the institution – hoists, stairlifts, high-backed chairs, walking frames, commodes, rails, bath seats – and the touch of the strangers who penetrate the domestic space is unmediated by the economy of altruism underlying the post-war welfare state.

3 The 'Gift' of Body Organs
Gurch Randhawa

The shift away from socialized forms of welfare over the past twenty years has changed the symbolic basis on which bodily parts are exchanged. Titmuss (1973) viewed the National Health Service which had been created in the post-war period as a vehicle for institutionalizing altruistic practices, notably the voluntary 'gift' of blood to strangers represented by the transfusion service. More recent advances in medical technology have made new forms of bodily tissue donation possible, including the transplantation of whole organs. Yet the excess of demand over supply is forcing a change from the principle of voluntarism on which 'opting-in' procurement arrangements have hitherto rested to one of presumed consent and the system of 'opting-out' adopted in other countries. This chapter will examine the implications of this transition within the context of late-twentieth-century multicultural Britain.

Recent advances in medical technology have offered new hope to patients who would otherwise have had to face the prospect of death. This is especially so in the area of transplantation. Following the transplantation of the cornea in 1905, the kidney was successfully transplanted in 1954 and the heart in 1967 (UKTSSA, 1994). As well as being able to transplant other major organs such as the liver, lung and pancreas, it is also possible to replace other body parts such as heart valves, bones and muscular tissue. Following a brief review of existing transplantation procedures, this chapter will address the adequacies of the existing procurement arrangements and the implications of introducing alternative policies.

The vast majority of organs for transplant come from deceased individuals, known as cadaveric donors. However, it is possible to donate some organs while living. The kidney is the most common as it is possible to live normally with one kidney. A part of a liver, lung or pancreas may also be donated.

Transplantation has succeeded in prolonging the lives of those fortunate enough to have received a body organ. What was once a rare and risky procedure for the privileged few has now become a well-established routine treatment and a positive option for those with organ failure. Despite this life-saving development, however, there are not enough organs to meet an ever-increasing demand. Patients for whom a transplant is the only realistic option for a healthy and pro-longed life are generally dependent on a suitable organ becoming available. This usually involves waiting for another patient to die and for the relative's consent for the organ to be used for transplantation. Waiting lists continue to grow, imposing physical, emotional and financial costs on patients, relatives and the health service alike (Randhawa, 1995). We are in a relatively rare position in relation to transplantation as opposed to other areas of health care – the expertise and financial resources exist but the organs for transplant do not.

The shortage of organs for transplant in the UK is very severe, with over 6,000 people throughout the UK currently awaiting a suitable organ for transplantation (UKTSSA, 1997). According to the United Kingdom Transplant Support Service Authority (UKTSSA), a special health authority operating within the NHS, the situation will reach crisis level unless measures are taken to address this problem (UKTSSA, 1997). Organs are procured in the UK on a voluntary basis based upon the principle of altruism. Titmuss (1973) had advocated such a 'gift' system in the area of blood donation previously. However, as will be seen, due to the diminishing supply of transplant organs, the basis of a system on notions of regulated social reciprocity is under growing pressure from demands for a system based on the manage-ment of individual obligation. This transition in policy, it is supposed, will increase the number of organs procured.

VOLUNTARISM/OPTING-IN

Donor cards

To procure organs from a deceased person, the UK, along with some other countries, currently employs what might broadly be termed an 'opting-in' legal system. Other countries which operate under a similar statute are Germany, the Netherlands, Italy, Canada, Australia and New Zealand. This system relies upon voluntarism and is seen in prac-tice with the use of donor cards and the recently introduced NHS Organ Donor Register. Carrying a donor card or being on the Donor Register serves only as an indication of an individual's wishes, but organs cannot be taken from a donor without relatives' permission (Randhawa, 1995). The Human Tissue Act 1961 permits use of parts of bodies of deceased individuals for the purposes of transplantation (New *et al.*, 1994).

Patients who are normally considered for cadaveric donation are those who have suffered some form of cerebrovascular accident (brain damage) commonly as a result of a road accident. Organs can only be removed once it has been confirmed that a patient is brain-stem dead. According to the UKTSSA, this is an irreversible state which occurs when all brain activity stops. The Authority states that, whereas a ventilator can keep the blood circulating after death, and this allows organs to be used for transplantation, a patient who is brain-stem dead cannot recover (UKTSSA, 1994).

Application of brain-stem death criteria is essential to the practice of organ transplantation as it enables medical staff to declare death before the cessation of blood circulation. Transplantation depends on the fact that an individual can be declared dead while many of the organs remain alive and healthy. Most transplantable organs, including hearts, lungs, livers, and pancreases, become unusable if they are not removed before the donor's circulation stops (Hunsicker, 1991).

Once brain-stem death has been confirmed in a potential donor the medical staff may seek to establish whether the patient indicated a wish to become a donor and then request permission for organs from the relatives. If the relatives agree to donation, the local Transplant Co-ordinator is contacted. The Co-ordinator explains the procedures involved to the family and spends time counselling them. A computer database of all patients awaiting an organ transplant, maintained by the UKTSSA, is accessed by the Co-ordinator to identify suitable patients (UKTSSA, 1995).

Donated organs are matched to patients by characteristics such as tissue type, blood group, age and weight. For kidneys the most important factor is the tissue type which is more difficult to match than blood grouping. The more accurate the match the better the chances of success. When patients and their locations have been identified, the doctors at the relevant hospitals are asked to confirm acceptance of the organ. A team of specialist surgeons is called to the donor's hospital to carry out the surgery and preserve the organs for transport to the transplant hospital. The organ is transported as soon as possible and transplanted immediately (UKTSSA, 1994).

As stated previously, the carrying of a donor card or being on the donor register serves only as an indicator of an individual's wishes.

Consent from next-of-kin is still required. There remains considerable controversy, however, over the issue of who needs to give explicit consent for donation of cadaveric organs and tissues. The sense in which one's body is 'owned' by family members after death is open, potentially, to challenge in circumstances where other lives could be saved if organs are reused. This debate is fuelled by the large gap between the number of individuals waiting for organs for transplantation and the numbers that are currently retrieved from cadaveric donors. Over the last ten years (1986–1996), the waiting list for organ transplants has risen by over 50 per cent from 3937 to 6441. However, in the same period, the number of donors has risen by only ten per cent from 817 to 895 (UKTSSA, 1997). It is clear that the number of donors is inadequate to meet the number of potential recipients.

For the voluntary system to be effective, either a donor card must be found on the body of the deceased at or shortly after the time of death, or the deceased person's name must be on the Organ Donor Register. The register is aimed at providing a more efficient method of discovering whether a deceased person wanted to donate her or his organs. It can be accessed by the Transplant Co-ordinators to check potential donors.

To address the problem of lost cards, the Departments of Health and Transport arranged for all driving licences issued or renewed from March 1993 to contain a box to record the holder's willingness to donate. Additionally, since October 1994, all new driving licence application forms have recorded the applicant's willingness to donate. The names collected from these forms have then been entered onto the NHS Organ Donor Register.

As a means of raising public awareness, the indirect impact of the donor card and Register cannot be underestimated (New *et al.*, 1994). In recent years, governments have mounted national publicity campaigns to boost the uptake of donor cards and ultimately increase donation rates. There was a 42 per cent increase in the number of kidney donations in Britain in 1984, which coincided with a six-month media campaign by the Department of Health and Social Security to highlight the donor card system (Lewis and Snell, 1986). Such publicity can not only affect card carrying directly but it can also have indirect effects on donation by initiating debate and increasing awareness about the dilemmas associated with the success of transplantation, principally the shortage of organ donors (Randhawa, 1995).

Raising awareness was also the aim of the publicity campaign conducted by the Department of Health in March 1993. A television advertisement was broadcast throughout the month, urging people to discuss organ donation with their relatives. A leaflet accompanying the campaign attempted to address some of the specific concerns which are thought to cause relatives to refuse consent. However, evaluation suggested that, despite a huge increase in the demand for donor cards and publicity leaflets, the campaign failed to achieve any significant change either in attitudes to donation on the part of the general public or the extent to which the issues it raised were discussed among family members. Furthermore, no impact on donation rates was demonstrated in the following six-month period (New *et al.*, 1994).

In March 1996, the Department of Health launched a national publicity campaign encouraging people to join the Organ Donor Register. Full-page advertisements were placed in national newspapers and prime-time television advertising was also used.

Commendable as such publicity campaigns are, they appear to have done little to overcome the problem of targeting those individuals resistant to the concept of donation. Consequently, they tend to have little impact on the overall level of potential donors as any increase in support for existing schemes tends to occur amongst people already predisposed towards donation. The key problem to be addressed is how to promote card carrying or signing on the Donor Register amongst those members of the public whose relatives would otherwise have refused consent (New *et al.*, 1994).

With transplant surgery becoming an increasingly favoured treatment option there has been increased pressure from health agencies to procure a far greater number of organs. This has led to the development of further initiatives, routine enquiry and required request, which retain the principle of voluntarism.

Routine enquiry

The procedure of routine enquiry is well established in the United States. It seeks to overcome the reluctance of those health professionals who may not themselves advocate donation. It requires the professionals involved to ascertain from family members the donor status of those who have met, or are about to meet, the definition of brain death.

Eighteen states have legislated for routine enquiry. Indeed, the US Congress has made the implementation of routine enquiry arrangements a condition of payment under their health insurance schemes (Medicare and Medicaid), and they are required as a condition of certification by the Joint Commission on the Accreditation of Healthcare Organizations (New *et al.*, 1994).

Required request

Required request is also common practice in the USA and involves staff ascertaining the donor status of all patients admitted to hospital. The development of these arrangements by hospitals was encouraged by the Omnibus (Budget) Reconciliation Act 1986. As is the case for routine enquiry, this Act provides that failure on the part of hospitals to adopt required request policies will lead to the denial of Medicare and Medicaid reimbursements from the Health Care Finance Authority (New *et al.*, 1994). Twenty-six US states have adopted this type of policy.

A recent estimate in the USA suggests that whilst 200,000 persons are declared brain-dead each year, organs are only harvested from 2,000. The combined need for hearts, lungs, and kidneys, is estimated at over 50,000 (Schwartz, 1985). Would required request procedures provide a solution to the disparity between supply of and demand for organs in the UK? In an audit undertaken in 1991, it was estimated that brain-stem criteria could be applied in an approximate 2,300 cases (Gore *et al.*, 1992). If this pattern were to continue in future years required request procedure may provide a partial solution to alleviating some of the pressure from the transplant waiting lists.

In the UK required request was considered in the 1980s by the Department of Health and Social Security, but rejected in favour of a policy of better disseminated information concerning donation and an extension of the donor card system.

Although there was an initial increase over time in the number of procured organs, evaluation of routine enquiry and required request programmes has shown little, if any, increase in organ procurement rates in the USA (New *et al.*, 1994). One reason for this, it is suggested, is the lack of institutional commitment to ensuring that the required request procedures are followed (McDonald, 1990). The United States experience illustrates that simply to enact required request legislation is not enough. It is vital to have adequately trained and qualified personnel (Randhawa, 1997).

RELIGION AND CADAVERIC TRANSPLANTATION

Although the implementation of appropriate procurement arrangements is an important factor in increasing the number of organs, there is a growing literature on the importance of religion in the decision to donate organs (American Council on Transplantation, 1985; Evans and Manninen, 1988; Wakeford and Stepney, 1989; Prottas and Batten, 1989; Callender, 1989; Kyriakides *et al.*, 1993; Spina *et al.*, 1993; Carlisle, 1995). All but one of the main religions practised in the UK support organ donation in principle, although in some there are varying strands of belief, as indicated below:

Religion	*Position on organ donation*
• Buddhism	No prohibition against organ transplants (Rees, 1990).
• Christianity	Organ donation acceptable provided prior consent obtained either from donor while alive and/or the donor's next of kin after death (Scorsone, 1990).
• Hinduism	Nothing in Hindu scriptures to indicate that organs cannot be donated to alleviate the suffering of other people, although some Hindu commentators have proposed that donation only acceptable if desire to donate overtly expressed prior to death (Trivedi, 1990).
• Islam	Recent 'fatwa' (edict) from Muslim Law Council states that it is permissible to donate organs and accepts brain-stem death as an acceptable diagnosis (Carlisle, 1995).
• Jehovah's Witnesses	No prohibition against organ transplants (New *et al.*, 1994) (though receipt of blood is forbidden).
• Judaism	Varied Jewish position on donation, although according to one leading authority, Orthodox Judaism is not opposed to the removal of organs from cadavers provided prior consent obtained either from donor while alive and/or the donor's next of kin after death (Weiss, 1988).
• Rastafarians	Oppose transplantation (Andrews and McIntosh, 1992).
• Sikhism	No prohibition against organ transplants (Rees, 1990).

A number of international studies suggest that people are frequently influenced in their decision about whether or not to donate an organ by the position their religion adopts towards such issues (Callender, 1989; Kyriakides *et al.*, 1993; Spina *et al.*, 1993). Although this has not been widely researched in the UK, the author has been involved in a pilot study to examine the attitudes of a representative sample of the UK's Asian population towards organ donation and transplantation. The findings suggest that, far from acting as a barrier to donation, those respondents who were aware of the position their religion took on organ donation and transplantation were more likely to feel positively about these issues (Randhawa, 1998). This highlights the importance of disseminating relevant information through the appropriate channels.

DISCUSSION

Numerous measures have been taken in the UK to reduce the organ shortage, some of which raise serious ethical and moral concerns. Dramatic appeals for donor organs have been made by prominent politicians and celebrity figures. In 1985, Britain closely followed the case of Ben Hardwick, a young child who died after a second liver transplant paid for by an appeal on the television programme *That's Life* (Muir, 1993). A more recent case was that of four-year-old Laura Davies who required a heart and lung transplant (Ellis, 1993). A mass of publicity surrounded her fading health and she eventually received a transplant in the United States where suitable organs had become available. All the related travel and medical costs were paid for by funds raised from the public, together with a donation from King Fahd of Saudi Arabia. The problem with such high-profile media appeals is that they benefit only a tiny minority of the total number of patients on transplant waiting lists. Additionally, public appeals of this nature have very short-term goals and are directed to help an individual in need by relying upon the personalized altruism of members of the public or wealthy benefactors such as King Fahd. Within a voluntaristic framework, however, the alternative is to seek more effectively to harness the institutionalized altruism of the NHS envisaged by Titmuss (1973), by encouraging all members of the public to consider organ donation, not only for the individual in the media spotlight but for the thousands of other individuals requiring or likely to require a transplant in the future – thereby contributing to the long term health of the population.

There is widespread agreement that a dead person cannot be harmed by the removal of organs and tissues for transplantation, and consideration of the public and personal good is commonly seen to outweigh that of due respect to the dead. The major ethical issues involved in the retrieval of cadaveric organs and tissues for transplantation have centred around the relative priority of the desires of the deceased when alive and of the next of kin after death (Hunsicker, 1991; Randhawa, 1997).

Such issues only come under public scrutiny because it is widely assumed that any risks attaching to the removal of organs from a donor who is brain-dead yet whose heart is still beating are far outweighed by the benefits derived from such an intervention. The social gains of organ transplantation are substantial and frequently underestimated by the public. The overall one-year graft survival for all organs now exceeds 60 per cent, with the most common transplants having one-year graft survival of 75–90 per cent. For most organs, the five-year graft survival is in excess of 60 per cent (UKTSSA, 1997). In the absence of transplantation, candidates for heart, liver, and lung transplants would be expected to die within one year. A successful transplant in these cases is therefore equivalent to prolongation of life. Given the quality of post-operative rehabilitation, the majority of successful recipients are able to resume employment and pursue a moderately active lifestyle.

For patients with renal failure, kidney transplantation is the only alternative to life-long dialysis (Hooker, 1994a; 1994b). Dialysis involves attachment to a machine for approximately four hours, three to four times a week – a treatment which carries emotional, physical and financial costs for the patient and is expensive for the health authority to provide. So far as the patient is concerned, there is convincing evidence that transplantation leads to better quality of life and rehabilitation than dialysis (Hunsicker, 1991).

The voluntary system, in its various forms, has its drawbacks. Where next-of-kin fail to search for (or even deliberately conceal) a donor card, the wishes of the donor card holder may be frustrated. The vetoing by relatives of organ or tissue removal may frustrate an individual's desire, in life, to become a donor. The donation of body organs after death entails considerations which do not apply to gifts of bodily tissue (such as blood) or organs by living donors. The ideal of the unilateral gift celebrated by Titmuss (1973) in his study of blood donation systems takes on altogether more complex dimensions: the intentions of the donor must necessarily be retrospectively rather than contemporaneously determined; the wishes and proprietal claims of third parties – that is to say, relatives – may intrude upon the transaction; and the moment at which donation occurs will be determined,

not by the donor, but often, for example, by the medical professionals
to whom it may fall to diagnose when death has occurred.

If the voluntary system is to be maintained, measures need to be
taken to attract more voluntary donors. In addition to the proposed
use of the driving licence to boost prospective donors, professional
awareness also needs raising. For example, more sophisticated
information about the mechanics of brain-stem death might be provided in nursing and medical training. There is a need, too, for further
investigation into the reasons why potential sources of organs, such as
intensive care units, are not adequately used. Many patients who
might become donors do not reach these units as some doctors prefer
to care for the dying on the wards without embarking on positive
pressure ventilation. Whilst this is legitimate, and in line with the principle that therapy should not be directed with extrinsic interests in
mind, it carries the problem that patients who are not on ventilators
cannot be suitable donors.

It has been argued that the most important factor in determining
whether organs are made available for transplantation is the difficulty
some doctors feel in approaching relatives whose only interest (as is
theirs) is in the survival of the potential donor (Clark and Whitfield,
1981). The highly-charged emotional circumstances surrounding
death, for relatives and staff alike, are not ideal conditions under
which to make a request for organs. Yet the most important determinant of the frequency of organ donation is the willingness of
medical and nursing staff caring for potential donors to initiate this
process and to undertake the considerable extra work that this entails
(Jennett and Hessett, 1981).

Although the circumstances of the request may not be appropriate
(assuming that they ever could be), the question is whether the feelings of the next-of-kin about a dead body are to be given priority over
the life or improved health of a 'stranger'. Harris (1993) is in doubt
that the duty to save life is paramount.

> If you doubt this claim just ask whether someone would be entitled
> to cause the death of another merely because they found him
> offensive or because this other individual had otherwise damaged
> their sensibilities, or whether that individual's continued existence
> would damage their sensibilities. These would be poor justifications
> for murder or manslaughter and so they are in the context of
> cadaver donations also. For it is clear, as it is, that for want of an
> organ, an individual will die, then the failure to give those bodily

products or permit them to be given causes death as sure as shooting. (Harris, 1993: 120)

ALTERNATIVES TO VOLUNTARISM

Presumed consent/opting-out

Unfortunately, the demand for transplant organs far exceeds the supply, and the situation is getting worse. Alternative organ procurement systems such as routine enquiry, required request, and presumed consent (also known as opting-out) have been implemented in other countries. Any shift in policy would represent a change in the principles governing the exchange of body organs after death. Whereas on the one hand, opting-in relies upon the virtues of voluntarism and the notion of a 'gift' (Titmuss, 1973), presumed consent depends on affirmative action on the part of the individual to prevent their organs being used for transplantation.

The problem with legislation based on a requirement for prior permission is that the number of organs made available in this way fails to match existing demands. A more efficient and practical way of meeting the demand could be to implement an 'opting-out' system. This would allow the medical authorities to use organs from any cadaver, except where specifically vetoed in advance by the deceased.

Presumed consent is a highly controversial proposal and many countries have been reluctant to make such provision in the face of opposition from a significant proportion of the population. Attempts to enact such legislation in the UK have always failed. In February 1984, a scheme was debated in Parliament which would have enabled people to be considered as prospective donors unless an objection – or wish to 'opt-out' – was recorded. There would be no need to consult the next of kin. Strong opposition, not least in the form of letters to MPs, led to the plan being shelved. The proposal was criticized on principle as an infringement of personal liberty, although people were also concerned as to whether records would be maintained accurately (Lamb, 1990). The latest attempt to legalize 'opting-out' in 1993, the Transplantation of Human Organs Bill, failed for many of the same reasons.

Other countries such as Austria, Belgium, Finland, France, Norway, Singapore, Spain, and Switzerland have privileged the need of sick patients and introduced contracting-out arrangements. In most countries with presumed consent, though, the practice of transplant teams is not to proceed until the family has agreed to the procedure, even though this is not required by law (New *et al.*, 1994). The problem with this is that it reintroduces the issue of obtaining prior consent and determining from whom this should be obtained.

Presumed consent is defended on the grounds that it could result in a marked reduction in transplant waiting lists yet enable people to opt out on religious or moral grounds (Lamb, 1990). In Singapore, where a system of presumed consent is in operation, Muslim citizens are excluded (Soh and Lim, 1991).

Counter-arguments are that only those in higher socio-economic groups and with higher levels of education would be able to exercise autonomy in their presumption of donation, and the situation may occur where the poor and the poorly educated – because they would not be aware of their rights or might be less able procedurally to exercise them – would not have the same autonomy. We could also reach the stage where patients close to death would be looked upon solely or primarily as potential sources of organ donation (Lamb, 1990).

Routine salvaging, with presumed consent, may take place before it becomes known that an individual did not wish to become a donor, perhaps overriding deeply felt objections to post-mortem donation. In reality, none of the systems currently in operation around the world can guarantee that an individual's wishes will be respected.

Assuming widespread commitment to organ donation and public trust in the concept of brain death and its application, this system could theoretically make a dramatic impact on the shortage of donor organs. It would also require the involvement of health professionals to identify those who could be donors, and an efficient organ procurement and distribution network.

If new procurement arrangements were to be adopted in the UK they would require statutory change, raising similar problems to those which bedevilled previous awareness campaigns around donor cards.

Commercialization

Trading in organs has been reported around the world and is widespread in certain countries. In Hong Kong, there have been reports of sales of kidneys extracted from executed prisoners from China (Meek, 1992). In India, where the government's cadaveric organ procurement programme has only been recently established, the buying and selling of organs has been rife for many years. Over 70,000 patients are diagnosed each year as requiring a kidney transplant (more than 10 times the entire kidney transplant waiting list in the UK). In 1989, nearly all of the 2,000 kidney transplants carried out in India involved living donors (Meek, 1992). However, in 1994, the Transplantation of Human Organs Bill was introduced which prohibits the commercial use of organs (Nandan, 1994).

Western countries have not been immune from this practice, either. There have been reports of people paying large sums of money in order to move to the top of transplant waiting lists in the United States (Lamb, 1990). During the late 1980s in the UK, there was mass condemnation of organ selling when reports surfaced of four Turkish peasants being brought to the country to act as live kidney donors in return for payment. As a result of this, the Government introduced the Human Organ Transplants Act (1989) which made it a criminal offence to make or receive any payment for organs removed from a dead or living person intended for transplantation into another person, whether in the UK or elsewhere (New *et al.*, 1994).

It has been argued that the sale of organs is justifiable as it would increase the supply (Lamb, 1990). The practice is also defended on the grounds that individuals own their bodies and have the right to do as they wish with their own body parts. Yet even in countries that profess to promote free choice, there are laws restricting individuals' jurisdiction over their own bodies. These include prostitution, limits on abortion, controls on boxers who fail certain medical tests, health and safety regulations at work and participation in dangerous experiments (Lamb, 1990).

The arguments opposing organ trading are compelling. In the free market where profit is the key objective, the usual standards of medical screening may well not be rigorously applied (Lamb, 1990; Sells, 1990). What is more, once a market in organs is introduced, the moral basis of the transactions involved is altered: donations cease to have the characteristics of a gift. This was precisely the concern expressed by Titmuss (1973) when analysing the US commercial system of blood donation in comparison to the UK's voluntary system.

Allowing markets in organs may predispose to the 'slippery slope' down which commercialization may slide and the ultimate sacrifice whereby a person may sell all their transplantable organs, and therefore their life, in return for their family's financial well-being (Sells, 1990). Markets in organs divide society, where the donors are always poor, and the recipients always rich. There have been reports of post-operative deaths from HIV transmission at the time of

transplantation (Sells, 1990). Additionally, if one is to part with something as close to our identity as an organ, many of us would prefer to
do so out of a concern for community or altruism rather than for a
money price. This in essence was the moral position supported by
Titmuss (1973) and it remains the case that, in a very literal sense,
donating an organ or blood is giving the gift of life itself.

There is opposition, too, from medical professionals on an ethical
point. Surgeons are guided by the principle that operations should
only be performed for therapeutic reasons. A financial reward does
not represent a therapeutic indication for surgery (Kilbrandon, 1968).

Xenotransplantation

The recent proposal for the use of animal organs for transplant (xenotransplantation), recently reviewed by the Department of Health,
eliminates the issues surrounding any transition from voluntarism to
presumed consent but introduces previously unimagined ethical
dilemmas. These developments in the organ procurement arena
remain under the media spotlight and are open to increasing scrutiny
as public interest in the bounds of medical science grows, with stories
of animal cloning and, ultimately, the possibility of cloning humans.

The early 1960s saw the first breakthrough in xenotransplantation,
when a patient survived nine months with a kidney from a chim-
panzee. Five other patients who underwent the same procedure died
within days. Liver transplantation was also attempted from chim-
panzee to human but was unsuccessful. In the early 1980s a baboon
heart was transplanted into a baby girl known as 'Baby Fae'; this also
failed after 20 days (Schwartz, 1985).

The most recent development in xenotransplantation has been the
use of a pig as a 'donor'. The pig has been identified as a suitable
organ donor for humans on size and anatomical grounds. Research is
being carried out in Cambridge, England and New Jersey, USA,
where it is hoped that the strong human immunological response to
foreign tissue can be overcome with genetically altered pigs. The idea
is to 'trick' the human immunological response into thinking the pig's
heart is its own (Koechlin, 1996).

The justification for xenotransplantation is that if it is morally
defensible to use animals for food then using them as a potential
supply of organs is acceptable. Clearly, this is controversial and raises
ethical issues. The defence of xenotransplantation rests on the
assumption that the ethical issues involved in the breeding of animals

for food and those involved in the breeding of animals for organs are the same. I would argue that they are separate and should be considered on their own merits. The undertaking of one practice does not necessarily legitimize the other. The breeding of animals for food is a controversial issue in Britain which arouses strong emotions. Some would want to argue that neither practice is necessary for human health and survival, as alternatives are available in both cases (see also the contribution by Parry and Parry, Chapter 9 in this volume).

Others have argued that whilst it is generally believed to be morally acceptable to kill animals for food, this is under circumstances which offer us alternatives. No one has to eat pork to survive – indeed, there are arguably cheaper and healthier sources of food available. In the case of organ transplantation, however, particularly of hearts and livers, there are no alternatives for a significant proportion of people who would otherwise die. Under these circumstances, those who wish to deny the use of animal organs for transplantation must provide even more compelling arguments than those who would wish to deny their use for food (New *et al.*, 1994).

The UK has a multi-faith population and it is important to recognize the views of different religious groups. For some religions, certain animals are considered sacred; thus organs from these animals would be unacceptable. For example, in Hinduism the cow is sacred, whereas among Jews and Muslims the pig is considered unclean (Randhawa and Darr, 1997).

Medical hurdles, such as hyperacute rejection and the spread of new diseases in humans, also remain to be surmounted. As mentioned previously, a Cambridge research team has made progress in the former area by using genetically altered pigs but is still struggling to overcome the latter problem. The research into the transfer of diseases from one species to another is well documented. Common examples include influenza viruses. These have their origins in pigs, ducks, and chickens, which act as reservoirs for the diseases. Most worrying of all is research in Central Africa which suggests that AIDS resulted from the monkey virus being transferred into humans (Koechlin, 1996).

The financial gains from xenotransplantation, which are considerable, are as likely to influence scientists as ethical concerns. This has parallels to the dangers of commercialization discussed earlier and raises in a broader context questions about the extent to which the profit motive can be compatible with the public interest in matters of health care. Large pharmaceutical companies, such as Novartis and

Imutran in Europe and Alexion and Nextran in the United States, are investing millions of pounds into xenotransplantation research. Profits from xenotransplantation have been projected to be as high as US$5 billion in 2010 (Koechlin, 1996).

In 1996, the UK's Department of Health set up an Advisory Group on the Ethics of Xenotransplantation. Their recent findings have indicated that xenotransplantation is permissible on ethical grounds but that there are still medical concerns that need to be researched further (Advisory Group on the Ethics of Xenotransplantation, 1997). The Nuffield Council on Bioethics has also considered the issue and raised no objection (Rogers, 1996). However, as was highlighted in the case of BSE, careful scrutiny of the membership of these advisory groups is required. Some governmental advisors with business and agricultural interests had a vested stake in the treatment and eradication of BSE; thus it was unclear whose interests were actually met by their recommendations (McKie *et al.*, 1996). Those with connections to pharmaceutical companies and surgical teams potentially involved in xenotransplantation may also find it difficult to offer an impartial opinion.

Whilst xenotransplantation would undoubtedly increase the supply of organs for human use, there is an argument for delaying further work in this area. With the risk of a variety of diseases spreading into humans, coupled with the ethics of xenotransplantation, I have argued elsewhere that existing organ procurement arrangements should be reviewed in the light of programmes used elsewhere in the world (Randhawa, 1996). Titmuss (1973) did not have to consider the impact of technological advances, specifically the use of animal parts, nor the contested notion of animal rights, but throughout his analysis he emphasized the altruistic nature of donation. Certainly, for my part, I would hope that such a principle can ultimately be retained and that solutions based on donations between humans can be sustained.

CONCLUSION

At present, public policy in respect of transplantation relies on voluntarism and the need for consent in the UK, whereas in some countries there has been a transition from voluntaristic to opting-out frameworks in which the 'gift' of a body organ is made. The number of organs available for transplantation seems set to decrease. Improved road safety campaigns have already resulted in better safety equipment (e.g. car air-bags, compulsory use of crash helmets for motor cyclists, and the increasing use of safety helmets for cyclists). These measures have led to the halving of the number of deaths from road traffic accidents over the last 25 years in the UK. Medical improvements in the treatment and prevention of stroke have also had a positive effect in reducing the number of stroke deaths in the UK by over 50 per cent since 1970 (Advisory Group on the Ethics of Xenotransplantation, 1997). At the same time, the gap between the number of organs available for transplantation and the number of potential recipients grows as the prevalence of kidney failure, heart disease, and related illnesses continues to rise.

Every attempt to change the principle of voluntarism on which public policy in the UK rests has been rejected in recent years. This leads to a curious anomaly in the UK – and, indeed, in many other countries. On the one hand, a post-mortem may be ordered without the consent of the next-of-kin where this is deemed necessary to establish the cause of death, either in the interests of medical science or in the course of a criminal inquiry. On the other hand, cadaver transplants, which could save the lives or improve the health of sick individuals, cannot be ordered but require the consent of the next-of-kin. Yet a post-mortem may equally well be considered as a violation of the body of the deceased and involves also the removal, albeit sometimes only temporarily, of bodily organs.

Thus, the removal of the need for consent is not without precedent. State ownership of bodies after death for the sole purpose of harvesting them for transplantable organs would obviate the need for consent either from individuals or the next-of-kin (Harris, 1993).

The NHS Organ Donor Register, to which every Transplant Co-ordinator has instant access, presently consists of the names of donors who have given their express consent. Although it is not current practice, the accuracy of the Register could be improved by regularly requesting registered individuals, in writing, to reaffirm (or reconsider) their donor status. The introduction of the Donor Register is primarily intended to save lives, but it also offers potential efficiency savings by reducing waiting times for operations. To date, there are four million people signed up on the Donor Register and with an ongoing publicity campaign it is to be hoped that this will rise substantially.

If the Register is successful, a marked reduction in transplant waiting lists, and, specifically, in the number of patients on renal dialysis would ensue. This in the long run would be highly cost-effective, saving millions of pounds each year as the cost of a transplant is cheaper than maintaining a patient on a dialysis machine. As a general rule, the cost of a successful transplant plus one year of post-operative therapy amounts to less than the cost of one year of the cheapest form of chronic dialysis. After the first year of post-operative therapy, the costs are negligible (Conference of European Health Ministers, 1987).

The harvesting of organs for transplantation has been developed within a framework of voluntary donation. Public education campaigns around the critical shortages of organs for transplantation invariably emphasize the altruism involved in 'giving the gift of life.' Alongside this attempt at mass public involvement, there is a need for the Department of Health to develop an information strategy directed at raising awareness amongst the public and health professionals alike of the benefits of organ transplants and the need for additional donors. Information made available to health professionals about the current status of, and possible developments in, public procurement policies might form part of such a programme. After all, government action and inaction directly affect the process and outcome of medical care for potential organ donors and patients with organ failure. Additional efforts to train staff in initiating and carrying through the process of organ request may also do much to enhance the donation of vital organs (Randhawa, 1997).

Titmuss (1973) saw the welfare state in general, and the system of blood donation in particular, as removing key elements of human welfare provision from the marketplace and restoring the 'gift relationship'. This has occurred to some extent in the case of organ donation in that commercial markets for human organs are banned in Western countries, with such legislation being implemented slowly worldwide. However, what we are now seeing in many countries is the positive right to give as (advocated by Titmuss) being replaced by the case for a negative right which may be waived. The future nature of organ procurement systems remains uncertain, with the on-going scientific advances, which on the one hand enable us 'unnaturally' to prolong human life and on the other, 'unnaturally' to exploit the organs of non-human creatures, likely to have a great influence.

4 Bodies and Dualism
Alison Assiter

LIBERALISM AND THE DISEMBODIED SELF

Rights-based language is used in a number of contexts in the contemporary world – it is used in debates about informed consent in medical ethics; debates about citizenship and work; debates about abortion or euthanasia. In all of these contexts, the notion of the individual as an autonomous, responsible entity, possessing rights to life and liberty, is taken for granted. What is often forgotten is that classically, the above subject – the liberal self – is assumed to be disembodied. In this chapter, I wish to outline the classical liberal position, and then to describe and critically analyse one of the feminist responses to the perspective. The response I would like to examine is the perspective in epistemology that takes the notion of embodied women's experience as an epistemological starting point. I shall argue that this perspective remains inside the dualist outlook of the liberal view. I will then go on, in the final section of the paper, to argue that the feminist outlook described reinforces a subordinate position for women in policies on caring for others.

In classical social contract theory, the individual political subject – the subject of political and legal rights, the subject that enters into the contract, the individual of classical liberal theory, the citizen – is constructed in opposition to the private, conjugal and familial sphere. On certain versions of classical liberal theory, represented in one form, this century, by Sartre's conception of the freely choosing, autonomous self, and much earlier by Kant's 'noumenal' self, the subject becomes literally disembodied. The needy, desiring, reproducing self is something to be transcended when one operates as an ethical being, as a self that is truly autonomous and free. Some theorists in the tradition represent the body as something dirty, an inconvenient obstruction that is to be transcended if one is to function in a truly rational or truly moral fashion. Descartes (1985) is probably the most famous in this respect. He clearly sees the body as alien, as outside the self. Metaphors like a cage, a prison, a swamp are used by

63

Descartes to describe his body. Indeed, another, more famous image in Descartes compares the body to a watch. The difference between a living and a dead person is just like that between a watch that is wound up versus one that is unwound. Much earlier, in a similar vein, Plato had said this of his body:

> '[it is] a source of countless distractions by reason of the mere requirement of food ... [it is] liable also to diseases which impede us in the pursuit of truth: it fills us full of loves, lusts and fears ... . of all kinds, and useless foolery and in very truth, as men say, takes away from us the power of thinking at all. Whence come wars and fightings and factions. Whence but from the body and the lusts of the body?' (Plato, 1948, 66).

In general, Plato viewed the body with disgust. It is part of the region of the changeable; it is excluded from and in opposition to the genuine self, the soul. In his later work, Plato developed the notion of the divided soul, but bodily elements continue to be depicted as inferior. (Plato, 1965)

Continuing this just for a moment, I think that it is significant that a number of feminist writers have also been susceptible to this negative thinking about the body. Simone de Beauvoir, for example, writing as recently as 1949, has this to say about women's bodies, including her own: 'she is absorption, suction, humus, pitch and glue ... inhibiting and viscous'. De Beauvoir sometimes associates herself very much with the negative dualist reading of Descartes: 'woman is her body ... but her body is something other than herself' (de Beauvoir, 1975: 189).

On the other hand, there are, it should be said, thinkers in the tradition who write much more positively about the body – for example, Nietzsche, Deleuze, Foucault.

In so far as classical liberal theorists have seen themselves as embodied, they have necessarily possessed male bodies. Civilized society is not supposed to concern itself with reproduction, but only with production. The task that, until recently (perhaps with a few exceptions, such as the notorious society where men participate in the task of having a baby), only women are able to perform is excluded from the domain of civil society; from the domain of citizenship. Carol Pateman has argued that the third element in the trilogy of liberty, equality and fraternity is often forgotten. She argues, in *The Disorder of Women* (Pateman, 1995), that liberalism is forged through the necessary subjection of women – of women's bodies. In the social contract story, sexual or conjugal right is natural: men's dominion over women is held to follow from the respective natures of the sexes. Eve's subordination is simply the subjection that every wife owes her husband. The individuals who make the social contract are men. Women are constructed as naturally deficient in a specifically political capacity, the capacity to 'create and maintain political right' (*ibid.*: 96). Civil society is the sphere of freedom, equality, individualism, reason, contract and impartial law. This sphere is separated, in classical liberal theory, from the 'private' world – from the world of ties of love, emotion and sexual passions – the world of women, but also the world of the body. The individuals who make the contract, in so far as they are embodied, have male bodies, but these are male bodies that lack emotion, love and passion.

One of the clearest exponents of this view of women's nature is Hegel. In Hegel's discussion of Antigone in *The Philosophy of Right* (Hegel, 1973), women are excluded from political life; from ethical life; from the public community. As the defenders of family interests, women become the enemy of the public community. In *The Phenomenology of Spirit*, Hegel (1977) constructs women as destined to give birth to children, to look after them and to attend to the household. Women, he argues, never make decisions or face choices. Hegel cannot therefore explain why Antigone chooses to defy her uncle and bury her brother. Women's interests, according to Hegel, are identified with those of the family, and women are destined, by nature, to express those interests. In *The Philosophy of Right*, Hegel argues that women are destined to give birth to children; effectively there is no split between their inclinations and their choices. Men, on Hegel's analysis, are necessarily constitutively attached to the polis, to the civic community, and their duties as citizens flow from this attachment. Women, by contrast, are necessarily attached to the family; and, within the family, for Hegel, there is no scope for choice or for rational reflection on conduct. Freud, too, argues that women are deficient in the basic moral law underpinning the social contract – a sense of justice (Freud, 1932).

There are two senses, then, of disengagement with 'the body' in classical liberalism. In one sense, the individual of classical liberal theory, the individual that participates in the body politic, has a male body. As an embodied male the individual is entitled to work and to engage in any other tasks for which the possession of a body may be a requirement in the political process. In another sense, however, the individual is disembodied: human identity is constructed, on the second reading, as transcendent mind or as transcendent reason. Descartes (1985) is usually invoked as responsible here, with his explicit articulation of mind/body dualism (I think that this is only partially true of Descartes himself). This is sometimes presented as a normative ideal – the better aspects of human identity are construed as the mental; those aspects that have to do with the functioning of reason. Then, nature, on some readings of Descartes again, is constructed as mindless, as alien. Animals, on readings of Descartes, are also mindless, mechanical things. (Again, I think that this reading of Descartes downplays the extent to which he idolized machines but that, again, is another story). In many readings of classical liberal theory, though, continuing the story, nature is seen as lack, as empty, passive and without a value of its own. It is this view of nature that justifies Locke's view that property is justified where one has mixed one's labour with it (Locke, 1924). Nature has no properties; it is 'unowned', and it cannot have a sense of self-ownership.

The disembodied individual of classical liberal theory is reinforced in Christianity, and especially in the early Protestant tradition. Early Protestant reformers made nature suspect, robbing it of its previous status as a source of religious inspiration. Protestantism was connected with attacks on magic, superstition and witchcraft (see Turner, 1996). Several writers have pointed to contemporary residues of this early modern denigration of the flesh. For example, there is the contemporary middle class obsession (reinforced in policy terms) with dieting, fitness, the dangers of smoking – arguably a hangover from the early Puritan desire to control the body and to curb its desires and excesses (see, for example, Ehrenreich, 1990). (This may, on the other hand, be read as deriving from a consumerist desire to maintain an 'attractive' body; a body that is seen to be desirable to others. On this reading, as well, however, the body is checked and controlled, as it is in the Puritan tradition.) Another example, from a very different area, of the separation of 'people' from bodies is the use of parts of bodies for medical experimentation without the consent of the people whose bodies are being experimented upon. There is also the defining of gay men as the repository of AIDS: gay men become defined through a certain type of bodily condition (see Mitchell, Chapter 8 in this volume).

Certain feminists have responded to the above picture by advocating, as an alternative to the liberal framework outlined, an ethic of care that focuses upon the qualities that derive from women's role in the 'private' sphere. Rather than being separate, autonomous, free and equal beings, care theorists emphasize the relational and embedded character of a person, deriving from the classical role of women in the private sphere, and the ethical qualities of caring and nurturing that might flow from such a model. Indeed, this perspective has been presented as offering a female ethic, as opposed to a male one (Gilligan, 1982). Instead of looking at this, however, I should like to look, in this chapter, at a certain feminist response to the picture in another domain – that of the epistemology that underlies the outlook.

'BODILY' FEMINIST STANDPOINT EPISTEMOLOGY

Some feminists have urged that the solution to the silencing of women and of the body in the political process is to effect a rethinking of the epistemology that underlies the theory. They argued, firstly, that the disembodied individual of classical liberal theory was also the 'subject' of Cartesian, positivist and many other types of epistemology. It is this 'subject' that purports to be gender-neutral, that claims to be merely a 'filler' for the S in the generic knowledge claim of the form 'S knows that P'. Instead of assuming this disembodied, disembedded subject as the knowing subject, the subject of liberalism, feminists have suggested that we should take up the standpoint of women. They have suggested that there is an epistemological standpoint or an outlook on the world that is specifically a women's or a 'feminist' outlook. Some of this writing has explicitly linked such an outlook with the body. Irigaray, for example, has talked of thinking 'through the body' and of 'writing the body' (Irigaray, 1974; 1977). Feminists have argued this in a number of ways. Lorraine Code, for example, one of the important contributors to this debate, put the point thus:

> Philosophers have tended to group philosophy with science as the most gender-neutral of disciplines. But feminist critiques reveal that this alleged neutrality masks a bias in favour of institutionally stereotypical masculine values into the fabric of the discipline – its methods, norms and contents. (Code, 1991: 26)

In her path-breaking work, Sandra Harding (1987) has produced extensive research documenting some of the ways in which this has been the case. She points to evidence of sex bias in what is presented as neutral scientific inquiry in the sociological and the biological sciences. For example, she suggests that, in biology, woman the gatherer played as significant a role as man the hunter in the origin of the species. Biological studies that omit this crucial fact about evolution, therefore, may be biased in any or all of the following ways: in the research questions asked; the hypotheses generated; the methods deployed; and the kinds of evidence accepted for knowledge claims.

One might accept the argument so far, however, and yet question Code's claim that there is a specific 'woman's' epistemological outlook. How have feminists justified this further claim?

There are a number of different kinds of argument deployed by feminists to justify the view that there is a woman's outlook on knowledge. At one extreme, as Code has pointed out, feminists like Firestone and Daly have argued that men and women have necessarily different cognitive capacities, based on sharply antithetical ways of experiencing the world. Firestone wrote of a 'subjective, intuitive, introverted' female response to the world, as contrasted with an objective, logical outlook (Firestone, 1971: 175). Others have pointed, in celebratory fashion, to research into brain function that reveals 'natural' female and male cognitive differences. This same research can be used either as Phil Hogan does in his column in *The Observer* to denigrate women ('Him Indoors', weekly column in 'Life' magazine, *The Observer*) or to celebrate female ways of knowing. The outlook that privileges 'female' qualities was used by the women of Greenham Common to suggest that women are more peace-loving than men and less prone to warfare.

This type of research has been questioned, however. Ruth Bleier, for example, has argued that the biology of the brain is 'shaped by an individual's environment' (Bleier, 1986: 65). Instead of proposing that there is an outlook on the world which necessarily connects with being a woman, another group of feminists therefore have looked to contingent connections between being a woman and seeing the world in a certain way. The major candidate for such claims is women's experience. Some feminists have argued along the following lines: the 'subject' of philosophical or sociological or other knowledge claims, historically, has been male. This fact about the knowing subject means that characteristics normally associated with masculinity have influenced the sorts of research questions asked; the methods used; and the interpretation of the results. Dorothy Smith, arguing for a women's outlook in social research, suggests that the sociological methods associated with Weber – rationality – should be contrasted with 'another voice' in sociology, which is more emotional and connected to the heart (Smith, 1988). Smith, in other words, is continuing the effective association of women with the body. Rationality, certainly in the Kantian tradition, is seen to be transcendent of the emotional, embedded, particular self.

Some such feminists have drawn on the very influential work of Nancy Chodorow (1978) who argues that female mothering produces and reproduces women whose deep sense of self is relational, whilst that of men is not. Drawing on theories of childhood socialization and psychoanalytic theory, Chodorow describes the reproduction in women, over generations, of qualities associated with mothering (Chodorow, 1978). Chodorow's work has been both extensively quoted and heavily criticized. I am both sympathetic to the idea that there are common features of the experience and practice of mothering which may be reproduced in little girls, and conscious of the vastly different circumstance of any two mothers, in my own area of Haringey. My son's school contains mothers who are of South Asian origin, who attempt to provide their children with a combination of cultural experiences; mothers of Kurdish refugee children; mothers who are single parents; mothers who have Italian, Greek, Cypriot, African, and many more, origins. That group of mothers are all alike in that their children attend the same school. In other respects, though, the group is very diverse. How much more diverse, then, must be the experiences of mothers and their mothering behaviour and beliefs across continents and over centuries?

Feminists, recognizing the difficulties involved in describing 'mothering' as the uniform shared experience of women, have tended to look instead to sets of values that have traditionally been associated with 'femininity' and 'masculinity'. An interesting example of this sort of reasoning is the article by Janice Moulton on what she called the 'Adversary Paradigm'. 'Under the adversary paradigm', she wrote, 'it is assumed that the only, or at any rate, the best, way of evaluating work in philosophy is to subject it to the strongest or most extreme opposition' (Moulton, 1983, p. 153). She suggests that this model of philosophical reasoning both accepts a positive view of aggressive behaviour and is based on the perception that aggression is 'natural' and good for males and neither of these things for women. It is possible therefore, to generalize from Moulton's work and suggest that there is an epistemological outlook, derived from a non-aggressive form of reasoning that is common to all women. Sheila Ruth (Ruth, 1979) describes mainstream philosophy in its content, method and practice as male, masculine and masculinist. Instead, an alternative outlook on the world, deriving from women's experience, would emphasize emotion and connectedness.

One of the motivations for this focus on women's experience, as Jean Grimshaw points out in her widely acclaimed book (Grimshaw, 1986) is that many women experienced a sense of discrepancy between some official (and often male) definition of their identity – who they are supposed to be – and their feelings. One example she gave was women's actual experience of sex as compared with the views of 'experts' on the subject. Another important example – originally documented by Ehrenreich and English (1978) – is the domination of male 'experts' in theories of motherhood and childrearing. Yet, again, it is hard to find common experiences of women across cultures or even indeed in one area. Grimshaw pointed out, however, some of the difficulties involved in focusing in this way upon women's experience. She writes: 'One is never just a man or a woman. One is young or old, sick or healthy'. Experience, she pointed out, 'does not come neatly in segments, such that it is always possible to abstract what it is due to "being a woman" from that which is due to being married, being middle-class and so on (Grimshaw, 1986: 85). A further important point made by Grimshaw is that feminists have coined certain concepts, such as 'sexual harassment' which, she argues, perform a double function. On the one hand this term suggests a realignment of the concept of 'harassment', but it also points out that certain behaviours are intrusive and coercive. This double function, she argues, would be unintelligible on the assumption of male and female realities. Grimshaw was referring to the idea of men and women inhabiting radically different worlds, which emerged from the view of Dale Spender and others that there are 'male and female languages' (Spender, 1980). But the point applies also to the notion of male and female ways of knowing: from whose perspective would we set out to understand the double function of the term? It has to be from both perspectives.

The central difficulty feminists have found with the notion of experience is that it is very difficult to come up with some experience that is genuinely shared by all women. What would or could it be? Judith Grant has extended this point (Grant, 1993). She points out that none of the qualities usually said to be shared by all women like emotion and connectedness or lack of aggression need be specifically associated with women until feminists name them as such. If that is the position, however, the argument becomes circular: feminists suggest that there is a woman's experience, which provides the ground for a specific woman's way of knowing. Yet experience is ascribed to women on the basis of this very claim about a woman's way of knowing.

An alternative to focusing on women's experience is to suggest that there is a 'perspective' on the world which derives in some way from the fact of women's powerlessness relative to the position of men. Commonly, the approach draws on Lukascian Marxism, and an analogy is posed between the positioning of women as a group and that of the proletariat in Marxism. Bat Ami Bar On, for example, puts the view that knowledge is 'perspectival' and the perspectives of socially marginalized groups are more revealing than those of others. Bar On draws on the work of earlier feminist writers who had intimated that there was an 'intrinsic connection between the degree of oppression suffered and approximation to the truth' (Bar On, 1993). Robin Morgan, in 1971, for example, had suggested that revolution must be made by those who are the most oppressed – whom she described at the time as 'black, brown and white women' (Morgan, 1971: 84). (It is interesting that it was possible, in the western world at that time, to locate these women all in one group.) Slightly later, Ann Ferguson, in *Woman as a New Revolutionary Class in the US*, (Ferguson, 1979) following Shulamith Firestone, had argued that women form a revolutionary class. Other feminists, notably Nancy Hartstock and Sandra Harding made the connection between oppression and epistemological standpoint explicit.

A version of this kind of argument is put by Anna Yeatman, who paints a picture of a 'contestatory politics' where socially marginal subjects continually push against the walls of established subjects and established hegemonic knowledges (Yeatman, 1994).

Bar On argues, however, that there is a significant difference between the Marxian proletariat and women as a group. The pro-letariat is both socially marginal in relation to the capitalist class and in the centre stage of capitalist production. Social marginality, she argues, is a function of economic centrality. I have outlined several problematic features of the association of women with the Lukacsian proletariat, in my book *Enlightened Women* (Assiter, 1996). One of the critical points I made there is that, for Lukacs, truth is equated with knowledge of the world. This true understanding of the world, for him, will be revealed when the working class brings about social-ism, because it is only then, for him, that the ideological blinkers on knowledge will be removed. But the working class may not bring about socialism. The truth of the theory is made to rest upon a poss-ibility that may not become actual. Harding's particular version of standpoint theory is not quite parallel with Lukacsian Marxism here for she does not argue that women have access to a truth which men do not. Yet her theory, and that of other standpoint theorists, is open to the objection that women's standpoint may not reveal gaps in the dominant one: women may, and often have, wholly imbibed the dominant view. Women's experience might fit the dominant paradigm.

I am wholly in sympathy with the argument that the values, interests, beliefs, indeed the identity of the knowing subject influence the sort of research questions asked, the type of evidence that is accepted, and therefore the justification of claims to know. I accept that what Harding, following Kuhn, has labelled the context of discovery is indeed relevant in these ways. But this is entirely different from endorsing the further claim that the sex of the knower is epistemologically significant. Why is my sex so particularly important when it comes to the justification and the truth of my claims to knowledge? Why is my sex so much more significant than my professional status; my location in North London; the particular circumstances of my life; my most cherished beliefs and values, and so on? Feminists have provided Freudian or other psychoanalytic explanations for the emphasis placed on sex: sexual difference is said to be a deep-seated identification, forged, in a range of ways, into our very being, entrenched in our unconscious, in a way that the other qualities I mentioned are not. A baby is labelled male or female, and occasionally wrongly – see the case studies of Robert Stoller (Stoller, 1984) – at the moment of its birth. Sexual difference is deep-seated baggage from which it is very difficult for us to distance ourselves. Sexual difference is constantly reinforced through the different stages of socialization – in school, for example. Mixed schools in the UK used to have separate entrances. Even today, when the entrances are no longer used in this way and when many schools make an explicit attempt to break down behavioural sexual differences, the differences, nonetheless, manifest themselves very early on in all sorts of ways.

SOME REFLECTIONS

Some of the above criticisms of the epistemological approach will be familiar. As one writer has put it: the margins (the women's standpoint) is not a shared space (Griffiths, 1995). Others, in a very familiar criticism, have criticized the 'essentialism' of the outlook. It is supposed to propose an essential nature of women, that purports to render change impossible. Essence, however, can be understood in a range of ways: from the Aristotelian unchanging substance that persists through change through to a nominal essence account where in essence is the set of qualities by means of which we name the thing what it is. On the latter view, essence is not unchanging.

I see nothing wrong in supposing that there is a Lockean 'real essence' to women – a causal substrate, shared by all women, which is responsible for the set of 'secondary' properties on the basis of which we name women as such. The problem with some individuals whose sex is indeterminate is that they were sometimes mistakenly assigned to the female sex. My argument against certain forms of 'essentialist' feminism, then, is firstly, that I think that the above feminists are actually wrong in their view of what the essence is – it cannot be the experience of mothering, because many women do not mother; nor should it be, except in a historically relative sense, a set of qualities that flow from women's marginal status, because such qualities are essential only in societies and historical periods where woman is marginal. Women, anyway, are never marginal in the same ways. The real essence will actually consist in the set of biological properties that are sufficient for categorizing someone as female.

The other component of the argument, though, concerns the conclusions that are drawn from the idea of essence. I have been suggesting, here, that there are no grounds for assuming that an epistemological outlook flows from one's identity as a woman. Further, the supposition that there is such an outlook confirms the position of women in the philosophical imaginary as embodied, and correspondingly men as disembodied. This is disadvantageous both for women and men.

It seems to me, then, that the attempt to found an epistemology on sexual difference has not been helpful for feminists. It has rested, I believe, on a form of Cartesian dualism. Descartes, on common readings, artificially separated the 'I' – the rational, thinking, believing 'subject' – from the body – the sensual, emotional 'thing'. Feminist dualist epistemologists separate the 'I' of the history of epistemology – the rational, autonomous, 'universal' mind – from the embodied, emotional, sensuous female. In attempts to search for universal characteristics shared by these 'female' or feminist subjects, feminist epistemologists have retreated, inevitably to these Cartesian claims. I say 'inevitably' because it is inevitable, when you are attempting to find commonalities where it is in fact very difficult to do so – where, dare I say, none may exist – that you will revert to a cultural heritage which is, in many respects, dualist in the Cartesian sense. The woman's way of knowing becomes the way of knowing of embodied females, or of females identified as bodies, whilst there remains a man's way of knowing which will continue to be as it is expressed in the liberal tradition. Many of the candidates identified in the above examples of shared features or experiences of women are experiences of them largely as 'disminded', to coin a parallel expression to that of disembodied. None of the types of experience or the common features mentioned in the literature involve the use of any higher cognitive faculty. A non dualist approach will be either unitary – there is one and only one type of knowing subject – or it will be plural: there is a diversity and range of types of knowing subject.

I would argue, indeed, that there are other dualisms that parallel the liberal mind/body; male/female dualism. Any conceptualization that characterizes a certain group as 'other' in relation to a mainstream grouping is reinforcing this framework. One example of this is the expression 'minority groupings' that Avtah Brah coins in her book: *Cartographies of Diaspora: Contesting Identities* (Brah, 1997). She refers to a conference that took place at the University of California, Berkeley, in 1986. The aim of the conference was to sanction the concept of 'minority discourse', and the project was conceived of as one of 'marginalizing the centre' and 'displacing the core/periphery model'. She signals the importance of this event and of the political discourse it suggests and she emphasizes that many of the contributors to the conference suggested that a minority location 'is not a question of essence but a question of position, subject position that in the final analysis can be defined only in political terms'. In other words, she is sympathetic to the political project, as indeed, am I to the intention behind the early feminist examples I have discussed. However, she says 'I am less than convinced about the use of the term "minority" discourse' (Brah, 1997: 188). Her argument is that the there is a tendency for the term 'minority' to be used to refer to racialized or ethnicized groupings, and it can be used as an alibi for pathologized representations of these groupings.

Whenever we employ the 'marginal' or the 'lesser' expression in a pair of binary opposites in a political or value laden context, then, we are opening ourselves to that grouping being presented in the terms in which women and bodies in general have been depicted in classical liberal theory. I do not want to deny that it is possible to turn a term on its head, as the Black Power movement did in the USA, and as the gay and lesbian movement has done in the Western world. However, it is not insignificant, given the liberal history that I have outlined above, that the negative stereotypes of black people, of gays and lesbians, of women, of animals, relate to sexualized and bodily image. The image of the black man as oversexualized; that of the gay man as the repository of AIDS; each relates to bodily image. It is, moreover, a bodily image that somehow suggests that the person is purely a body; that he has no higher mental abilities.

In her recent book *Bodies that Matter* Judith Butler (Butler, 1993) has reached a similar conclusion. She writes that binaries such as male/female, mind/body and form/matter form part of the 'phallogo-centric' symbolic that produces the latter constituent of the pair as the former's 'outside' – its 'other'. She suggests that it is the 'cultural symbolic' that assumes such binaries that brings about the exclusion of femininity and the female from metaphysics and from the symbolic domain itself. She symbolically identifies woman/'matter'/the body with the Derridean 'supplement' – the excess that cannot be symbolized, or the Wittgensteinean 'that of which we cannot speak'. I concur with some of her characterization of the problem, but I would very much demur from Butler's conclusion that woman cannot be identified at all – that there is no such thing as women.

TOWARDS A SOLUTION

In the end, a possible solution to the problem I have outlined, I suggest, involves the development of an alternative philosophical imaginary to the dualist perspective – one that is neither liberal nor attempts to turn around some negatively defined 'other' and valorize that 'other'. The dualist thinking outlined stems from a logic and metaphysics of 'A' and 'not A', where the 'not A' is invariably characterized by virtue of its not being 'A', as with 'man'/'woman' – i.e. 'not man'. An alternative logic and metaphysic would emphasize the idea of 'becoming' as fundamental. Rather than identities being fixed and determinate, with clear boundaries, rather identity would be fluid, with the capacity for change and development. Such a metaphysic would allow for identities that contain others within them, and for a more fluid boundary between male and female.

Some people have suggested turning to Spinoza for an alternative model of identity to that of Descartes (see, for example, Moira Gatens, 1996). Spinoza writes that there is only one substance, which is single and indivisible; body and mind become expressions of the attributes of substance. We might also turn, in Brah's words again, to a 'multi-axial performative conception of power'. This would allow that a grouping that is constructed as a minority in one context may be in a majority in another. It would also allow for the extension of identity. Butler, for example, has suggested that people should try out new sexualities in a 'game of masks' (Butler, 1993).

Another dimension of the solution may be to do what I have argued elsewhere, and separate out the determination of identity from the values that are significant. The epistemological outlook I have, for example, and the values that I uphold, may have nothing to do with my identity as a woman. Further, it is important to remember that each one of us, in so far as we are human beings, is an embodied agent and a minded body – there are points of commonality between men and women; between gays and heterosexuals; between majority and minority groupings. The most significant point of commonality, I would suggest, is that all of us are human beings with certain basic bodily needs. Some of those needs are not being met for significant numbers of people in the world. (I have developed an argument for the existence of objective basic needs in Assiter, 1990; but see also Doyal and Gough, 1991).

DUALISM AND CARE

I should like to argue, in the remainder of this chapter, that this feminist epistemological outlook actually reinforces stereotypical and negative norms of what is acceptable for women in policy terms. The specific area that I shall look at, necessarily in cursory fashion, is community care. Feminist epistemologists, as we have seen, laudably attempted to transcend the individualizing and implicitly masculine perspective of early liberal political theory and epistemology. I will argue, however, that their attempt did not succeed.

Writers and researchers on the subject of community care have suggested that the development of policies in Britain on the subject dates from the 1950s (Finch, 1990). The sorts of argument provided for the policy framework turned on the need for 'clients' of care services to live in circumstances as much like those of 'normal' life as possible. Large-scale institutions would be replaced by smaller localized forms of care. The motivation for such policies was double-edged – it was partly financial, as the costs of institutional care were high (see Walker, 1982) – but it was also 'humanitarian'. In the 1970s (Finch, 1990) care 'in' the community began to be replaced by care 'by' the community: policies emphasized that care is the responsibility of 'everyone' in the community – voluntary organizations, friends and relatives (Walker, 1982; Parker, 1985).

In its original form, community care had envisaged 'a significant role for public services in maintaining highly dependent people outside large institutions' (Baldwin and Twigg 1991: 118). However, as the years of Conservative government in Britain rolled by, this commitment metamorphosed into an emphasis on the providing of care 'by the community'. Feminist critics argued that this form of care usually meant primarily family care (Parker, 1985) and this, in turn, invariably entailed care by women (Ungerson, 1987; Finch and Groves, 1983). There was little or no financial or practical forms of support for such women (Finch and Groves, 1980).

Drawing on the small-scale piece of research by Claire Ungerson in the early 1980s (Ungerson, 1987), I will argue in the next section of the chapter that the language used by those providing care reflects that of a number of the types of justification given, in the previous section, for a woman's epistemological outlook on the world. Ungerson interviewed a small number (nineteen in all) of carers from the Canterbury area. She argues that the history of each individual is significant in the conceptualization each one gives of the process of caring and in their respective approaches to the enactment of the process. I should like to discuss two of the 'attitudes' to approaches to care shown by some of the women (of the nineteen, fifteen were women) in the sample. The most obvious is the 'mothering' model, demonstrated clearly by one woman Ungerson identifies as Mrs Mitchell, who cares for her husband. Ungerson quotes Mrs Mitchell: 'we had a very stormy marriage, but now I love looking after him. Now I've got another baby; it's the same thing really. I take a long time over his toilet. I take great pleasure in doing all these things for him' (*ibid.*: 114). Another woman found it difficult to construct a conception of the caring role for herself; she had hated looking after her babies; she had found 'the nappy business ..... revolting' (*ibid.*: 115). These women had, in very different ways, internalized the Chodorow model of being a woman. One found the adoption of the maternal role in the caring relationship easy, whilst the other had difficulty taking it on. Neither had any difficulty, seeing it as a relevant and pertinent model for the caring relationship. The model of care that each had internalized suggested that the identity of each of the carers (each in her very different way) was partially but significantly constructed, as Chodorow had argued, through the model of motherhood. Another writer on community care, Graham (1983), suggested that women's experience of caring involves both labour and love. The most readily available model here, for many women, is that of mothering. It is certainly difficult to generalize from the very small sample of women researched by Ungerson. However, there is a conceptual point at issue, here, as well as the empirical one. It is not surprising that the feminist epistemologists, if they were looking for commonalities amongst the experience of women, should have drawn on the mothering model. It is clearly not the case that all women are mothers, and it is even more clearly not true that women take on the mothering role all their lives. However, whilst the maternal model need not be the one deployed either by the feminist epistemologists or by the female carers of adults, it is one that is readily available, from media images, norms, common ways of thinking. This is true even if the model is not, for particular women, derived from direct experience.

Those feminist epistemologists, in other words, who draw on Chodorow's work to suggest that it provides an outlook on the world that is preferable to that of the individualist, purportedly gender-neutral, yet effectively masculine model, are reinforcing the very gender stereotype that condemns women to a role that lies outside the 'public' domain and outside certain constructions of citizenship. They are reinforcing the idea that the primary role for women lies in the private, family arena, acting as a mother.

The feminist epistemologists who drew on Chodorow were not, of course, suggesting that there is one epistemological outlook on the world that derives from women's 'mothering' role, and another 'superior' perspective that reflects the public world of paid work. On the contrary, the suggestion is that the view that stems from women's mothering role should become the norm for all: that if everyone were to adopt it, then it would reveal gaps, partialities in the classical liberal view. This was certainly the intention. Yet the perspective effectively draws – inevitably, I have suggested – on the very area of women's experience that is precisely that of the classical liberal view, but in inverted form. Instead of challenging the public/private split, the feminist epistemologists have embraced it, but embraced its underside. This, however, does nothing for those feminists who are attempting to challenge the split and nothing for those feminist policy analysts and activists who argue for an extension of the domain of citizenship, and of welfare policies, into the activities traditionally located in the 'private' sphere.

There are some in the Ungerson sample whose perspective on care fails, on the surface, to fit onto any of the versions of the epistemological perspective outlined above. Whilst some of the men, for example, justified what they were doing in terms of 'love', several of the women, by contrast, suggested that they were only able to perform the task – of caring for a husband or a parent – if they cut themselves off from their feelings. Instead they described their role in normative terms: it was their 'duty'. They saw themselves as carrying out the role out of 'obligation', and were only able to do it if they suppressed their love for the person for whom they were caring. On the surface, this looks like disconfirmation of the view that there is an analogy between the language of caring and the women's epistemological outlook. Yet, on closer inspection, we can see that it could be argued to involve an internalization of the perspective that women are socially marginal – that it is woman's role, once again, to be immersed in the private sphere, carrying out some sort of caring function. This marginality required them to take on the role; it gave them an identity, from which an outlook on the world emerged. Some of the female carers in the sample gave up paid work in order to carry out their caring role.

The feminist epistemologists who argue for a female 'standpoint' or outlook on the world, then, are effectively contributing to the confining of women to the private domestic realm, and to the view that caring in the community should be seen to be a woman's function.

But there is another dimension to the argument. Jenny Morris has criticized the research of Ungerson on the ground that it excludes the 'cared for' from its parameters. Ungerson wrote: 'my interest in carers and the work that they do arises out of my own biography. The fact that my mother was a carer' (Ungerson 1987: 1). Morris counters: 'Lois Keith, a disabled feminist, commented on Ungerson's inability to see herself as potentially a person who needs physical care' (Morris, 1991: 155). Here we have another example of a dualism that excludes, by negative definition, a certain grouping. The person cared for becomes the 'body' that has to be looked after in the caring relationship. But the feminist epistemologists who emphasize the shared bodily experience of women are surely doing nothing to overcome this. If, as I have suggested, on the perspective, women become effectively 'disminded', are the feminist epistemologists not playing into the hands of those who would identify the 'cared for' in terms of their bodily needs, rather than as people with desires, wishes of their own?

I believe that the agenda of the present government in Britain resonates with the earlier perspective on community care. Tony Blair and New Labour have embraced some of the assumptions of communitarianism. In an article in the journal *Prospect*, Tony Blair says:

'we need to fashion a new social order to meet the anxiety and insecurity people feel about the breakdown of traditional norms and institutions, and the fragmentation of families and communities' (Blair, 1996: 11). Communitarianism, as Beatrix Campbell has put it, 'has prospered handsomely in Britain under the patronage of the new boys in the Labour leadership' (Campbell, 1996: 48). Communitarianism is viewed by Blair and New Labour in the UK, and by several similarly placed individuals in the USA, as the solution to the moral disintegration that they see to be manifest in the contemporary world.

Communitarians argue that political thinking involves interpreting shared understandings bearing upon the political life of a community. This is in contrast to the liberal view that there are universal principles based upon an abstract consideration of an individual's needs and wants. Communities, for the communitarian, can be communities of place, of memory, or they can be grounded in 'psychological sharings' like, for example, friendship. Communities, for the communitarian, provide a narrative through which we live our lives: our identities are formed through them, and we find our value systems embedded in them. The liberal individual – the abstract person – is, it is argued, too thin a notion on which to pin any real conception of an individual life, it is too fragile to provide a conception of a real person making real choices in real situations. Communitarians are critical of the 'abstract individualism' of liberalism, which ignores the family altogether. Instead, they emphasize the importance of individuals being members of communities, for their sense of themselves, and for the values they see to be important. Individuals are indeed embodied creatures for the communitarian.

Communities range over such things as the family, the locality, the nation and, fundamentally for New Labour, the workplace. Work is one 'positive' community that is supposed to provide a person with a role, an identity and a set of values. Work, however, once again, is seen to be wholly antithetical to what goes on in the classical 'private' sphere. Individuals are supposed to be gradually helped out of the 'dependency' of the private realm into the bright light of the autonomy of the workplace. Despite their commitment to communities, and their admission of the importance of the role of the family, communitarians, and New Labour in the UK, are reinforcing the antithesis between the public and the private. Therefore, although they purport to escape the dualism of the earlier perspective, in fact they reinforce it by locating the divide between 'civic' activities and the family exactly where it has always been located. Caring, archetypically, in the sense of caring for a child is not seen to be work. This resonates with the earlier, and ongoing, perspective that care 'in' the community is good, whilst care in 'institutions' is bad. It further resonates with the dualism of the epistemological perspective and with the implicit downplaying, once again, of the body, which is identified symbolically with 'woman' and 'feminine' activities.

Furthermore, whilst the communitarian accepts the existence of communities, he or she plays down the conflicts within each community, and specifically, as one dimension of this, of the differential role played by women and men within them. Communitarianism idealizes and homogenizes each community. The model of community articulated by Blair and others may be different in intention, but it resonates with that described in the early 1980s by Elizabeth Wilson, in the following terms: 'the "community" is an ideological portmanteau word for a reactionary, conservative ideology that oppresses women by silently confining them to the private sphere without as much as ever mentioning them' (Wilson, 1982: 55). The 'welfare to work' programme effectively silences carers; it removes them from the public domain and from the rights that flow from citizenship. It identifies women, once again, with the 'bodily' dimension in the mind/body polarity.

Mothering, typically, in the welfare-to-work programme, is not seen to be work. The feminist epistemologists, whilst their intentions are radically different from those of New Labour and of similar programmes elsewhere, effectively lend support to such programmes. They do so through homogenizing women and through emphasizing 'feminine' qualities that traditionally have been undervalued. The feminist epistemologists, policies advocating care in the community and New Labour each reinforce traditional liberal assumptions about women lying 'outside' the domain of citizenship, of rights and autonomy.

An alternative policy on caring might be, as Finch argued, promoting different models for the care of dependent people, and providing a range of residential facilities. However, this has to be pluralist in focus, and is not brought about by policies that focus on work to the detriment of caring responsibilities and by failing to recognize the work that is involved in caring. It must, furthermore, contrary to Finch's own suggestion, allow that there is a choice, for both carer and cared for, about the type of care, and about where the caring takes place. Sometimes the family might be the appropriate place for it. All of us, to different degrees, need to be cared for. For those whose needs are greater than those of the majority, to be denied the right to choose who carries it out (in a reciprocal fashion), and where it is done, is a very great infringement of their rights and autonomy and of their identity as a person.

CONCLUSION

I have argued, in this chapter, that feminist epistemologists who emphasize qualities shared by all women reinforce traditional liberal assumptions about women as 'other', as 'disminded' bodily creatures. Thus, although they escape the picture of humans as disembodied that characterizes much liberal theory, they remain, I have argued, within liberal premises by valorizing the qualities traditionally left out of the picture, rather than through revising the dualist assumptions of traditional liberalism. The work of these feminist epistemologists, I have argued, resonates with two recent policies on care: each policy gives the responsibility for caring to women. I have suggested, although this has not been argued in detail, that an alternative outlook might involve a different set of metaphysical and logical assumptions. Such a metaphysic might appear to be far removed from policies on care; yet it is surely testimony to the power of the dualist ontology that it was difficult for feminist epistemologists to think outside its frame of reference. One has only to think how recent is the dualist division of individuals into heterosexual types and homosexuals, to recognize that dualisms of this kind are not facts of nature, and that it may require philosophical thinking, at a level of abstraction that challenges the basic premises of the debate, to escape the 'imaginary' that informs so much present policy making.

5 Bodily Metaphors and Welfare Regimes

Hartley Dean

Discussions of welfare policy and social justice lend themselves to the use of bodily metaphors. There is a compelling 'organic analogy' (Turner, 1991: 9) that is often drawn between the human body as an organic system and a society which sustains itself through systematic welfare provision. Social policy has in the past been defined as the manifestation 'of society's will to survive as an organic whole' (Titmuss, 1963: 39) or, with a slightly different emphasis, as 'that which is centred on institutions that create integration and discourage alienation' (Boulding, 1967: 7). The contemporary concern of European social policy with combating 'social exclusion' (e.g. Commission of the European Communities, 1993) represents in many ways a new Durkheimian preoccupation with functionalist notions of integration and solidarity (Levitas, 1996) which are implicitly predicated on notions of social wholeness and the body social.

A corollary of the organic analogy is the medical metaphor: the humane objectives of social well-being or integration entail, more than the treatment of individual symptoms, but healing for the causes of social ills. The holistic approach which characterized the development of British social policy both during the earliest debates about its future (e.g. Webb and Webb, 1909) and at its height in the 1960s (e.g. Seebohm, 1968) was one which emphasized the systematic prevention, treatment and relief of social problems. William Beveridge, architect of the British post-war welfare settlement, had compared his scientific approach to state intervention to that of a surgeon whose knowledge is directed to the growth, functioning and development of the complex human organism and whose skills lay in addressing the ills suffered by that organism (see Silburn, 1995: 85). It might also be argued that, just as surgeons have tended in the modern era increasingly to specialize in the treatment of a single area of the body and have often been concerned with the removal, modification or replacement of specific organs rather than with the functioning of the body as a whole, in time

83

policy intervention in the field of welfare became similarly specialized and lacking in co-ordination or breadth of vision.

A variety of politically, religiously and critically informed conceptions of social welfare and social justice call – more or less explicitly – upon bodily metaphors as a means to defend the functionality of solidaristic or altruistic practices. Anthropologists, such as Mary Douglas (1978), have argued that the human body furnishes systems of 'natural symbols' through which to conceptualize social realities. Although she does not extend her analysis to consider different kinds of welfare system, Douglas has sought to distinguish between different systems of natural symbols and I shall return to discuss her taxonomy later in this chapter. However, in one of these systems, she notes, 'the favourite metaphors of statecraft will harp upon the flow of blood in the arteries, sustenance and restoration of strength' (*ibid.*: 16). I should like briefly to cite three striking examples of this; particular instances in which blood and the body's circulatory system have been used to discuss the way in which life chances flow within the body of humanity.

The first example is provided by the Fabian academic, Richard Titmuss, who in his celebrated study of blood transfusion services (1973), drew upon the deep symbolism of voluntary blood donation to develop a wider discussion about altruism, welfare and the 'right to give'. Although industrial capitalism extinguished the gift-exchanges which had characterized earlier community based societies, the development of the welfare state reflected the renaissance of the theme of the gift. In a complex and anomic society, according to Titmuss, social policy can achieve a unity between the needs of strangers and our personal needs for identity through participation; a means to satisfy certain 'ultra obligations' which are human, not contractual in nature.

The second example, which I have discussed elsewhere (Dean and Khan, 1997), relates to the Islamic principle of *Zakat*; a central pillar of Islamic faith propounded by sixth-century Quranic authority and one which, Muslims would say, requires no renaissance. *Zakat* is the religious duty owed by Muslims to give a proportion of their wealth for the benefit of more needy members of the Muslim community. *Zakat* is an unconditional act of faith, not a circumscribed legal obligation, and it constitutes precisely the kind of 'ultra-obligation' of which Titmuss has spoken. Muslims often invoke a metaphor to help conceptualize *Zakat*, likening it to a self-healing process which taps the parts of the body where the blood is congested and transfers it to those parts which are weak or anaemic (Hussain, 1947: 137): *Zakat* ensures the health of the Muslim community by ensuring the circulation of wealth and preventing hoarding, exploitation and social conflict.

In spite of its powerful sense of social justice, Islam is in other ways inimical to Western notions of human rights, and the third example upon which I shall call is a critical analysis offered by Michael Ignatieff (1994), in which he dismisses Islam for failing, in his estimation, to reconcile its appeal to solidarity with the need for individual human freedom. Yet Ignatieff also attacks the failures of modern welfare citizenship and the overweening authority of the very mechanisms which Titmuss had celebrated. The language in which he does so employs the same metaphor of blood circulation: he laments the impersonal nature of our social belonging and the fact that 'the moral relations which exist between my income and the needs of strangers at my door pass through the arteries of the state' (*ibid.*: 141).

These three commentaries on social welfare, though mutually opposed, have recourse to the same bodily metaphor and share certain moral assumptions. The purpose of this chapter is to explore the possibility that different approaches to welfare and social policy, supported by other moral assumptions, may correspond to different kinds of bodily metaphor. In so doing, I hope to lay the foundations for a more extended kind of taxonomy than that proposed by Douglas. First, however, I shall explore the philosophical and religious roots of bodily metaphors, and then their relevance to competing political projects and different kinds of welfare regime.

PHILOSOPHICAL AND RELIGIOUS ROOTS

In this section, I shall seek principally to define and briefly to discuss four philosophically or religiously inspired traditions: conservative, puritanical, utilitarian and moral-universalist.

From Plato to the Enlightenment

Probably the oldest application of a bodily metaphor to questions of statecraft was furnished some two and a half thousand years ago by Plato, who contended that good governance requires, not democracy, but rational rule: the 'body politic' should consist, like the human body, of three parts. According to Plato (1974), the body is composed of the head, which is the seat of reason and should demonstrate wisdom;

the chest, which is the source of will and should display courage; and the abdomen, which is the seat of appetite and must be subject to temperance. The ideal state should correspondingly consist of three classes or castes: wise rulers, courageous warriors and obedient labourers.

The legacy of Plato may be detected, on the one hand in the link (through Hellenism and mysticism) with religions such as Hinduism, Buddhism and Confuscianism, and on the other with conservative strands of Christian theology. The synthesis between neo-Platonism and Christianity in the third century has been accredited to St. Augustine. Augustine's anti-democratic belief in predetermined statuses and his vision of ecclesiastical power over the Christian believer (Held, 1987: ch.2) had elements in common with Plato's vision of the political power of the philosopher king over the variously classified members of the Athenian state. Although the body of Christ was the original metaphor for the Church, in the centuries which followed the focus of this essentially Platonic metaphor became in a sense inverted: rather than the rational outer harmony of the social body assuring the good order of its individual members, the inner spiritual harmony of individual members was the guarantee of good order in the social body. The actual body of the believer became the object of ascetic regulation as the means for managing the individual inner spirit (Turner, 1983). Even before the development of administrative state power, according to Foucault (1981), such religious practices as the confession and absolution of the sins of the flesh represented an emergent technology of social discipline.

Parallel to Plato's rationalism there has been another ancient philosophical tradition, namely Aristotelian empiricism. Empiricism, ostensibly, has less need for the rationalist device of the metaphor, since it seeks to depend for knowledge directly upon the body's own senses. However, it is through different modes of reconciliation between rationalist and empiricist world views that different meanings have attached to the human body. The Renaissance in Europe in the fourteenth and fifteenth centuries initiated a separation between science and secular administration on the one hand and religion and the church on the other. It ushered in both a new secular individualism and a new religiosity. The latter culminated in the Protestant Reformation; the former, ultimately, in the Enlightenment.

Much has been made of the relationship between religion (especially Protestantism) and the development of capitalism (Weber, 1904;

Tawney, 1926). Certainly, the Judaeo-Christian tradition furnished a basis, first, for the ideological individualism which characterizes capitalism (MacPherson, 1962); and secondly for what Marx (1845) regarded as the self-alienation of the members of civil society from their own 'social humanity'. The extreme of these tendencies was epitomized by such Reformation figures as Luther and Calvin, whose theology was not merely puritanical but essentially anti-humanist. The philosophy which is alleged to have driven the great entrepreneurs of early capitalism was one which reviled the human body while refusing to countenance a social body.

It must be remembered, however, that the Protestant Reformation did not extinguish either absolutism or Catholicism in Western Europe. It has been argued that the emergence of baroque culture in the early seventeenth century signified 'an attempt to win the hearts and imaginations of the people in the interests of a hierarchical and authoritarian power bloc ..... or, more exactly, to defend the old order against individualism' (Turner, 1991: 27). In stark contrast to the repressive drabness of puritan culture, baroque brought an array of sensual, even erotic, imagery to church art and public architecture. Through the 'culture of the spectacle' (*ibid.*: 28), the baroque elites sought to refine feudal disciplinary techniques (cf. Foucault, 1977) and sustain conservative ideological traditions. Though the life and pleasures of the body were celebrated, it remained spectacularly vulnerable, not only to death, but to pain and pollution.

From the Enlightenment to the welfare state

Of the new and radical philosophical traditions to emerge in the seventeenth and eighteenth centuries – before, during and after the period of the Enlightenment – it is important for my purposes to distinguish the tradition associated with Descartes from that associated with Kant (for an introduction to the essential elements of both traditions see Scruton, 1995, or, perhaps, Gaarder, 1996). It is to Descartes (1985; and see discussion in Assiter, Chapter 4 of this volume) that we customarily attribute the tradition of 'dualism': the idea that body and mind are in their essence distinctively different and separable. Though the mind stood above the 'base' impulses of the body, the human body itself he regarded as a highly complex machine or automaton. Within the Cartesian tradition, the appropriate metaphor for the social whole is characteristically mechanistic (or, more recently perhaps, cybernetic) rather than organic.

Descartes, though a rationalist, was to be an important influence on empiricist and liberal thinking in the seventeenth and eighteenth centuries and there is, arguably, a particular correspondence between the mechanistic model of the human body and the classic utilitarianism which would later inform the middle-class social reformers of the nineteenth century. Utilitarianism represented a subversion of classical liberalism, since it sought to subordinate the sovereign individual as if s/he were a perfectable mechanical part. Bentham, for example, was not only concerned to devise methods of social administration calculated to achieve the greatest good for the greatest number, but he regarded society as no more and no less than the sum of its components. In a passage redolent of Margaret Thatcher's (1988) celebrated remark two hundred years later – 'There is no such thing as society' – Bentham wrote 'The community is a fictitious body, composed of the individual persons who are considered as constituting as it were its members' (1789 – cited in Spicker, 1995: 19).

A rather different synthesis between rationalism and empiricism was provided by Kant (1959). He subscribed, like Descartes, to the idea that human beings are 'dual creatures', possessing both material bodies and reasoning minds. His concern, however, was that reason can become a prisoner of the causal relations to which the natural world subjects our bodies unless it has regard to an inner moral law. Free will depends on moral choices which transcend self-interest; it depends on the voluntary observance of the categorical imperative that humanity, whether in one's own person or in the person of any other, is an end in itself and not only a means. The notion of a universal moral law has provided a central justification for conceptions of social justice and social democracy in the twentieth century.

It is important to emphasize that Kantian thinking is not the only source of moral–universalism. Not only, as we have seen, does Islam provide a very much older example of a moral-universalist premise, but the Marxian concept of social humanity (though it may eschew such fetishized bourgeois categories as 'justice' or 'equity' – see Pashukanis, 1978) has provided an alternative source of moral–universalist political discourse. In practice, nonetheless, the moral discourses of the social liberals, social democrats and even Fabians who have championed universal welfare owe more to Kantian premises than to Marx. Though moral–universalist discourses do not necessarily have recourse to bodily metaphors (as we shall later see), the point for the purposes of this chapter is that they do lend themselves especially to the more elaborate and explicit kinds of organic bodily metaphor which I have already discussed.

COMPETING POLITICAL PROJECTS

In this section I shall discuss the political movements which in varying degrees equate with the philosophical traditions identified above. First, however, it is necessary to examine the way in which the body enters politics.

Politics and the body

For Foucault, the body has been central to the exercise of power. In antiquity, it is supposed, the father of the family had power of life and death over children and slaves; in the middle ages the sovereign retained the power of life and death over his subjects for the purposes of defending his own person and authority; in the modern era, according to Foucault, 'the ancient right to *take* life or *let* live was replaced by a power to *foster* life or *disallow* it' (1981: 138). From around the seventeenth century onwards the modern political state has been concerned, with ever-increasing sophistication, with the *administration* of life and the body. However, there have been two forms of power over bodies. The first is concerned with the body of the individual, its capabilities, its usefulness and its docility: this form of power is concerned with the refinement of disciplinary procedures and techniques, and with what Foucault calls 'the anatomo-politics of the human body' (*ibid.*: 139). The second is concerned with populations of bodies and their propensity for propogation, mortality and morbidity: this form of power is concerned with regulatory controls and a 'bio-politics of the population'.

The substance of social policy is very much dedicated to 'anatomo-politics', but the form and context of welfare intervention has been determined by movements in the dimension of 'bio-politics'. Drawing both on Foucault and Donzelot (1980) I have argued elsewhere (Dean, 1991) that the development of the welfare state in Britain is intelligible in relation to the history of three intersecting discourses. Although I wish now to reconsider that analysis, the three discourses I then identified were:

1. paternalistic/humanitarian/pro-populationist discourse;
2. repressive/'Malthusian'/anti-populationist discourse;
3. utilitarian/philanthropic/'self-help' discourse.

Pro-populationist discourse has been evident in such essentially conservative measures as the development in the eighteenth century of the Speenhamland system of relief, which supplemented the wages of labourers in proportion to the size of their families, but also in the introduction of pro-natalist family allowances in 1945. Anti-populationist discourse has been evident in the introduction of puritanical workhouse regimes in the nineteenth century and the punitive work-testing of social security benefits throughout the twentieth century. The third of the discourses is that which has been evident in the development of the detailed case management techniques and legal frameworks which came to characterize the modern welfare state. It is a discourse appropriate to Foucault's category of 'anatomo-politics' and to the development or refinement of administrative and disciplinary techniques in place of coercive and violent methods of social control. It is important to emphasize, however, (more clearly perhaps than I have before) that this discourse, which found particular expression in the organized middle-class philanthropy of the nineteenth century, had different strands or facets. One, indeed, is essentially utilitarian and may be called in aid of a limited welfare state which attends to the failing or dysfunctional components of society. The other is essentially Fabian or social-democratic and may be called in aid of a more universal, preventive welfare state which ensures the organic self-regulation of society as a whole.

The limitation of this analysis is that it fails to locate these discourses in relation to the actual political struggles which gave birth to different kinds of nation-state and the ways in which class conflicts have been institutionalized or accommodated. Michael Mann (1987) has elaborated a distinction between two different approaches to the containment of the substantive challenges to the old ruling classes mounted both by the new middle class (or bourgeoisie) and the working class (or proletariat). The absolutist strategy, according to Mann, required that the despotic power of the monarch should be exercised partly through selective tactical repression, but also through 'divide and rule' negotiations with powerful corporate groups in society. The constitutionalist strategy required the development of civil citizenship and a limited political franchise. In some countries these two strategies have either conflicted with each other, or have been successfully combined. Mann's argument is that, from the nineteenth century onwards, constitutionalist strategies took different paths – liberalism in the USA and Fabian-reformism in Britain;

absolutist strategies (such as in Germany) achieved 'modernization' through the introduction of civil legal codes to facilitate capitalist economic development and the concession of limited social rights to organized labour; where strategies conflicted (as in France), political alliances were eventually achieved in order to effect compromise, while, where stategies combined (as in Scandinavian countries), a kind of corporatist reformism flourished.

I wish to argue that it is possible to articulate Mann's distinction between absolutist and constitutionalist strategies with Foucault's (1977; 1981) distinction between the coercive power relations which characterized the *ancien régimes* and the disciplinary power relations which characterize modern nation-states. I also wish to argue that it is possible to map the philosophical/religious traditions (with the different meanings which they attach to the human body) on to this broad analysis.

Moral repertoires

A rather unsatisfactory precedent for the kind of taxonomy which I propose to develop has been furnished by Marquand (1996) who has rightly claimed that, to understand the dynamics of the ideologies that have featured in recent political history, we need to do more than distinguish between individualism and collectivism: we also need to have regard to the moral bases of political strategy. He distinguishes between what he calls 'hedonist' or 'passive' approaches on the one hand and 'moral' or 'active' approaches on the other. In this way Marquand generates a fourfold taxonomy by which he seeks to characterize different phases in recent British political history. His concern is to distinguish, for example, what he would characterize as the moral-collectivism of Tawney from the hedonistic-collectivism of Tony Crosland, and the moral-individualism of Gladstone from the hedonistic individualism of Nigel Lawson. The problem is that, as with all Weberian ideal-type analyses, the models never exactly fit or else they fail to accommodate important exceptions. Additionally, Marquand operates with his own notion of 'morality' which does not account for the different kinds of moral position which flow from the competing philosophical and religious traditions that I have outlined in the previous section of this chapter.

An altogether more persuasive account of the moral dimension within the policy-making process has been provided by Claus Offe. Offe has made the point that state welfare and 'the welfare

transaction' are regulated by 'moral and political intuitions about rights
and duties, and arguments that activate or invalidate these intuitions'
(1993: 235). He argues that there are different moral repertoires upon
which society may draw in order to validate any particular pattern of
rights and obligations. Offe identifies three such repertoires, corresponding (at least approximately) to three of the four philosophical
traditions which I have identified. The first is the utilitarian moral
position which may defend welfare on the basis of a calculus of second
order material benefits (such as economic efficiency) and the avoidance
of collective evils (such as epidemics or social unrest). The second is the
conservative moral position which defends welfare on the basis of a
particular set of external preferences and draws on the principle of solidarity (a term having particular meaning in the context of Catholic
doctrine – see Spicker 1991) exclusively to protect the welfare of a
defined community: Offe calls this the 'communitarian' position and,
though he clearly had in mind the kind of communitarianism associated
with continental European Christian Democracy, it is a moral position
which has at least some resonance with the brand of communitarianism
more recently advocated within the US and the UK, for example, by
Etzioni (1994). The third is 'the Kantian solution' which defends
welfare in terms of a principled commitment to universal and inclusive
rights and obligations. The fourth moral repertoire to which Offe might
have referred is the puritanical, moral authoritarian position which
would only countenance welfare interventions in order to deter certain
behaviours or to enforce others.

It is possible, therefore, to construct a taxonomy which does not
characterize the views of politicians, but which does characterize the
different moral repertoires on which political discourse may draw in
relation to issues of social justice (for a more developed account, see
Dean with Melrose 1998). It is a taxonomy constituted by two axes,
each corresponding to the related dimensions or continua that have
been discussed above (see Figure 5.1). The horizontal axis encompasses the classic individualism–collectivism dimension signalled,
as we have seen, by Marquand, but overlays this with Foucault's bio-
political dimension, schematically defined in terms of the distinction
between anti- and pro-populationist discourse. The vertical axis
encompasses Mann's distinction between the absolutist and constitutionalist strategic trajectories whose legacies have constituted
different approaches to welfare, but overlays this with Foucault's
anatomo-political dimension, schematically defined in terms of the
distinction between coercive and disciplinary societies.

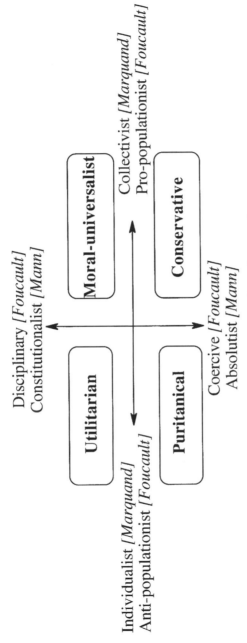

Figure 5.1   A taxonomy of moral repertoires

In the next section, I shall add another conceptual layer to this taxonomy. It is important now to emphasize, however, that the taxonomy is no more than an heuristic device and one which is specific to the cultural and political traditions of the Western world. When one seeks to locate political parties or individual thinkers on welfare in relation to this model it becomes immediately apparent that their thinking tends to represent a synthesis drawn from more than one of the quadrants illustrated in Figure 5.1. The Beveridge model of welfare, for example, though driven by a social-liberal interpretation of Kantian moral-universalism, was also significantly influenced by elements of both conservatism and utilitarianism (Silburn, 1995). To take another example, the British Conservative Party under the leadership of Margaret Thatcher (see Gamble, 1988), although conservative by name, did not correspond at all with the classic continental European mould of Christian Democracy, but exhibited both a radical utilitarian or 'neo-liberal' tendency and an essentially puritanical or moral-authoritarian influence (or what is often, confusingly, called a 'neo-conservative' tendency, see Roche, 1992).

CLASSIFYING WELFARE REGIMES

This section will discuss the classification of welfare-state regimes before presenting a taxonomy of the bodily metaphors appropriate to such regimes.

Welfare-state regimes

The most influential taxonomy of capitalist welfare-state 'regimes' is that provided by Esping-Andersen (1990). It corresponds (and was probably a seminal influence upon) Offe's taxonomy of moral repertoires in so far that it defines three ideal-type regimes: liberal, conservative and social-democratic. Esping-Andersen's approach is empirically driven to the extent that he classifies 'clusters' of countries within the OECD using two indices: the first, a measure of 'decommodification', contrasts the varying extent to which social security provision in different countries will allow aged, sick or unemployed workers to live independently of the labour market; the second, a measure of 'stratification', contrasts the varying degrees to which social security provision in different countries is selective as opposed to universal.

Liberal regimes, such as the USA, are characterized by low levels of de-commodification and high levels of selectivity. They are what Mishra (1977) had previously termed 'residual' welfare states in which the levels of welfare provision are generally low, the conditions of entitlement are strict and preference is given to occupational and private forms of welfare. Conservative regimes, such as Germany or France, are characterized by medium levels of both de-commodification and selectivity. They are 'corporatist' welfare states in which policy is negotiated between major corporate interest groups (classically, between capital, labour and the state), with a strong emphasis on social insurance and family allowances. State support for marginalized social groups may be selective or poor and the influence of Catholicism may mean that ideological support for the traditional family precludes or constrains the development of social and child care provision (but see Lewis, 1992b). Social democratic regimes, such as Sweden, are characterized by high levels of de-commodification and low levels of selectivity. They are 'universalist' in the sense that generous social insurance provision is combined with policies to achieve full employment and extensive social and child care services.

While Esping-Andersen's analysis has been of seminal importance, it has two important weaknesses. First, as Esping-Andersen himself acknowledges, many countries are in fact 'hybrids' which combine features of different regimes but, more importantly, it is actually quite difficult to see how some welfare regimes fit within his typology. The typology is too narrowly conceived and fails to account for the different ways in which welfare states have been developing or responding in the context of global economic change. Calling again on Offe (1984), it has been argued that, as Western nations compete with each other for economic growth, there is an inherent and self-paralysing contradiction between welfare capitalism's commodifying and de-commodifying tendencies. Neither a return to laissez-faire liberalism nor a vigorous reassertion of social democracy can address the paralysis and the likely response is a process of 'administrative re-commodification'. Offe leaves us to speculate about the forms which administrative recommodification may take, but quite clearly it entails, not the withdrawal of the state, but its vigorous involvement in supply-side investment and in the creation and regulation of markets: a strategy which might, *inter alia*, entail elements of moral authoritarianism and the use of extensive state intervention in order to change individual behaviour. In Britain, this may be exemplified, on the one hand, in the introduction to state-funded health, education and social care systems of internal market mechanisms and pervasive managerial controls (Taylor-Gooby and Lawson, 1993), and on the other, in such acts as the creation of a massive state bureaucracy to enforce the payment of child maintenance by 'absent' fathers (Dean, 1995). The second weakness of Esping-Andersen's typology is exposed by feminist critiques such as that by Langan and Ostner (1991). They point out that his theory of decommodification fails to take account of the way in which women are decommodified by their position within families. What is more, familial ideology plays as much of a part as class ideology in determining the selectivity of welfare benefits.

Together, these two criticisms suggest there is a missing element to Esping-Andersen's original analysis, and I wish tentatively to suggest a fourth type of welfare regime, the moral authoritarian regime. I do not pretend that a 'pure' example of a moral authoritarian regime is to be found, any more in fact that it easy to identify strictly 'pure' examples of any of Esping-Andersen's other welfare regimes. However, if we are to engage with this kind of analysis for its heuristic validity, rather than its empirical exactitude, regime types – like the moral repertoires discussed above – represent the spectrum of options from which actual welfare regimes are synthesized. In this context, it is possible to envisage a welfare state which gives precedence to moral–authoritarian interventionist principles; to the control of individual behaviour; to the promotion of patriarchal family values, labour discipline and responsible consumption; to the suppression of depravity.

Bodily metaphors

The correspondence between regime types and the moral repertoires I have discussed should be evident, but my purpose now is to relate this analysis back to the issue of bodily metaphors and to different constructions of the body in relation to welfare. Douglas, to whom I have already referred, has generated her own taxonomy of social systems in which 'the image of the body is used in different ways to reflect and enhance each person's experience of society' (1973: 16). It is a fourfold taxonomy which can be loosely mapped within the pattern of the wider taxonomy which this chapter is developing. Corresponding, I would argue, to the Kantian moral–universalist repertoire and to the social-democratic welfare regime is a system described by Douglas in which the body is conceived as an organ of communication: a system that is concerned with effective functioning, with the relationship between the head and the subordinate organs and/or with central control and circulatory systems. The metaphor is that of the organic body. Corresponding, I would argue, to the conservative moral repertoire and the corporatist welfare regime is a system described by Douglas in which the body is seen as a vehicle of life: a system that is therefore preoccupied with vulnerability to pollution, corruption and invasion and the need to maintain corporate integrity. The metaphor is that of the vulnerable body. Corresponding, I would argue, to the utilitarian moral repertoire and the liberal/residual welfare regime is a system described by Douglas in which the body is pragmatically regarded: a system that is very practical about the deployment of the body and unconcerned by controversies about spirit and matter. The metaphor is that of the mechanical body. Finally, corresponding, I would argue, to the puritanical moral repertoire and the moral-authoritarian welfare regime is a system described by Douglas in which the body is irrelevant matter: a system in which life is seen as spiritual and undifferentiated and the body as a symbol of evil. The metaphor is that of the reviled body.

I must emphasize that the interpretation which I am placing on Douglas's scheme is somewhat reductionist in nature and is not in every respect consistent with the complexity and detail of her work. The value of Douglas's insights is such that it is worth critically exploring the theoretical model which she articulates. Douglas is known for developing a cultural typology model based on two dimensions which she defines as 'grid' and 'group'. The concept of grid relates to the extent to which systems of classification in society are shared or private, to which a society employs common rituals as a means to negotiate social reality, to which (borrowing from Bernstein) codes of discourse are restricted or elaborated. The concept of group relates to the extent to which individuals in society are controlled by other people's pressure or to which they are able to exert pressure on others, to which people are integrated through group social relations or alienated from them.

For a rather different purpose, I have attempted elsewhere (Dean and Melrose, 1997) to articulate Douglas's concepts of grid and group with Giddens's (1990; 1991) characterization of late modernity and, in particular, the use he makes of the notions of reflexivity and anxiety. There is an ambiguity or tension in Douglas's framework between explanations for differences between groups within societies and explanations for differences between different kinds of society or different historical phases. Giddens in contrast is concerned with the

impact of social processes: with the reflexivity which is required of
individuals under conditions of modernity in order that they might
place trust in abstract technical and administrative systems and maintain social relations across increasingly indefinite spans of time and
space; with the anxiety that is entailed in the maintenance of self-
identity and ontological security in a society that is increasingly
characterized by social, economic and environmental risk and
uncertainty (cf. Beck, 1992). Where Douglas is describing the ways in
which some individuals, groups or societies may depend less on ritual
and more on elaborated communicative codes, Giddens speaks of
reflexivity. Where Douglas is describing the ways in which some
individuals, groups or societies are less bounded by collective power
and more alienated, Giddens speaks of loss of ontological security.

By incorporating Douglas's and Giddens's respective theoretical
distinctions as intersecting dimensions or continua, it is possible to
construct the schematic taxonomy set out in Figure 5.2. As is the case
with the taxonomy of moral repertoires in Figure 5.1, this is an
abstract heuristic representation. Its purpose is to convey the sense in
which there is a variety of bodily metaphors appropriate to capitalist
welfare regimes. In one sense this representation is very narrow in
that it does not purport to describe the nature of the different societies concerned, merely the characteristics which inform different
developments in relation to welfare policy. In another sense, the representation is very broad: the metaphors reflect more than different
political attitudes towards welfare and social justice, but contradictions or tensions which are inherent to late modernity. In any event,
this remains a two-dimensional representation, whereas an adequate
model would need to encompass better other dimensions (including
and especially gender) and to accommodate or locate a wider spectrum of alternative approaches to welfare (for example, socialist,
radical democratic and ecological approaches).

CONCLUSIONS

In the introductory section of this chapter it was suggested or implied,
not only that the organic metaphor is the strongest and most persuasive metaphor for the defence of social justice, but that it has
relevance well beyond the narrow limits of Western Judaeo-Christian
societies, and that it provides a language through which to debate the
efficacy of a developed welfare state. It should now also be clear that,

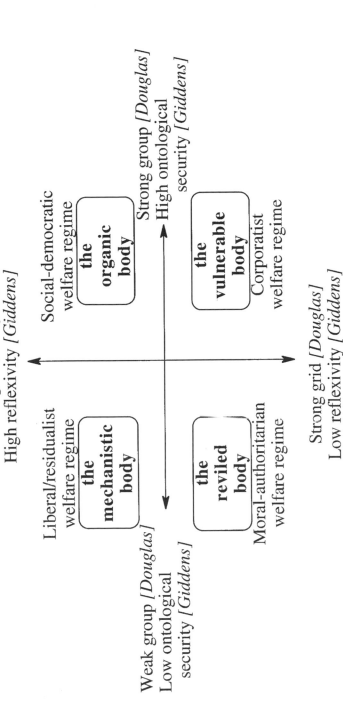

Weak grid [*Douglas*]
High reflexivity [*Giddens*]

Strong group [*Douglas*]
High ontological security [*Giddens*]

Social-democratic welfare regime

the organic body

Corporatist welfare regime

the vulnerable body

Liberal/residualist welfare regime

the mechanistic body

Moral-authoritarian welfare regime

the reviled body

Strong grid [*Douglas*]
Low reflexivity [*Giddens*]

Weak group [*Douglas*]
Low ontological security [*Giddens*]

Figure 5.2   A taxonomy of bodily metaphors and corresponding social welfare regimes

to the extent that the organic metaphor once had particular resonance for the development of the social democratic welfare state, it is not the only metaphor of relevance to social policy. The evolution of welfare capitalism has been tempered by many influences and incorporates a synthesis of symbolic associations.

Mishra (1990) has argued that in capitalist society the development of state welfare is achieving a certain irreversible maturity, tempered by a more pluralistic approach than hitherto: the implication is that there is a tendency to convergence between different welfare regimes. Against this view, and specifically at the European level, writers like Leibfried (1993) identify competing tendencies in the development of welfare and, in particular, a tension between the prospect of 'Europeanization from the top down' as opposed to 'Americanization from the bottom up'. The former tendency would entail the substantive imposition through the EU of essentially corporatist welfare mechanisms; the latter would result from formal provision to apply minimum standards across Europe and a dilution of welfare to a common minimal level. In either scenario, it is the social-democratic welfare model that is eclipsed.

This book has already discussed the emergence of a discourse of the 'independent body' (see Introduction and Chapter 1). This we have associated with the ideological ascendancy of the New Right and, in Britain at least, a degree of 'Americanization' in social policy. Applying the taxonomy elaborated in Figures 5.1 and 5.2 above, it is now possible to explore this further. The discourse of the independent body is one which does not draw on moral–universalist or conservative moral repertoires, but may draw on utilitarian or puritanical repertoires. The metaphors appropriate to both social-democratic *and* corporatist welfare regimes are beginning to lose their purchase.

It is striking that, within the discourse of advocates of the social-democratic tradition, the organic metaphor is now seldom if ever used. Such recent documents as the Report of the Commission on Social Justice (CSJ, 1994) is devoid of bodily metaphors. This report, which represented one of the influences on the thinking and policies of the British Labour Party, draws its principal metaphors from the discourses of finance and economics: the strategy proposed is an 'investors' stategy' (*ibid.*: Ch.3), calculated to enhance the nation's 'social capital' (*ibid.*: Ch.7). Notions of organic interdependence and self-regulation seem largely to have disappeared from the political discourse of the left.

To the extent that elements of corporatism had once been evident within the British welfare state, as well as in continental Europe, the age of such tripartite bodies as the National Economic Development Council and the Manpower Services Commission has passed (Kingdom, 1991: 423–5) and are unlikely to be resurrected. While Britain's corporatist European partners were debating (largely rhetorically) the need for measures to protect against 'social exclusion', the British Conservative government in the 1980s and '90s continued to dispute definitions of the (arguably) much narrower concept of 'poverty' and whether indeed poverty, let alone social exclusion, existed (Oppenheim and Harker, 1996: Ch.1).

At the time of writing, it remains to be seen exactly how the notion of social exclusion, with all its resonance with the metaphors of the vulnerable body and the corporate whole, might take hold in British political discourse. The New Labour government, elected in May 1997, has created a special 'Social Exclusion Unit' to co-ordinate initiatives across departments. In its rhetoric, however, the government draws upon an ambiguous mixture of neo-liberalism (the inheritance of the Thatcher/Reagan orthodoxy) and a narrowly conccived neo-conservative communitarianism (indicative of a new Blair/Clinton orthodoxy – see Jordan, 1998). During his election campaign, the New Labour Prime Minister had pledged 'a new government to bind the wounds of a fractured society' (*The Guardian*, 16.4.97), but such fleeting dalliances with the metaphor of the vulnerable body are generally eclipsed by the more 'disciplined' emphasis exemplified in New Labour's revised constitution, which calls for a community in which 'the rights we enjoy reflect the duties we owe' (Clause 4 (IV)).

Meanwhile, the moral repertoires on which the discourse of the independent body is drawing are capable of furnishing, on the one hand, the metaphor of the mechanistic body and, on the other, the metaphor of the reviled body. The increasingly ascendant liberal/residual welfare model is concerned pragmatically to eliminate defects from the functioning of the social/economic machine: the individual bodies of, for example, aged or disabled people, are like redundant or faulty cogs which, if they are to function at all, should be maintained independently. The task of the state is to ensure efficient (i.e. minimal) but accountable forms of independent or self-regulating informal provision. Current social policies also exhibit elements of a moral–authoritarian regime which is pre-occupied with idle bodies, with bodies that are unclean or out of control, with the correction of unacceptable bodily impulses. Here, the task of the state is to enforce labour discipline, family responsibilities and moral values.

The analysis offered in this chapter is as speculative as it is abstract. Its value, however, is that it invites further reflection, not only about the ways in which social policy impact upon embodied human actors, but about the way that human actors' perceptions of their own and others' bodies may be reflected in the discourse and substance of social policy.

6 Body–Mind Expertise: Notes on the Polarization of Health Care Discourse

John Paley

The argument of this chapter is that it is possible to identify a politics of expertise in current debates about health care, and that this politics is bound up with a view of the relation between mind and body which is still inherently Cartesian. To illustrate this theme, I shall focus initially on the rhetoric associated with 'new' nursing, turning to the contrast with medicine in the second half. I shall be making much of what we may legitimately call nursing's 'rediscovery of the mind', which I think can be regarded as a solution to two related problems. In the first place, it functions as an academic ideology supporting the discipline's recent arrival in the university sector through Project 2000. Second, it articulates a division of labour vis-à-vis medicine, whereby the body is assigned to the medical profession, while the mind becomes the province of nursing. However, it is clear that, despite the discourse of professional autonomy, medicine remains the dominant partner, and that the latent function of nursing is still to co-opt the patient into the most recent version of the 'medical model', the mind being (as it were) simply the point of entry.

In passing, it is worth noting that nursing is, on the face of it, moving in the opposite direction to social work (see Ellis, Chapter 2 in this volume). For whereas social work has refocused the 'psycho-social gaze', typical of the 1960s and 1970s, on to the physical domain of the body, nursing has switched attention from the body to the social and the psychic. I think this difference is more apparent than real. For one thing, social work's pretensions to psychological and sociological expertise were also associated with its reorganization as a university discipline; and it seems that nursing has adopted the same sort of tactic. But we must not forget that there is a symbiotic relation between nursing and medicine, and that the two professions have always been engaged in an unwitting conspiracy. To this extent, the 'new' nursing cannot be taken entirely on its own terms, independently of the way in which it serves to buttress the discourse of medicalization. 'Nursing is to medicine as social work is to …'. This is an equation that has no solution.

HOLISM AND DUALISM

The new nursing represents itself as a site of resistance to the medicalization of illness, and as a form of practice whose field is the embodied person rather than the body of the patient. A consensus has gradually been built around this imagery, culminating in a flood of published material during the 1980s and 1990s, and in the emergence of 'caring' as the concept central to nursing's professional identity and, for some of the discipline's more sophisticated academic writers, its ontology (Benner, 1984; Benner and Wrubel, 1989). While this orthodoxy is not without its critics, the principal objections to it are largely pragmatic. It is argued that the 'holistic' approach to nursing which it implies is overly ambitious and potentially invasive (Reed and Ground, 1997), and that the ethical imperative of 'caring' takes no account of either the bureaucratic environment in which health care is practised or the professional dynamics, the pervasive imbalance of power between nursing and medicine (Bowden 1997). The current position could perhaps be summarized, though no doubt over-simplified, by noting that the holistic paradigm is barely questioned as a philosophy of nursing, but that its weakness as a politics and policy of health care is reluctantly acknowledged.

In referring to the 'holistic paradigm', I am signalling that nursing's achievement in building this consensus should not be underestimated. It is not, in fact, a paradigm in the classic sense associated with Kuhn (1977) since, despite Benner's efforts, it lacks universally recognized exemplars, and falls well short of other requirements for a disciplinary matrix. However, it is entrenched as a form of discourse, and it may be that a version of it will prove both coherent and powerful enough to act as a unifying force, a way of thinking and doing which can realistically inform nursing practice. It is not my intention, in this chapter, to cast doubt on that possibility (about which I remain non-committal). The argument is simply that, in its current forms, it remains bound by the gravitational pull of medical orthodoxy, unable even to achieve escape velocity. Far from providing a genuine alternative to the 'medical model', and the body/mind dualism with which that model is identified, the holistic paradigm merely serves to confirm and reinforce both.

That the medicalization of health and illness is identified with dualism is an article of faith in the nursing literature. The 'old' nursing accepted medicine's construction of the patient as a psychologically inert body, whose hypothetical status as a person was irrelevant to care and treatment. This, the 'defining feature of the old model', could be 'traced to its Cartesian inheritance' (Reed and Ground, 1997) since Descartes's account of the relation between mind and body was designed to render the latter amenable to scientific study and intervention. In contrast, therefore, the holistic paradigm – at least by implication, and as a rule explicitly – declares itself to be anti-dualist.

However, it is not always clear what precise form this anti-dualism takes, though it is reasonable to assume that many of the currently fashionable strategies for avoiding dualism, which can be found in the philosophical literature, are not what is intended. Among the strategies I have in mind are reductionism, eliminative materialism and different versions of the mind-brain identity thesis (Macdonald, 1989). To adopt any of these strategies is certainly to reject ontological dualism, the idea that the mind is a different, immaterial, kind of substance. In Ryle's terms, it is to reject the view that minds are 'not merely ghosts harnessed to machines … [but] themselves … spectral machines' (Ryle, 1964). However, this does not entail that they are not machines of another sort, and these philosophical accounts of the mind identify it, in various ways, with the brain, the central nervous system, or neurophysiological functions. None of which can keep at bay the kind of mechanism that holistic nursing resists (Benner and Wrubel, 1989), 'mind' itself having been, to all intents and purposes, abolished.

Ditching ontological dualism, then, only sets an agenda (as McCulloch, 1995, points out, 'vanishingly little is settled when immaterialism is rejected'). Questions about the exact nature of the relation between body and mind remain unanswered; and adopting a view in which the concept of the person is logically primitive (Strawson, 1964) or in which Dasein is 'ontologically prior' to the body (Heidegger, 1962) does not in itself answer them, although it does place limits on mechanism. A person still has a mind and a body even if, philosophically, she can no longer be regarded as an aggregate of the two; and there are still numerous intractable problems concerning what we can say about the relation between body, mind and self (see Bermúdez *et al.*, 1995, for an impressive series of philosophical and psychological papers on self-consciousness and bodily awareness). So rejecting Cartesianism, even making the idea of a person 'primordial', does not get us all that far.

Much of the nursing literature opts out at this point, and suggests only that 'holistic approaches to nursing care focus on the patient as a whole person, as someone with biological, social and psychological needs' (Reed and Ground, 1997), as if Descartes had unaccountably overlooked the fact that people have minds as well as bodies; and as if, in identifying body and mind as different kinds of substance, he was committed to believing that the one has no effect on the other. As it happens, although Descartes was unable to explain, adequately, *how* the mind and body interact, he went out of his way to draw attention to the fact *that* they do, commenting perceptively on one's awareness of the body, the ways in which it limits experience, and the influence that the mind, in its turn, exerts over corporeal states and occurrences (Gaukroger, 1995).

Crudely, then, where 'old' nursing followed medicine in focusing the 'gaze' on the body, letting the mind take care of itself, the holistic paradigm fastens on the psycho-social dimensions of the patient's illness, and claims them for its own. If ontological dualism has been abandoned, it has been replaced by methodological dualism. This is an idea that I will trace through several sites of discourse in health care; but we can see it, in the first instance, as the basis for a division of labour in which medicine gets the body and nursing gets the mind. The social and psychological needs of the patient having been recognized, they are separated out – methodologically, not ontologically – from the biological needs, and formally constituted as the proper object of nursing's professional activity. When nurses speak of the 'autonomy' of their profession, this is essentially what they mean. Without methodological dualism, there would be no place to stand, although (as we shall see) this independence of medicine is largely notional.

THE ELISION OF THE BODY

Medicine is assigned the body, and performs literal and metaphorical operations upon it. Nursing is allocated the mind and, to use what has come to occupy the space of a technical term, *cares*. The word has a long history (Dean and Bolton, 1980) but, as Dunlop (1994) argues, it has an 'emergent' sense which has become associated with the holistic paradigm. According to Dunlop (and hers, incidentally, is one of the more thoughtful essays on this topic) the emergent sense 'seems to involve a form of love', an idea which broadly reflects Bowden's (1997) philosophical contribution, which examines the 'ethics of caring' in the context of motherhood, friendship, nursing and citizenship. In common with many authors (Gilligan, 1982; Noddings, 1984), Bowden sees caring as the basis for a feminist ethics of interdependence, opposed to the ethics of autonomy that is usually associated with Kant, but which could also be linked to Nietzsche, Sartre, or Kierkegaard. This line of thought is certainly worth pursuing, but here my primary interest is in the role played by caring in the specifically nursing literature.

The starkest feature of that literature is the way in which it 'etherealizes the body', to quote both Dunlop (1994) and Reed and Ground (1997). Dunlop caricatures this perspective as 'a tendency to lose the bedpan', and its most extreme version can probably be found in Watson (1979 and 1988), who construes virtually every biophysical need in terms of its psycho-social correlates, while laying greatest emphasis on the 'spiritual', and what she calls the 'transpersonal', aspects of nursing care. In fact, 'etherealization of the body' is close to being a misnomer, since what strikes the reader of this corpus of writing most forcefully is that the body has largely disappeared from view. Indeed, O'Connell and Duffy (1978), reviewing five years' worth of published material in *Nursing Research*, found hardly any studies of the physical dimensions of care; and my strong impression is that the situation has not changed. Almost every study of 'caring', whether theoretical or empirical, depicts it as a form of personal relationship – involving support, solicitude, respect, empathy, trust, communication, and all the other humanistic clichés – from which the dirty, oily and gritty bits have been expunged (see Kyle, 1995, for a recent review confirming this picture). We should perhaps speak of the 'elision of the body', rather than its etherealization.

The point, of course, is that this elision has become identified with nursing, in a sense epitomized by Leininger's (1984) assertion, 'caring is nursing, and nursing is caring'. Though other writers are nervous about so bold an equation, most readily sign up to weaker versions of the same thesis, caring being variously described as the 'essence' of nursing (another Leininger formulation), 'essential' to nursing or, at the very least, 'central' to nursing. It is often conceded that such claims make differentiating between nursing and certain other professions – social work is an obvious example – somewhat problematic;

but so great is the discipline's obsession with definitions, that the search for the right nuance continues. On the same theme, there are also numerous attempts to define 'caring' itself, and to identify its components systematically. In that the results of these investigations are usually banal – of a kind that would be replicated by any decent thesaurus – it is tempting to ascribe an almost magical belief in the power of 'naming' to those who undertake them. At any rate, sterile exercises of this sort soak up a lot of academic energy. Their significance, for my argument, is that they represent what might be called a discourse of disembodiment, or perhaps a discourse of mind-independent-of-the-body, inherent in the dematerialized concept of caring to which the nursing literature has wedded itself.

THE ETHEREALIZATION OF EVIDENCE

The methodological dualism to which I have referred is equally appar-ent in the context of research strategies. Just as caring has come to preside over the conceptual framework of nursing, its function that of an academic and professional mantra, so the research literature has been progressively infiltrated by an approach which claims to have a unique affinity with the discipline: phenomenology.

The phenomenological tradition is usually said to originate with Husserl, and includes Heidegger and Merleau-Ponty among its more significant figures. Most nurse writers appeal either to Heidegger or to Husserl, recognizing that their approaches, nominally belonging to the same 'school', were very different. Given the intrinsic difficulty of the works of both thinkers, they are standardly read through other authors, philosophical commentators on the one hand, and estab-lished nurse writers on the other. However, it is noticeable that there is hardly any acknowledgement of the influence each has already exerted in the social sciences. Husserl's ideas, for example, were sub-stantially modified by Schutz (1972) and passed on to American social theorists, emerging in various guises such as phenomenological sociology (Berger and Luckmann, 1967), ethnomethodology (Garfinkel, 1967), and symbolic interactionism (Blumer, 1969). Meanwhile, Heidegger's thought was taken up by an assortment of social scientific writers, especially in sociology and geography (Hägerstrand, 1973; de Certeau, 1984; Bourdieu, 1990; Thrift, 1996). Giddens (1984) is perhaps the best known example of a social theorist whose work is explicitly indebted to Heidegger's ontology.

The neglect of these intellectual bloodlines has had unfortunate consequences. Both philosophers are normally taken to be representatives of a 'humanistic' movement that is opposed to empiricism and positivism in the social sciences. In Husserl's case, this is certainly wrong, as his views on science in general are almost classically positivist (Bell, 1990). Philosophy, in Husserl's work, was to become a 'rigorous science' in that it would begin by ridding itself of all unexamined assumptions, and make no claims that were not absolutely guaranteed. The phenomenological reduction achieves the first part of this programme by putting on hold every assumption that is normally made in the 'natural attitude' – the habits of mind which are characteristic of everyday understanding, but which are also the basis of scientific activity – including common sense beliefs about the nature and existence of things in the 'outer world'. This move leads to 'transcendental idealism', and to a methodological solipsism so profound that it is impossible to see how the everyday world can be reconstituted from the material available to the transcendental ego (even Schutz gave up the attempt). For all that, nurse researchers seem to imagine that the phenomenological epoché, or 'bracketing', is itself a social research technique, and that Husserl's ideas imply a methodology in which the 'phenomenon' can only be accessed 'through prereflective descriptions of it, in the person's own words' (Jasper, 1994). This misconception has helped to produce an entire genre in nursing research – 'lived experience research', as we might call it – which restricts itself to a narrow band of subjectivity completely divorced from any concern about what happens in the real, physical world. Despite the use of Husserl's vocabulary, despite the appeals to his authority, there is no connection at all between this research genre and the philosophy of transcendental idealism (Paley, 1997).

Other lived-experience researchers invoke Heidegger as the intellectual source for the approach (there is, in practice, little to choose between the methods adopted by each group); but this case is far more subtle and interesting. The writers on Heidegger most frequently cited in the nursing literature (Dreyfus, 1994; Taylor, 1985) emphasize that 'when we try to understand the cultural world, we are dealing with interpretations and interpretations of interpretations' (Taylor, 1985); so it may not be surprising that nurse researchers have fastened on this idea, and translated it into a programme whose only concern is to examine people's accounts of their experience, which is to say their interpretations of the circumstances in which they find themselves. However, I have suggested elsewhere (Paley, 1998) that this is not the only, and arguably not the most plausible, reading of Heidegger. Certainly, it is not the reading that Giddens would assent to. Giddens (and he is not alone) derives from Heidegger's work an ontology of distributed social practices which are 'at the root of the constitution of both subject and social object' (Giddens, 1984); and structuration theory provides, in the idea of the 'duality of structure', a sociological translation of Heidegger's 'peculiar union of being in the world with the being of Dasein'. An extended discussion would clearly be out of place here, so I shall simply add the observation that it is extremely difficult to identify, in the nursing literature, any reasoning which leads from Heidegger's 'bedrock' of practices, constitutive of both self and world, to a style of research which is concerned exclusively with the question, 'What is this or that kind of experience like?' (van Manen, 1990).

Most significantly, nurse writers claim to find a fit between lived experience research, as vindicated (on their reading) by Husserl or Heidegger, and their understanding of nursing as a profession. For, whereas medicine is apparently obliged to treat persons as objects, independently of social context, nursing aspires to the holistic perspective. This natural affinity between nursing and phenomenology is expressed in a variety of ways. For example, phenomenology is said to foster understanding (Munhall, 1994); to value whole persons who create personal meanings (Taylor, 1994); to emphasize uniqueness and diversity (Wilson and Hutchinson, 1991); to allow for multiple levels of meaning within the practice of nursing (Reeder, 1985). All of which is summarized, perhaps, in Reeder's idea of 'nursing as an "active ontology"'. As with 'caring', then, a deliberate attempt has been made to *identify* nursing with a particular expression of subjectivity. And if the adoption of caring represents a vote for disembodiment, for the 'etherealization of the body', phenomenology – at least in the nursing literature – represents a vote for the 'etherealization of evidence'.

I have come across a paper that dramatizes this choice more effectively than any other. It is not, in itself, a particularly important contribution, and its authors are not big names in the field; but, appearing in a major journal, its very ordinariness carries a significance which a more overtly challenging and provocative piece would lack, the kind of significance which only a routine editorial decision can confirm (see Hacking, 1990, for an extended justification of the idea that it is the ordinary, unremarked texts that most clearly demonstrate the degree to which a certain vision has taken hold).

The main aim of Rose *et al.* (1995) is to illustrate phenomenology functioning as a nursing research method. One of the authors herself carried out a phenomenological study of 'caring in the lived experience of intensive care nurses', and the tribulations of her research serve as the main focus of the discussion. Halfway through the paper, reference is made to an earlier article (Baker *et al.*, 1992), which comments on the problem of 'method slurring'. This is the unfortunate tendency of nursing researchers to lump together concepts and techniques drawn from phenomenology and grounded theory – which, Baker *et al.* suggest, cannot be combined (let alone 'blended') because their purposes and presuppositions are entirely different. It happens that Jayne Beeby encountered this problem in her own study of caring. She had originally planned to conduct 'lived experience' interviews with nurses from an intensive therapy unit, and also to observe these same nurses at work, 'to match what they said with what they did'. However, 'she found the two sources of data incompatible.' There follows a long quotation in which Beeby explains her dilemma. At this point, it will perhaps be most revealing to let the author speak for herself.

> I tried to do triangulation between my field notes and my interview transcriptions to see if I could cross-check in terms of reliability. In qualitative research you can do that but in phenomenology I found that you couldn't because of the difference between first person experience and third person experience, which is what the participant observation gave me. I was stuck with these two sets of data ... I felt morally I could not show the nurses the data from my observations because I'd chosen phenomenology. I couldn't hold up a mirror and say but look what you do ... I decided to abandon my observation data because I felt a moral obligation to my participants not to disturb or upset them because they had shared with me something quite vital. I can't discredit what they told me because that is what they truly believed, that was caring, for them. (Rose *et al.*, 1995: 1127)

Collectively, the authors then observe:

> Jayne's attempt at method slurring raised an ethical dilemma. As a practising nurse she had identified a problem in relation to patient care. Yet she felt morally unable to disturb or upset the participants. Had she done so she would also have endangered her research. She chose to be true to phenomenology. However, had

her research design remained consistent with the philosophical underpinnings of phenomenology in the first place, she would not have encountered this dilemma. This example supports the view that method slurring may lead to methodological inconsistency and, at worst, ethical dilemmas in professional practice. Remaining true to the methodology ensures academic rigour in this respect. (Rose *et al.*, 1995: 1127)

Faced with physical evidence ('what they did') which contradicts the lived experience accounts ('what they said'), Beeby 'abandons' the physical evidence. In doing so, she not only resolves the 'ethical dilemma' (I confess to not being fully clear what this is) but also achieves methodological consistency and rigour. The suppression of data as methodological heroism, the withholding of evidence as moral triumph. But, in the context of my argument, something else as well. A clear choice in favour of the code of subjectivity, which reduces the 'phenomenon' to the perceived, the intentional, the imagined. I have not found a better illustration of the 'etherealization of evidence', nor – given that Beeby's topic was 'caring' – a more transparent example of collapsing physical activity into its mental accoutrements.

THE THEOLOGY OF EVIDENCE-BASED MEDICINE

If nursing discourse has been purging the mind of bodily residues, the discourse of medicine has been engaged in a mirror operation, excluding mind from the array of bodies which it subjects to the medical 'gaze'. Both these moves count as works of purification (Latour, 1993), an idea to which I shall return. However, the body which remains after the purifying is not the same as the body which existed beforehand. It is hardly possible that it could be; for the pre-purification body was at least connected to the mind, whereas what I have proposed to call methodological dualism pushes them, determinedly, apart. In this respect, it is deeply ironic that methodological dualism represents a more radical separation of minds and bodies than even Descartes would have countenanced. And here I should add that the use of the plural, 'bodies', is not arbitrary. The subject of the medical 'gaze' is now, not so much a singular anatomical and physiological entity, as a plurality of countable objects.

Evidenced-based medicine can fairly claim to be the official theology of the NHS. It 'emphasizes the need to move beyond clinical experience and physiological principles to rigorous evaluations of the consequences of clinical actions' (Oxman *et al.*, 1993). A self-styled 'paradigm shift' (Evidence-Based Medicine Working Group, 1992), the 'new' medicine shifts the clinician's attention away from 'pathophysiologic rationale', which is to say the 'internal workings' of the patient's body, and focuses it instead on a statistical expression of the effects of intervention. This move explicitly transforms the grounds of clinical decision making, substituting a calculus of treatment outcomes for the 'traditional' understanding of bodily mechanisms. The 'old' paradigm, it is said, was organized around the assumption that a training in physiology and pathology, the 'basic mechanisms' of corporeal functioning, supplemented by the individual's clinical experience, was an adequate basis for diagnosis and treatment. That assumption can now be seen to be misconceived: clinical experience is re-interpreted as 'unsystematic observation', while pathophysiological principles are regarded as unreliable. The new paradigm overturns the tradition, and replaces it with statistical evidence drawn from randomized controlled trials.

In the course of this revolution, patients become bodies, and bodies become numbers. By the same token, 'mind' is pushed beyond the clinical horizon. The 'old' medicine may have concentrated on the body, but it acknowledged that the patient was 'minded' and this fact was frequently, indeed standardly, taken into account. There was a space for the idea that non-clinical factors were implicated in clinical decision making, and these non-clinical factors revolved around an understanding of the person behind the patient, and the relationship which he or she enjoyed with the medical practitioner. In the 'new' medicine they are given token recognition, but simultaneously marginalized. The object of medical discourse is no longer the patient, or even the patient's body, but an array of statistically significant figures. At the same time, the clinician's own mental function – judgement, experience, professional instinct – has been displaced by a new form of objectivity, one which resides in computation and meta-analytic texts. The discourse in which specific judgements are made about particular cases has given way to a discourse in which quantifications of risk, and likely outcome, are read off from systematic reviews, and applied to all members of the class to which the case belongs. This is not, we might say, medicine as expertise but medicine as calculus. It need hardly be added that a calculus is far more amenable to budgetary considerations than clinical judgement, and that this shift in medical discourse is closely associated with the stampede towards managerialism dictated by the NHS reforms.

At any rate, the mirror image is a double one. As the new nursing elides the body of both nurse and patient, placing a mind-to-mind relationship – borrowed from humanistic psychology – at the centre of its ideology of caring, so medicine denudes both patient and clinician of the mental states and processes that were formerly essential to their encounter. Each distances itself from the embodied-person-as-patient, taking a step backwards in opposite directions. But there is, of course, a further parallel; and again it takes the form of a mirroring. Earlier, I described nursing's adoption of what it calls phenomenology, and observed that this research 'paradigm' is said to have a special affinity with the profession (correctly, in that caring and phenomenology both honour the code of subjectivity). I can now add that the new medicine also has its favoured research method, the 'gold standard' of randomized controlled trials (Sackett *et al.*, 1996). The difference is that, while phenomenology has only an 'affinity' for 'caring', the RCT has driven the whole evidence-based medicine revolution.

That much is evident without further comment, as is the fact that the numbers yielded by the RCT, or by a meta-analysis of RCTs, are precisely those which form the object of the practitioner's clinical 'gaze'. However, it can also be noted that, while nursing phenomenologists label 'positivist' everything which is not phenomenology, evidence-based medicine relegates all that is not RCT to the status of anecdote. There is, at the heart of the evidence-based movement, a bid to redefine what counts as evidence. It is overt in the published league tables, which place the RCT at the top, lesser forms of experimental method in the play-off positions, peer opinion lower still, and anecdotes at the bottom. This is evidence recast as 'Evidence'. It is almost aggressively one-dimensional, permitting no other axes of merit. With a single gesture, it sweeps entire genres of research off the board; for, as a question posed by the Centre for Evidence-Based Medicine puts it: 'if you're reading about treatment and it's not a randomized controlled trial why are you wasting your time?'

In defensive mode, writers on evidence-based medicine note that it is 'not restricted to randomized trials and meta-analyses' (Sackett *et al.*, 1996), although the small print reveals that, when asking questions about therapy (as opposed to, say, diagnosis and prognosis), 'we should try to avoid the non-experimental approaches'. However, it is a moot point whether *sotto voce* qualifications of even this modest kind are likely to be heard against the general background noise, as medical discourse is buried in what Hacking (1990) calls the 'avalanche of numbers'. If there was ever a time when the belief that science and rampant quantification go together – and in nursing this belief amounts to a prejudice – for the health service disciplines, that time is now. Nursing's apprehensions on this score, almost a paranoia, are further intensified by the fact that access to patient bodies, for the purposes of research, is more tightly controlled than ever. One does not need to dispute the ethical propriety of this in order to recognize, in the arrangements for NHS research funding, in the R&D screening procedures recently imposed by trusts, and in the operations of local research ethics committees, a formidable barrier. Indeed, since LRECs pay even more attention to method than they do to ethics *per se* – on the entirely defensible grounds that it is hardly ethical to expose patients to poorly designed protocols – it is fair to say that all health-related research proposals are now vetted methodologically at least twice, and usually three times. And, since the bodies which do the vetting are all dominated by the medical profession, it is perhaps not surprising if nurses feel that the cards are stacked against them. The 'mirror image' developments in professional discourse to which I have been drawing attention are not matched by a corresponding equality in the dynamics of professional power.

There is another irony in all this. The discourse of nursing research is organized round a bivalency, a simple choice between positivism and phenomenology. Of course, in philosophical terms, this is a mid-century anachronism. In both the natural and social sciences, and whether it is taken as a descriptive or a normative account of scientific activity, positivism is discredited; while phenomenology, as I noted earlier, has gone through a series of translations and transformations during its adoption by the social sciences. Yet, between them, nursing and medicine have contrived to turn a choice between anachronistic alternatives into a kind of self-fulfilling prophecy, with nurses opting for phenomenology and the medical profession committing itself to a Bayesian form of positivism. And this at the very moment when, in the philosophy of science, a new realism (Hacking, 1983, Leplin, 1984; Bhaskar, 1986; Archer, 1995, Pawson and Tilley, 1997) has become entrenched. In any case, I doubt whether we can make sense of embodiment – from which both medicine and nursing are in flight – without a realist theory of some kind.

MIND AND MEANING

Meanwhile, the patient. Or rather, since the new medicine reads the body as a matrix of probabilities and propensities, the person subject to risk (that is, all of us). For writers such as Englehardt (1986) and Sherwin (1992), the cognitive authority of medicine conditions reality, so we can perhaps expect methodological dualism to be associated with a subtle shift in our experience of the relation between mind and body. The calculus of risk assigns all bodies to categories governed by diet, habit, and lifestyle; and these categories are activated by a discourse of public health and health promotion, already subject to critique in a growing sociological literature (Bunton and Macdonald, 1992; Petersen and Lupton, 1996). From the individual perspective, this discourse implies a form of management in which the body is 'regulated' by the mind, no doubt in the interests of social control (Castel, 1991). Metaphorically, the mind becomes a middle manager, responsible for supervision, quality control, scheduling, progress chasing, and disciplinary procedures, in an effort to roll 'healthy lifestyles' off the production line. Subjectively, as a majority of us can probably testify, this involves determined, but frequently unsuccessful, exercises in will power. Indeed, one might say that it reduces the mind's executive capacity to one of 'will', an idea rendered problematic by the fact that (as regular failure suggests) we do not have the least idea how to exercise this faculty routinely. The recalcitrant body confronts a bemused mind, whose only resort is the mirage of internal straining, combined with endless New Year resolutions.

To this extent, I would like to say, methodological dualism is an interesting example of 'de-skilling', translated from the sphere of work, and reinscribed as a characteristic of mind/body interaction. Indeed, I am almost tempted to describe it as a Taylorism of individual faculties, though that idea presupposes a philosophy of mind which I have insufficient space to justify. Still, a move of this kind would be a logical, and perhaps inevitable, extension of the Taylorization of bodily care, depicted in the other chapters of this book. The reorganization of tasks, roles and functions can hardly be completed satisfactorily without a corresponding fragmentation of the raw material – the patient – on which the newly defined skills are brought to bear.

A similar enfeebling – or at least passivity – is typical of nursing's contribution to the polarization of health care discourse. But here the imagery is different. Where the new medicine offers mind a picture of itself as a sort of helpless, non-executive director, the new nursing presents us with a television news reader reporting on events in distant places. In this image, the body is a far-away country of which we know little, except that it is a problem we could do without. In phenomenological studies, the condition of the body is little more than a brute fact; and in the starting question, 'What is this or that kind of experience like?', the subject of reference ('this' or 'that') almost always coincides with an established diagnostic category. Inevitably, then, the respondent is confined to reading data from the screen: a reading which is, at best, only a subjective annotation of the objective circumstances defined by health care professionals. The 'meaning' of the illness, for the patient, is limited to its psychosocial consequences which, once the nurse has understood what they are, elicit an extravagant form of sympathy (a remark that I shall want to qualify, in one respect, a little later).

In saying this, I do not mean to cast doubt on the potential value, in psychological terms, of empathy or compassion. My intention is, rather, to suggest that the holistic paradigm reduces mind to a receptacle for 'meaning' and that, *ipso facto*, it restricts the idea of 'meaning' to 'something in the mind'. Despite the rhetoric, this position has distinctly Cartesian echoes, though it misses out on Descartes' insistence that the mind has a more intimate relationship with the body than this function would, on the face of it, imply. For one thing, it renders the idea of psychosomatic conditions virtually unintelligible, and makes nonsense of the view that states of mind can, in other ways, be implicated in states of the body. However, in order to show that the new nursing does sanction this kind of passivity and that, in doing so, it co-opts the patient into the latest version of the medical model, I will have to look briefly at an example.

The example I have chosen is a paper by Benner and her colleagues (Benner *et al.*, 1994). Benner is an important and influential writer, and her philosophical views have had a significant impact on nursing theory. Hers is one of the more sophisticated versions of the phenomenological approach to nursing studies, and her appropriation of Heidegger and Merleau-Ponty (Benner and Wrubel, 1989) is the basis for a (partly) persuasive account of holism, which actively distances itself from Cartesian dualism. Any view that Benner adopts, therefore, is likely to have much wider resonance; and this is one reason why it is worth devoting attention to her work.

The paper reports a series of interviews conducted with people who have asthma. The analysis of interview material begins with an assignment of the respondents into one of four categories, which are then collapsed into two. These two summary categories reflect different 'self-described relationships to the illness'. People in the first category exhibit 'non-acceptance and adversarial themes', while those in the second demonstrate acceptance (in some cases they have made a transition from 'less accepting and more control-oriented relationships to the illness'). The *non-accepters* are said to have 'an either extremely objective or extremely subjective view of the disease as external to the self, or in the mind'; while *accepters* describe 'illness experience in terms that are neither highly objective – that is, personal experiences and feelings are described – nor extremely subjective – that is, the illness is not described as internally caused by thoughts, feelings, or attitudes' (Benner *et al.*, 1994). It should be noted, however, that non-accepters alternate between these two views: they do not hold to one or the other exclusively.

At first sight, the difference between the two groups appears to involve a question of identity. In point of fact, the non-accepters do seem disinclined to see asthma as part of how they define themselves, saying things like: 'I hate to think of it as controlling my life'; I don't want it to be up there as part of my life'; '[asthma is] like a bad college roommate that I could never adjust to'; and so on. According to Benner, though, the essential difference is that accepters believe their condition must be 'cared for', while non-accepters resist this idea – for example, they vary the medication prescribed, or leave off completely, and (when in 'extremely subjective' mood) undertake informal experiments in controlling the illness mentally, by attempting to 'will it away', 'psych it away', or 'pray it away'. All of which contrasts with 'a more relational and situated position of acceptance', acknowledging 'the limits of control', and making possible a 'more humane self-reliance and interdependence'.

It is noticeable that the basic distinction carries a strong normative loading. Accepters have got it right, while non-accepters have fallen foul of the false, Kantian, imperative towards autonomy. Throughout the paper, moreover, the 'personal meanings' involved in acceptance are associated with 'taking medications' and increasing control over asthma 'through rigorous Western medical treatment'. So it is hard to avoid the sense that acceptance of the illness is, at the same time, acceptance of medicine's view of it, and that the 'interdependence' which Benner recommends largely involves health care professionals. Effectively, then, the classification is another version of the distinction between compliance and non-compliance; and the 'limits of control' are those defined by the orthodox medical view of the disease. Implicitly, the body is a site of medical expertise, while nursing expertise is confined to an analysis of the patient's subjective annotations. However, since (in this example) the non-accepter's view goes beyond a description of the psycho-social consequence of the illness – it challenges not only the orthodox aetiology but also conventional treatment – she is offered, not just sympathy, but a philosophical explanation of why the subjective account is wrong. This does not count as resistance to the medical model; nor does it count as independent practice. It is, instead, a discourse in which the patient is co-opted, and in which mind becomes a repository of true (or false) 'meanings', compatible (or incompatible) with the role of 'manager' assigned to it by medicine.

PURIFICATION AND EMBODIMENT

This role is not, by any means, the only conceivable one, even in the experience of illness; and we might think that a robust concept of embodiment would incorporate other possibilities. Benner, in the example just outlined, does not think much of the informal theories of mind/body interaction proposed by some asthmatics. Neither do I; but the existence of one implausible psychological theory does not necessarily discredit all theories of this type (in the same way that the existence of an implausible physical theory would not imply that all physical theories could be discounted). On the face of it, a view of the person which somehow integrates mind and body is likely to ascribe greater powers to the mind than a view which regards body and mind as 'separate'. Popularly, many alternative and complementary approaches to healing claim that the integration of body and mind is a metaphysical truth underpinning their success, and that this belief in integration is what distinguishes such therapies from conventional medicine. In principle, and for anyone who is broadly anti-dualist, this should not look unreasonable.

If some complementary approaches invoke a mechanism akin to 'conscious control', or at any rate a particular state of mind, as the key element in healing – and they do – then it may be easier to see how this could be possible on an 'integrated' view than on a Cartesian view. For if mind and body really are 'integrated' (whatever this turns out to mean), then mind must be somehow implicated in health and illness. Rather more cautiously, the mind might well have a role which conventional medicine overlooks, and which Cartesians would find difficult to account for. I am not competent to assess Eastern approaches; but in the Western tradition, I would cite gestalt therapy (Perls *et al.*, 1973), the Alexander Technique (Alexander, 1923;

Barlow, 1973), hypnosis (Laurence and Perry, 1988; Braude, 1991), and certain approaches to pain, developed by people with chronic illness (Wendell, 1996; see also Horn and Munafò, 1997) as particularly significant in this respect. It strikes me that a genuine anti-dualism, even in nursing, would be open to such ideas, rather than trying to exclude them from the range of what is thinkable – which is what Benner, wittingly or otherwise, contrives to do in the case of asthma.

In saying this, I am not making a general pitch for alternative and complementary forms of medicine. I am interested in the examples I have just referred to because, in various ways, they imply a relation between mind and body which is in stark contrast to the 'managerial' view (the same can possibly be said of psychoneuroimmunology; see Pitts, 1996, for example). Their significance lies, not just in the notion that the mind can learn to exercise a form of control which goes beyond the limits defined by medicine, but in the idea that one's awareness of the body can also be enhanced, a concept for which methodological dualism provides little or no scope. Indeed, the polarization of mind and body in health care discourse formally sanctions the view that mind has no privileged access to corporeal information, even in principle. One's knowledge of the body is delegated to medicine, with kinaesthetic, proprioceptive, or other forms of 'internal awareness' being dismissed as hearsay. Hence, the numerous accounts of people reporting symptoms which medical practitioners declare to be impossible, but which are subsequently validated (see James, 1993, for a particularly graphic example in the recent history of multiple sclerosis). It is certainly true that our own culture does not have an extensive proprioceptive vocabulary; but as long as dualism – in any of its guises – defines what the experience of illness can be, it is not likely that we will acquire one. The allocation of body and mind to different spheres of expertise serves to reinforce their mutual alienation and ensures that, short of recourse to alternative health care practices (Saks, 1992), most people never secure access to the experiences and language which might help them to overcome it.

As I noted earlier, methodological dualism brings to mind Latour's (1993) discussion of the 'modern constitution', with its rigid distinction between 'nature' and 'society'. 'We have never been modern', Latour says, meaning that 'modernity' has never been more than a fiction. The world is, and always has been, built of networks of things and people. Its constituents are hybrids, resisting any understanding that would reduce them to the 'natural', the 'social', the 'artefactual', or even 'discourse'. That this insight applies to health care seems to me evident. In Latour's terms, people are body/mind hybrids, just as the other constituents of the world are nature/society hybrids; and the polarization of mind and body, characteristic of health care discourse, I see as one of the 'purification' devices Latour is trying to dismantle. Latour thinks of this dismantling as a form of empowerment, freeing us from the dominant either/or of the scientific and the social, the objective and the subjective, the technological and the human (see also Haraway, 1991, where a similar view is linked to an idiosyncratic interpretation of feminism).

I would accept a modest version of this claim for a robust concept of embodiment. By 'a robust concept', I mean one which is rather more than a superficial alternative to Cartesianism. Minds and bodies do not confine themselves to sending each other the occasional postcard. Mind is not limited to giving body lectures on what counts as a healthier lifestyle. The question of how body and mind interact (just as importantly, how they might be capable of interacting) has a legitimate place at the centre of health care discourse; and I have no doubt that putting it there will turn out to be an act of empowerment as well.

7 Labouring Bodies: Mothers and Maternity Policy

Fiona Brooks and Helen Lomax

Bodies do not emerge out of discourses and institutions; they emerge out of other bodies, specifically women's bodies. (Frank, 1991: 49)

In recent years, an intense and highly polarized debate has developed around the control of pregnancy and childbirth. The choice has been presented in terms of two opposing forms of maternity care: the medical model and its apparent antithesis, 'natural' childbirth. Whilst the medical model is characterized as the active technicological management of pregnancy and childbirth controlled by obstetricians, natural childbirth is represented as low intervention in a biologically determined process supported by midwifery care (Annandale and Clarke, 1996). The controversy over maternity care intensified in the early 1990s as it became apparent that any policy change would determine the future direction of both obstetrics and midwifery (Martin, 1987). This came with the publication of the Winterton Report in 1992, and the Department of Health's subsequent response, *Changing Childbirth*, published in 1993, which were intended to settle the debate around maternity care. Both were acclaimed by the midwifery profession, consumer pressure groups and social policy analysts as heralding a new dawn in women-centred maternity care (Jackson, 1996; Pascall, 1997).

Sociologists have already problematized the notion that a fusion of midwifery and natural childbirth represents an automatic prioritization of women's needs (Rothman, 1982; Arney, 1982; Arney and Neill, 1990). In this chapter we attempt to develop this critique further by suggesting that current policy on maternity care in the UK, including *Changing Childbirth*, represents not so much a radical departure from previous interventions as the continuing prioritization of the medical model and the negation of women's situated knowledge of birth

122

(Rothman, 1982; Annadale and Clarke, 1996). We suggest that maternity policy both continues to reflect the dominance of professional, medicalized discourses on the female body and serves as the means of their reproduction. Moreover, we argue that, by locating the female body in a culturally constructed conception of 'nature', the natural childbirth model similarly operates to prevent an account of childbirth based on women's actual and diverse embodied experiences.

Through an exploration of the dominant discourses surrounding the management of labour, pain control and women's expression of the experience of childbirth, we shall examine the argument that maternity policy fails to give credence to women's situated knowledge of birth. As a consequence, we suggest, women's embodied experiences remain unvoiced in maternity policy and care. The analysis is drawn from two studies exploring women's experiences of maternity care (Brooks, 1991; Lomax, 1995). The impetus for the chapter arose not only from a sense of connection between our two sets of data but also from our own experiences of pregnancy and childbirth which neither of us were able to locate within the natural childbirth discourse in the way we had expected. This led us to question the construction of dominant discourses of reproduction and childbirth, and the assumptions they made about women's embodied experience, and subsequently to explore their role in the formation of contemporary maternity policy.

THE FEMALE BODY, MEDICAL DISCOURSE AND CHILDBIRTH

Within the sociology of reproductive health, a central feature of analysis has been the identified failure of the medical profession to respond to the actual health needs of women. Instead, the profession has been seen to have created and sustained an influence over the reproductive process disproportionate to the value of medical knowledge and expertise for women's reproductive health (Barrett and Roberts, 1978: 41–2; Roberts, 1981). An important area of medical control to come under increasing criticism over the last two decades is that of maternity care (Garcia, 1984; Garcia *et al.*, 1990; Maternity Services Advisory Committee, 1984: 1; Flint, 1982). Dissatisfaction has been expressed with high levels of medical intervention, poor communication, and the depersonalized and fragmented nature of care

(Cartwright, 1979; MacIntyre, 1982; Walker, 1985). The evidence suggests that black and ethnic minority women are particularly disadvantaged by the maternity services (Bowes and Domokos, 1996). 'Medicalized' childbirth, it is argued, has transformed women into objectified, passive bodies processed by a system over which they have little control (Oakley, 1980; Rothman, 1987). Moreover, epidemiological studies would suggest that the improved health and survival rates for infants and mothers over the course of the century have more to do with social and economic change than the application of medical knowledge (Pascall, 1997: 171).

The origins of the medical model of childbirth and its product, the active management of birth, have been firmly located in Western cultural discourses concerning the female body. Feminist theorists have identified how the female body is always defined as the 'other' in Western scientific thought (Bordo, 1993; Keller, 1995):

> Women are so other to men, as blacks are to whites, as animals are to human beings, as death is to life – although different degrees of otherness are here involved. (Jordanova, 1989: 109)

On such a continuum of 'otherness', black and ethnic minority women's bodies are perhaps the most 'other' as evidenced, for example, by the use of black female slaves for gynaecological experimentation in nineteenth-century America (Daly, 1979). In the Cartesian dualism of Western philosophy, the female body became the representation of 'nature, emotionality, irrationality and sensuality' in contrast to the self-control apparently evidenced by the male body (Davis, 1997). Pregnancy and labour represent the female body at its most 'other', mysterious, potentially undisciplined and unpredictable, distant from the male body as the disciplined locus of rationality and self-control (Martin, 1987).

As a privileged discourse, Western biomedicine has played an influential role in the characterization of the female body as inherently pathological (Ehrenreich and English, 1978; Bleier, 1984; Keller, 1995; Jordanova, 1989; Walton and Fineman, 1996). Martin (1987) suggests that women's bodies in cultural definitions of sexuality and reproduction are more likely than men's to be fragmented and objectified in a medical lexicon which separates mind and body (1987: 21). She further suggests that the medical response to birth is firmly located in a mechanical metaphor of the body with female bodies, and more particularly the uterus, being regarded within obstetrics as a machine. The pregnant and labouring body in this paradigm becomes a corporeal object in need of being 'tamed and controlled by the (dis)embodied objective male scientist' (Keller, 1986). The ascription of unpredictability, coupled with the potential for pathology, provide justification for the extension of the medical gaze to all births (Arney, 1982: 100; Campbell and Porter, 1997). Labour becomes something to be monitored and controlled, each 'stage' of 'normal' labour adhering to a prescribed time with any 'deviations' managed artificially with technology, forceps, surgery or drugs. The regimentation inherent in medical approaches to childbirth makes the labouring body predictable, and hence disciplined and controlled.

The medical management of pain in labour through drug regimes is a further way of achieving a controlled and disciplined body that will not disrupt the order of the ward (Arney, 1982; Glaser and Strauss, 1967). Kirkham (1987) found that professional advice and support during labour, and particularly the decision to instigate the use of pain relief, functioned to ensure the user's passive compliance and hence the smooth running of the ward. Midwives felt their role to be one of suggesting or administering pain relief if they felt that the patient might become too distressed and pose a potential threat to the quiet ordering of the ward (Kirkham, 1987). In other words, the control over the decision-making process is clearly not in the hands of the users. Rather, the restriction of the medical response to pain relief is a vehicle for the machine model of embodiment, one that effectively negates the emotional experience of pain in labour (Bendelow and Williams, 1995). This has implications for the embodied agency of women in labour, as their subjective and emotional responses to pain are denied in the focus on ensuring pain relief.

In the medical model, then, the labouring body becomes a faceless vehicle conveying the foetus into 'obstetrically appropriate places' (Arney and Neill, 1990). At best, women's own accounts, or situated knowledge of their embodied experience, are viewed as a form of self-indulgence and, at worst, they are reduced to an irrelevance (Frank, 1991). Women's invisibility is further assured by the position of the foetus in medical discourse. Based as it is on individuality, foetal personhood creates an illusion of physical and psychological separation from the woman's body that devalues maternal dependence. In addition, the foetus in medical imagery is invariably male, imagery that results in a promotion of male bodily integrity and the invisibility of the mother's self and body (Oakley, 1980).

It is from a critique of the negation of the subjective experience of childbirth that the natural childbirth movement emerged in the 1930s

(Arney and Neill, 1990). This gave rise, in turn, to the second of the two dominant discourses shaping the expression of the embodied experience of childbirth.

NATURAL CHILDBIRTH: EMBODYING CONTROLLED AND MANAGED NATURE?

The discourse of natural childbirth privileges the role of the woman's psychological experience in determining the process and outcomes of birth (Arney and Neill, 1990). A useful articulation of the natural childbirth discourse is provided in a key text of the movement, Janet Balaskas's (1989) *New Active Birth: A Concise Guide to Natural Childbirth* (but see also Michael Odent's *Primal Health and Birth Re-Born*). Balaskas's book, which is intended as 'a manual for women and their birth partners', emphasizes 'uninhibited', 'active' birth. One way of achieving this, the author suggests, is through a regimen of yoga-based exercise during pregnancy. However, natural childbirth is more than just a simple health promotion message based on exercise. Its regimes are concerned with women re-educating their bodies to recapture instinctive childbearing:

> We can regain a link with our primitive female heritage by re-educating our bodies in the habits, movements and postures which are instinctive to the childbearing woman. (Balaskas, 1989: ix).

Consequently antenatal preparation becomes a process not so much of health education as what Balaskas terms a 'physical remembering' of a pre-historical, almost mystical past. In so doing, natural childbirth draws on an essentialist discourse of female embodiment (Lupton, 1994) which constitutes women as instinctive beings for whom childbirth is an opportunity to express natural womanly instincts (see Leboyer, 1977; Kitzinger, 1978). In this particular cultural construction of the female body, the defining category for the subjective experience of childbirth is ascribed to 'nature' (Frank, 1991; Sbisa, 1996).

As in the medical model, the pain of childbirth is an aspect of the corporeal body to be managed. In natural childbirth, however, it is the woman herself who must manage the pain through successful regression into her primitive being. In so doing, the pain experienced by the corporeal self becomes positive – 'life-affirming' – and transformed into a form of sexual fulfilment. Thus Balaskas argues that regression not only reduces pain but affords the labouring woman the most rewarding sexual experience of her life:

Many women say that the moment of birth was like the greatest orgasm they have ever experienced. (Balaskas, 1989: 94).

In contrast to the medical model, where control of pain is under the supervision and gaze of the obstetrician, the management of pain in natural childbirth must be achieved by the corporeal body of the woman (by secreting endorphins). The discourse of 'natural' labour is of birth as a sexual experience located in an apparent universality of female bio-logical connection to the forces of nature (Sbisa, 1996). Women's bodies undergo a process of sanctification during childbirth, with the uterus becoming a site of reverence rather than revulsion and pathology:

This great opening of the womb happens only once or a few times in your life. (Balaskas, 1989: 91)

Another parallel with the medical model is the way in which natural childbirth and its techniques of pain relief are justified in terms of the safety of the child. Using the active birth programme to cope with pain is a means of achieving a 'healthy end product':

The greatest advantage of being able to accept and tolerate the pain, and allowing nature to take its course without disturbing the whole process, is an alert, healthy, undamaged and vigorous baby at the end of the day. (Balaskas, 1989: 94)

Ironically, then, the same type of argument which is frequently used by obstetrics to justify intervention is used by exponents of natural childbirth to advocate non-intervention. So far from the counter-discourse of natural childbirth representing a radical challenge to the medicalization of pregnancy and childbirth, it merely reconstitutes the privileged discourse it purports to resist.

In the course of their implementation, the bodily techniques of natural childbirth have also been co-opted by the medical model. Rothman (1987) and Oakley (1982) provide empirical evidence for this process of co-option in their examination of 'prepared child-birth', a concept which, they suggest, has involved the socialization of women into a certain form of labour management. In order to labour appropriately, women must remain psychologically adjusted to the pregnancy and prepared for an active birth:

In order to give birth properly these days one must attend classes in it ... to learn how to do it actively. (Oakley, 1987)

Increasingly, the responsibility for learning has extended to the woman's partner, relatives or companions who have been transformed into 'birth partners' through their attendance at antenatal education classes. Both medical and non-medical attendants have thereby been assigned responsibility for supervising and maintaining women's adherence to the tenets of natural childbirth. The explanation for this subjection of women to bodily regimens may be that natural childbirth was not inspired by women's actual embodied experience or a wish to extend their control over the birth process. Rather, as evidenced by the work of Lamaze (1958) and Leboyer (1977), natural childbirth emerged out of the concerns of its key exponents with pain management, with the role of the woman's (male) partner or 'coach', and with the experience of the foetus (Mead, 1949; Rothman, 1987).

In both medical and natural childbirth discourses, therefore, the labouring body is a potential source of 'bodily contingency' (Frank, 1991) which requires regulation and control. In the former, this is achieved through medical regimens and the temporal ordering of labour into distinct stages, each managed by specific interventions. In the latter, the notion of prepared childbirth results in another strait-jacket constraining the pregnant and labouring body to achieve appropriate regression to a more primitive and instinctual state. This process of rendering women's bodies into symbols of nature to be revered is as problematic as the pathology of the medical model (Coward, 1989). The expression of women's own subjective and situated knowledge of childbirth (Sbisa, 1996) is, once again, subordinate to a dominant discourse of women's oppression. This time the construction of women as instinctive primitive bearers of children requires all aspects of the performance of the labouring body to conform to a definition of the feminine as natural, sexual and instinctive being.

MATERNITY POLICY: MAINTAINING DOMINANT DISCOURSES

The preceding sections have attempted to highlight how both the medical and natural childbirth discourses fail to give prominence to women's own embodied experiences. Instead it is professional or essentialist accounts which are privileged in each discourse. Maternity policy, we suggest, has maintained the privileged position of dominant discourses, offering a means of promoting obstetric discourses of the pregnant and labouring body and of regulating women's resistance. A review of maternity policy over the last thirty years provides a useful illustration of the ability of obstetrics to be 'rapidly reactive' and reconstitute its objective field to incorporate and, perhaps more importantly, to construct a version of women's subjectivity that is acceptable to obstetrics (Arney, 1982).

The debate over place of birth provides one of the most significant examples of the many tensions and debates surrounding the provision of maternity care (Wertz and Wertz, 1979; Romalis, 1981). Consideration of the approach adopted in government reports over the last twenty years provides an indication of the influence of medical definitions of childbirth, particularly in terms of the view of childbirth as a pathological event:

> We consider that the resources of modern medicine should be available to all mothers and babies and we think that sufficient facilities should be provided to allow 100% hospital delivery. The greater safety of hospital confinement for mother and child justifies this objective (Maternity Advisory Committee, 1970: para. 277).

Both the Peel Report (Maternity Advisory Committee, 1970) and, even more markedly, the later Short Report (1980) clearly subordinated the preferences of women to the demands of medicalized childbirth (Oakley, 1984: 220). However, in its response to the Short Report, the government acknowledged that the recommended levels of obstetric control were inappropriate and made it clear that health workers could not make executive decisions on women's behalf. The Maternity Services Advisory Committee to the Secretaries of State for Social Services was set up in the 1980s in the wake of the Short Report, in part as a response to:

> .... the groundswell of consumer complaints which alleged that the service was in the grip of technological advance, the victim of excessive pressure on hospitals and in dire need of humanising." (Munro [chair of the committee], 1985)

The remit of the Committee was to identify ways of raising the standard of maternity services. However, the focus was on reducing levels of consumer criticism by identifying ways of 'humanizing' the service within existing resources. Enhancing user control and actively developing strategies for increased participation in the decision-making process did not appear to be on the agenda.

The Committee reported its findings in 1984 in *Care During Childbirth*. Although its tone represented a shift away from the enforced compliance advocated by the Short Report, in essence the message was identical. The second of the three parts of the report completed by the Committee, 'Maternity care in action', devotes an entire chapter to home births. Tellingly, however, this is positioned immediately after the chapter on complications in labour rather than alongside the discussion of labour and birth. The text of the chapter provides further evidence of the negative stance of the Committee on home confinements:

> As unforeseen complications can occur in birth, every mother should be encouraged to have her baby in a maternity unit where emergency facilities are readily available ... . (Maternity Services Advisory Committee, 1984, part II: 23)

This policy statement by the Committee effectively represents a tacit acceptance of the medical definition of every birth as only being normal in retrospect (Romalis, 1981: 21). Rothman (1982) argues that it is the inherent emphasis on risk, an emphasis that moves to encompass more and more births as high risk, which serves to justify medical authority over childbirth. Furthermore, within the medical model, the judgement of what constitutes a high or low risk is only open to clinical definition. Alternative definitions, such as those offered by the woman herself, are ruled unscientific. This division between acceptable professional opinion and unacceptable lay preference is made explicit in the chapter on home births referred to above:

> Some mothers might prefer to have their babies at home despite the possible risks, feeling that these are outweighed by the benefits they perceive to themselves and their families. Doctors and midwives should discuss the reasons for each mother's preference, so that her final decision is an informed one. (Maternity Services Advisory Committee, 1984, part II: 23)

The recommendation that professionals 'discuss' with the woman her reasons for seeking a home birth suggests an attempt to dissuade her, presumably by informing her of the risks associated with this choice from an expert perspective.

As Oakley (1981) notes, there has been a tendency in government reports (notably the Peel and Short Reports) to take the view that women need only be adequately educated or informed to appreciate the benefits of a hospital delivery and the value of technological intervention. The authoritarian tone of the Short Report has been replaced by more subtle appeals to the power of professional persuasion. Arney and Neill (1990) argue that obstetric practice has been humanized by encompassing the notions of support and reduced intervention advanced by natural childbirth, thereby simultaneously extending medical surveillance to the mind as well as the body of the pregnant and labouring woman. The concept of 'informed choice' can be similarly interpreted as a means by which women's sources of information, thoughts and decision-making are subjected to medical scrutiny and validation.

A further noteworthy feature of maternity policy at this time is the construction of the midwife as a defender of hospital deliveries and advocate for medicalized definitions of childbirth. This is problematic inasmuch as the view of midwifery care as 'woman-centred' is frequently expounded in the professional literature. Moreover, both the Short Report and the Maternity Services Advisory Committee Report were published in or after a period when evidence had emerged which systematically demonstrated that home births were as safe or even safer than hospital deliveries (Hazell, 1975; Mehl, 1977; Tew, 1978). As Chalmers and Richards (1977) argue, supposedly scientific decisions are frequently based on medical fashion and institutional custom rather than any considered evaluation of the findings of controlled research studies. It may be concluded that the emphasis on hospital confinements says more about the dominance of obstetrics than it does about the actual safety of either hospital or home deliveries. Yet the dominance of medical definitions of normality and safety have had important implications for the nature of midwifery and for the involvement of women in the decision-making process.

Prior to 1993, government reports acknowledge the conflict between women and providers, and between their approaches to childbirth, although their recommendations have been clearly situated within the medical model. Although some concessions were made in the light of women's criticisms, reforms were limited to humanizing the face of, rather than radically changing, the system of medicalized maternity care (Graham and Oakley, 1981: 70). For example, partners were 'allowed' to be present during childbirth; the organization of antenatal clinics was made more user-friendly; and efforts were made to change professional attitudes, such as encouraging doctors to be 'less dogmatic about the needs of maternity patients' (Graham and Oakley, 1981: 70). However, humanizing care is not necessarily the same as changing power relationships, and the balance of power has remained with the professionals (Haire, 1972; Stacey, 1988: 243). The inspiration for changes in maternity care has been less an attempt to gain increased control for women, or even for patients as a whole, but frequently a response to 'vogue' theories such as maternal bonding (Critical Social Policy editorial 1982). As Stacey (1988) notes, reforms achieved in this way amount to no more than 'privileges' which can be revoked if the theory is discredited. Measures have also tended to be implemented piecemeal rather than as part of a concerted strategy to improve maternity services. Finally, humanizing care has been seen as a means of diluting and negating women's more radical demands. As Oakley (1981) notes in her analysis of the role of the consumer in government reports, the Short Report anticipated that women's demands for home birth and GP unit deliveries would be eradicated if consultant units were 'humanized' and mothers 'educated' about the need for intervention.

The problem with incremental reform is not so much the changes in themselves but their limited nature. Concessions have been made in the light of women's criticisms but institutional priorities remain undisturbed (Oakley, 1984). An evaluation of any move towards user-centred maternity care would need to consider not only attempts to humanize care but also changes oriented towards increasing women's control over the management of their care. Furthermore, it seems possible to conclude that the latter would involve a redefinition of the risks defined as attaching to pregnancy and childbirth within the medical model. It is with the apparent potential for such a radical reshaping of maternity care that we consider the latest expression of maternity policy, *Changing Childbirth* (Expert Maternity Group, 1993).

CHANGING CHILDBIRTH – HUMANIZING THE MEDICAL MODEL

Pregnancy is a long and special journey for a woman. It is a journey of dramatic physical, psychological and social change; of becoming a mother, of redefining family relationships and taking on the long-term responsibility for caring and cherishing a new born child. Generations of women have travelled the same route, but each journey is unique. (Expert Maternity Group, 1993: Part II)

The expert group responsible for *Changing Childbirth* was set up in 1992 in response to the Winterton Report (HMSO, 1992) which rejected the view of the Maternity Services Advisory Committee that all births should take place in hospital. In the light of the 1992 report, the expert group was set up to 'review policy on NHS maternity care, particularly during childbirth, and to make recommendations'. Three key principles of maternity care emerged from their deliberations. These were that women should be at the centre of decisions about their care; that services should be accessible to women; and that women should be involved in the planning and auditing of services.

Thus, on a first reading, *Changing Childbirth* appears to constitute a radical departure from previous policy interventions. The description of pregnancy and birth in the document as a 'unique' experience', 'a time of growth' and a 'journey' seems to embrace the terminology of the natural childbirth movement. Moreover, by clearly placing women at the centre of maternity care and stating that 'pregnancy is not a pathological process', the medical model of childbirth appears to have been rejected:

> Pregnancy is not a pathological process or a disease ... clinical care is too often delivered in a way which is determined by a model or pattern of care more appropriate to states of ill-health than to a physiological process which for the majority results in a normal and uncomplicated outcome. (Expert Maternity Group, 1993: Part II)

However, detailed textual analysis, particularly of the section dealing with the objectives of the report, indicates a high level of accommodation to the medical model. As we shall demonstrate, the document maintains a focus on the abnormal and privileges both the safety discourse and the view of pregnancy and childbirth as pathological. We therefore argue that, far from providing a platform for women's own situated knowledge of childbirth, instead *Changing Childbirth* creates a humanized vision of maternity care that is marked by continuity with, rather than departure from, previous interventions. *Changing Childbirth* not only fails to remove the labouring body from medical surveillance, it provides considerable credibility for a humanized obstetrics that comfortably incorporates the discourse of natural childbirth without challenging the privileged position of obstetrics (Arney and Neill, 1990). It is now the professional's role to manage childbirth so that the goal of childbirth as a 'positive, life enhancing experience' is achieved. The report is further limited by its reliance on the natural childbirth discourse for its woman-centred perspective. For example, as we discuss, the report draws almost exclusively on the view that, given the right care and the right social circumstances, women will be empowered by childbirth. Thus, the 'unique experience' of childbirth is not one different and unique for each individual woman but unique to women as primitive instinctual beings. Support for this interpretation of *Changing Childbirth* can be drawn from two areas: a consideration of the evidence base underpinning the report and the prominence given in the report to a discourse of safety.

THE EVIDENCE BASE: POWERFUL PROFESSIONALS AND MARGINALIZED MOTHERS

The publication of *Changing Childbirth* has been heralded by the midwifery profession as policy developed directly in line with women users' views and expectations of services (Summers *et al*:, 1997). However, closer scrutiny of the nature of the evidence on which its recommendations are based does not seem to support such an interpretation. Specifically, although on first reading the report appears to give credence to the views of women, analysis of the 'methods' section, and particularly the document's appendices, indicates a prioritization of 'expert evidence' and a downgrading of consumer 'opinion'.

   The report indicates that the evidence on which the recommendations were based was obtained from four sources: oral testimony from both professionals and women using the service; visits to maternity units; an 'expert' conference; and a MORI survey of women who had recently given birth. The list of contributors included in the appendices reveals that the panel did not give equal weight to the views of consumers, rather the evidence supporting the findings was derived almost entirely from maternity services representatives. Actual users of maternity services (listed as 'consumers') represent only three out of the 61 individuals and organizations to contribute. The remaining 58 are all professionals or organizations purporting to represent the service, the consumer, or both. While the latter two might claim to, or be seen to, represent women's interests, they also have their own distinct political identities and agendas. Membership of the expert group itself similarly comprised, principally, health service professionals drawn from NHS management. Exceptions were the President of the National Childbirth Trust, a management consultant, and a journalist. No members of the expert group were listed as consumers. The membership of the expert conference is even more dominated by professionals. The listed participants – the panel and invited speakers – are all professional representatives connected with maternity care. While, of course, many of these are women, some of whom will have experienced services as consumers, what is of interest here is that they are included in their capacity as professionals rather than as service users. With the exception of one editorial director, whose status as a 'mother of two children' is also mentioned, no woman appears to have been invited on the basis of her reproductive experience alone.

Further problems concern the way in which the Committee obtained evidence. It is apparent from the report that evidence from consumer groups was received in writing only whereas the representatives of professional organizations had the opportunity to present evidence in person. Moreover, while the evidence derived from women service users' situated knowledge of childbirth are described as 'stories', the accounts of professionals (or 'experts' according to the definition used in the report) represent testimony or evidence:

> The experts heard many stories illustrating ways in which sensitive and flexible professional care can enhance the experience and safety of pregnanacy and birth. (Expert Maternity Group, 1993: pp. 11–12)

Furthermore, as the above quotation illustrates, women's accounts were frequently used to endorse the value of professional input rather than as a means of identifying the direction of policy change.

The level of detail provided on the professional status of each of the representatives involved offers an interesting contrast to the lack of information about the MORI research. The report indicates only that this involved women who had recently given birth. It is not clear what information was obtained from respondents or, indeed, what numbers were involved, how the sample was drawn, or what its precise contribution to the final report was. Again, this discrepancy runs counter to the philosophy of the 'woman-centred' approach advocated in the report and represents a failure to engage fully with women's experiences of childbirth. Overall this imbalance between user and professional voices is somewhat at odds with the assertion made in the report that women should not only be at the centre of decisions about their own care but should be involved in policy and planning decisions about maternity service provision.

CHANGING CHILDBIRTH: THE PROMINENCE OF THE SAFETY DISCOURSE

The continued elevation of the medical discourse in *Changing Childbirth* can be illustrated by its treatment of the issue of safety:

Maternity services should support the mother, her baby and her family during this journey with a view to their safety but also to their long-term well-being. (Expert Maternity Group, 1993: Part II)

The document appears initially to problematize medicalized approaches to safety by pointing to empirical evidence identifying the safety of home deliveries (Tew, 1990) and by acknowledging the iatrogenic effect the dominance of the safety discourse has on the construction and delivery of maternity care:

The issue of safety, however, used as an over-riding principle, may become an excuse for unnecessary interventions and technological surveillance which detract from the experience of the mother. (Expert Maternity Group, 1993: 9)

Yet there remains a central emphasis in the report on medicalized definitions of safe maternity care. The first substantive chapter, which is concerned with defining and describing the principles of *Changing Childbirth*, has an initial section entitled 'Safety'. Expression of the notion of woman-centred care is qualified by issues of safety. While acknowledging the psycho-social aspects of labour, ultimately, the medicalized safety discourse remains unchallenged as the basis for professional decision-making in maternity care:

We believe, on the evidence that we have seen, that the service could be organised in a way which *does not jeopardise safety, yet is kinder, more welcoming and more supportive* to the women whose needs it is designed to meet. (Expert Maternity Group, 1993: Part II, our emphasis)

In addition, the report's final words on the issue privilege the continued prioritization of the medical model's safety discourse:

The issue of safety, encompassing as it does the emotional and physical well-being of the mother and baby, must remain the foundation of good maternity care. (Expert Maternity Group, 1993: 10)

So far from proposing a radical reorganization of care with the objective of empowering women to take the central place in the decision-making process, one of the primary concerns of the expert group is to make the service 'kinder'. The widespread conclusion of research into the efficacy of obstetrically-managed childbirth is that the benefits for woman and unborn child alike derive from its selective rather than universal application (Pascall, 1997). Yet the identification of safety as the foundation of maternity services suggests they are to be made user-friendlier rather than user-centred so as not to compromise medicalized approaches to safety.

CONCLUSION

In this chapter we have suggested that maternity policy, including the most recent initiative *Changing Childbirth*, represents a re-presenting of professional power and a humanizing of the medical model rather than a clearly identified alternative vision. The overriding influence in the construction of maternity policy is one that is external to the pregnant woman and functions to reinforce the dominant discourse of women's oppression:

> Embodiment is anything but a neutral constant in social life, representing instead the political principles of class and gender domination. (Frank, 1991: 42)

In both the dominant discourses influencing the construction of maternity policy, women are objectified as producers of children, and the body in childbirth is defined in terms of a potential for bodily contingency which consequently requires regulation and control. We suggest that both models function to prevent the construction of an account that is based, or even draws, upon women's actual embodied experience of birth. Further, both approaches universalize women's experiences such that any differences around, for example, class, 'race', religion, ethnicity, sexuality or disability are obscured and distorted. In doing so, they allow only for the expression of standardized acceptable accounts of the embodied experience of childbirth and consequently result in fixed responses to the pregnant and labouring body.

It has been suggested that the challenge for social policy is to forge connections between women's situated knowledge and professional practice. For example, in her new feminist analysis of social policy, Gillian Pascall (1997) is optimistic about the progressive intent of *Changing Childbirth* which she interprets as a response to a shift in the politics of childbirth towards consumers and away fom medicine. Inasmuch as both the Winterton Report and *Changing Childbirth* recommended a more central and powerful role for midwives, Pascall argues that: 'there is now a prospect of increasing women's choice as consumers and their role as service providers in maternity care' (188).

However, as we have suggested in this chapter, in order to construct new cultural elaborations of women's embodied experience of birth, there must first be a social recognition of women's right to generate their own knowledge about the experience of childbirth (Sbsia, 1996). In the context of the re-presentation of *Changing Childbirth* as *the solution* to women's problems with maternity care there is a very real danger that this may not now happen.

In conclusion, perhaps the ultimate danger of *Changing Childbirth* is not only that it negates women's experiences or gives too much prominence to a safety discourse. Rather, it is that its reception by consumer organizations, midwives and policy analysts as a radical and 'woman-centred' way forward is such that the conflict over maternity provision is now perceived to be resolved. As we illustrate in this chapter, given the ability of obstetrics to incorporate within its sphere of power any attempt to reform and reshape maternity provision, maternity policy must remain an actively contested arena.

8 Disciplinary Interventions and Resistances around 'Safer Sex'

Martin Mitchell

The recent interest in the relationship between the body and society in sociology has developed alongside an increased scrutiny of the construction and impact of social policies in many areas of health and social care. These developments have opened up the possibility of critically re-examining debates about the nature of subjectivity, while also attempting to reach an understanding of the ways in which state institutions actively intervene to shape and discipline our bodily practices and sense of self.

The advent of HIV and AIDS ushered in a new visibility for the bodies and sexual practices of those infected with the virus or deemed to be 'at risk' (Fitzpatrick et al., 1992; Watney, 1989). During the 1980s and early 1990s a great deal of interest was stimulated around the discourses of AIDS prevention and health education as different moral agendas collided (Treichler, 1987; Weeks, 1989). In particular, the 'gay community' resisted the intrusive threat of heterosexist policy interventions that tried to re-construct gay sexuality to the point of non-existence (Davies and Project SIGMA 1992).

More recently criticism within sociological analyses has focused on rationalistic and behavioural approaches to HIV/AIDS intervention strategies which produced restrictive definitions of 'safer sex' (Hart et al., 1992; Donovan et al., 1994; Boulton et al., 1995; Kippax, 1996). These criticisms allow the opportunity to draw on the more abstract debates within the sociology of the body and emotions (Burkitt, 1997; Williams and Bendelow, 1996), and to examine the deep physical, sexual and emotional significance of sexuality for gay men in the context of developing more appropriate and effective HIV/AIDS prevention strategies (Ames et al., 1995; Boulton et al., 1995; Parnell, 1996).

I will begin this chapter by briefly examining Foucault's theory of the relationship between discourses, subjectivity and the body, and then by discussing whether such a perspective leaves sufficient room for the body and emotions in terms of resistances to power that it identifies. Following similar criticisms of Foucault's deconstructive methodological approach, I then go on to outline the nature of my own discursive analysis of the gay community's response to HIV/AIDS discourses through the medium of the gay press. I argue that there is by no means one definitive meaning of 'safer sex', and that the gay community and gay press have acted to continually negotiate the meanings of 'risk' and 'safety' in changing medical, social and political circumstances. In fact these circumstances have provided the context for a recent transition in discourses around 'safer sex' and the way in which the 'gay community' has responded. During the late 1980s there was a shift from the repressive and puritanical discourses of the 'moral right', towards a more subtle 'rationalistic' disciplinary discourse in the 1990s concerned with public health and social efficiency. While the latter discourse may initially have appeared more positive, I suggest that the last decade has seen the development of a more critical, 'embodied' discourse that resulted from the lived experience of gay men in their sexual lives. It is this new discourse that has resisted both the repressive and rationalistic discourses that preceded it. Consequently, in terms of HIV/AIDS prevention, I argue that the most effective and appropriate strategies will be those that take account of this embodied discourse, that actively involve gay men, and that take account of the deep emotional and sexual significance of gay men's sexual practices in their everyday lives.

DISCOURSE, SUBJECTIVITY AND THE BODY

Generally speaking, most sociologists agree that our experiences of subjectivity and the body are socially constructed (e.g. Synnott, 1992). There are, however, differences in emphasis: firstly, in terms of the extent to which the body is either an active recipient of social processes, or simply inscribed by them (e.g. Crossley, 1996); secondly, in terms of the extent to which bodily experience is constituted within discourses (e.g. Jackson, 1993), represents some degree of physical and emotional resistance to discourse (e.g. Craib, 1995), or becomes visible only in the act of physical and embodied expression of discourses (e.g. Burkitt, 1997). The relevance of these debates is that they allow us to examine more closely the relationship between discourse, subjectivity and the body within Foucault's conception of the historical construction of sexuality (Foucault, 1981).

Foucault was particularly concerned to show that sexuality should not be described as a 'stubborn drive ... disobedient to power', but rather as 'an especially dense transfer point for relations of power' (Foucault, 1981: 103). In the *History of Sexuality* Foucault depicted a move away from the primacy of sovereignty, law, coercion and force (the power to take life) towards the new more effective and complex technologies of power which were positive and productive in seeking to foster life (power over life). This historical change in emphasis, however, was at the same time both productive and regulative (Burkitt, 1997: 50). Modern 'technologies of control' have been concerned increasingly with the 'normalization' of health and good function (Foucault, 1981: 147; Taylor, 1986: 75; Hekma *et al.*, 1995: 17). Consequently, one of Foucault's major contributions to social science has been to describe the ever more subtle disciplining of the body through forms of 'anatamo-politics' (Foucault, 1981: 139).

Following this model it would appear that we can only make sense of modern sexual subjectivities, and the disciplinary bodily experience of such subjectivities, by examining the discourses through which they are constituted. Here the initially absent subject is positioned through meaning systems which are ontologically prior to it (Jackson, 1993: 207), and there is a distinctive emphasis on the social aspects of the body and its historically relative nature (Williams and Bendelow, 1996: 127). Yet there is a danger of a kind of 'discursive reductionism' (Burkitt, 1997: 38). The *embodied* aspect of subjectivity is lost, and reduced to the ideas in people's heads. As Craib puts it, the 'sociological aspects of emotional life should not be mistaken for the whole of emotional life' (Craib, 1995: 155), otherwise we are left with little sense of the body as lived and acted, and only with a sense of it as 'inscribed' from without (Crossley, 1996: 99).

Within Foucault's methodological approach of 'geneaology' or 'archaeology' I believe that he sets out a useful framework for tracing the historical roots of various competing discourses, and of examining the 'sociological' aspects of their impact on sexual subjectivities (Foucault, 1978; Davidson, 1986). In doing so Foucault provides a way of detaching the normative and regulative power of 'truth' from dominant discourses and practices, or 'regimes of truth' (Foucault, 1980: 131). Yet despite Foucault's prescription that history should be susceptible to analysis 'in accordance with the intelligibility of struggles

... strategies and tactics' (Foucault, 1980: 114), his analyses differed from those in the Marxist or feminist traditions where revelation of the 'abuse' of power under a particular system was supposed to provide the basis for revolutionary struggle and the transcendence of current social relations (Callinicos, 1989: 62). Foucault was primarily concerned to map out the discourses he discovered, and frequently avoided any critical evaluation of the 'quality of power' or its effects/ affects (Taylor, 1986: 92). Without some conception of the bodily experience and *affectation* of discourse, and its possible *oppressive* effects [my italics], Foucault is left failing to account for the 'resist-ances' or 'subjugated knowledges' that he describes (Foucault, 1980: 133; Taylor, 1986: 95).

It is here that the relationship between the social and physical body as a site of *resistance* can be explored at two levels: firstly, at the level of social classes or groups, where the body acts as a source of political knowledge emerging from the self-definition and activity of people who 'feel' oppressed (Williams and Bendelow, 1996: 131) – an approach with much in common with feminist standpoint epistemol-ogies (Hartsock, 1983; Harding, 1987); and secondly, through the way the personal and emotional intersect with the political and social (Craib, 1995). We need to be aware of the way in which the 'subjective and political intersect', and of the 'fact of each person's uniqueness to language/discourse' (Hollway, 1989: 84). This is not just about the 'positionings' of people within discourses, but is about 'flesh and blood selves, actively bound in power relations' (Burkitt, 1997: 53–4).

ANALYSIS OF DISCOURSE AND SUBJECTIVITY IN THE CONTEXT OF HIV, AIDS AND 'SAFER SEX' AMONG GAY MEN

My own discursive research began in the early 1990s and was con-cerned with the construction of the meaning of 'safer sex', and the effect on gay men's sexuality and sexual practices. I attempted to examine the various discourses around issues of HIV, AIDS and 'safer sex' as they developed and changed during the 1980s and 1990s. I was particularly interested, on the one hand, simply to reveal what the competing discourses were. On the other hand, however, I wanted to explore the ways in which such discourses affected the interpretation of the illness and responses to it in terms of clinical control, social policies, and its effects on gay men's sexual practices and subjectivities.

The purpose of the research overall was not only to understand the processes involved in the formation of social policies around HIV/AIDS prevention strategies and their relationship to the constitution of subjectivity, but also to determine the best and most appropriate strategies from the point of view of the sexual lives of the gay men involved. This meant taking a 'standpoint' which was explicitly gay positive, and which was determined to be sensitive to the ways the moral, political, sexual and emotional aspects of sexuality intersect from the point of view of the group affected (Mitchell, 1992).

My initial research involved discursive analysis of all HIV/AIDS headlined and related articles, reports and letters (excluding arts and entertainment sections) from 209 issues of Capital Gay (CG), a London-based, free, weekly gay newspaper. The gay press was chosen for analysis because it had been highly significant in the monitoring of discourses on AIDS, and was central in developing a critical gay standpoint on the issues raised. It has also tended to act as a vehicle and residual for the expression of the experiences of the gay community. In order to gain an understanding of the subjective impact of the competing discourses that emerged, a small number of (ten) essay-type questionnaires were distributed by 'snowballing', and used to supplement the views expressed in the gay press. To increase representativeness, the views expressed in the questionnaires were further supported by evidence collected in other, larger-scale qualitative research.

Basing my analysis initially on the different 'phases' of the social response to AIDS identified by Weeks (1989: 3–8), I selected the periods 1982–83 and 1985. I then added an additional 'phase', January 1991–August 1992, to move beyond the period covered by Weeks. This initial analysis was subsequently updated through analysis of 75 issues of the Pink Paper (PP), a national, free, weekly gay newspaper, over the period January 1996–June 1997 (PP replaced CG since the former had ceased publication). All relevant articles were fully read, listed, summarized, and indexed according to the type and significance of the article (Mitchell, 1992: 12–16).

HIV/AIDS DISCOURSES IN THE UK

It was a particularly ironic coincidence that AIDS happened at the time of an 'especially fierce conflict between rival definitions of sexuality in the west' (Watney, 1990: 21). On the one side was a radical demand for an enlargement of the forms of sexuality and sexual relationships considered to be culturally legitimate. On the other were the voices of a largely secularized, yet nonetheless potent, Christian tradition which drew heavily on 'family' rhetoric. In so far as AIDS raised the reality of sexual diversity, and exposed sexual relationships and practices often previously seen as unmentionable, the disease served to threaten many of the 'most fundamental organizing categories for both individual and collective identities' (Watney, 1989: 69). AIDS came to symbolize not only a decline in sexual morality but also the moral decline of society more generally. In the early stages of the epidemic, the 'New Right' was largely successful in setting the terms of the debate, and this was reflected in increased hostility towards gay men and lesbians.

Yet from the very beginning the gay and lesbian community took part in all aspects of the management and control of HIV and AIDS, while also making interventions into biomedical science (Treichler, 1987) and social policy around AIDS prevention and health education (Weeks, 1989; Watney, 1990). Early on, the organizational skills that had been developed in the fight for lesbian and gay liberation, and which emphasized self-definition and self-help, came into play. As the intense media interest in AIDS began to decline during the 1990s, and the debates around AIDS became more 'professionalized', the gay press and gay community continued to intervene in the social policy decisions on health promotion and social care being made. As 'gay' sexuality was politicized through a repressive 'moral right' discourse, the gay community began to resist. The result was that the gay community survived the attempts to eradicate it through informed vigilance and the construction of its own alternative discourses.

THE DAWNING CRISIS AND THE EARLY CONSTRUCTION OF 'SAFER SEX'

AIDS first appeared as an embryonic issue in the UK gay press in the summer of 1982. This very early part of the crisis was most clearly marked by an awakening sense of anxiety about the possible effects of AIDS on the achievements of gay liberation, and on attitudes to gay sexuality. Headlines such as 'Please Keep a Sense of Proportion' (CG, 26 November 1982) and 'Don't Call It The Gay Cancer' (CG, 3 September 1982) were typical of the mood. Nonetheless, the overall response to the issue by the gay community was in stark contrast to widespread government indifference (Weeks, 1989: 4). By November 1982 an article entitled 'US Disease Hits London' (CG, 26 November 1982) reported that plans were already being laid for the establishment of the Terrence Higgins Trust after only the fourth death in the UK. The major watershed of concern, however, was reached in May 1983, with 72 relevant articles in the six months between May and October, compared to only nine in the equivalent period prior to May. It was at this time that Capital Gay identified AIDS as an issue for the whole gay community with its front page article 'AIDS Our First Dilemma' (CG, 6 May 1983).

Around the same time the first tentative steps were made towards the development of possible preventive health strategies. With a general lack of medical knowledge and insufficient research, the guidelines for safer sex at this time were often heuristic, and in many cases seemed impossibly restrictive. Guidelines issued by the Terrence Higgins Trust in early 1985 included such advice as to 'have sex with fewer men', and 'avoid sex with men who have had sex in high risk areas (especially the USA) in the last three years'. They went on to advise that 'since the virus has been found in saliva, perhaps the only safe sex is mutual masturbation, body rubbing and dry kissing' (CG, 1 March 1985).

It was eventually during 1985 that a number of medical advances, and the emergence of a massive self-help response (in the form of charities and organizations largely set up by gay men), combined to produce new dialogues and new guidelines around 'safer sex'. The identification of, and the production of a test for, the HIV virus led to heated debates about whether to take 'the test'. Around the same time new research indicated a link between anal sex (particularly receptive) and HIV transmission, while oral sex seemed to be relatively 'low risk'. It was this that led Capital Gay's writer on AIDS, Julian Meldrum, to announce: 'so there is such a thing as "safer sex"' (CG, 3 May 1985). While initially the Terrence Higgins Trust would not back the use of condoms ('AIDS Doctor Backs New Condom', CG, 6 December 1985), after further research it became clear that the issue was not so much whether condoms 'could hold viruses', but rather whether gay men could be 'taught and persuaded to use them properly' ('Meldrum On AIDS Special', CG, 1 November 1985). Increasingly discourses on AIDS in the gay community were couched in terms of 'risk activities' or 'safety', and by November 1985 the Terrence Higgins Trust had revised its guidelines to resemble much of what would be accepted today.

Clearly, within the gay community itself, the issue of AIDS had been couched very much in terms of the pragmatics of safer sex. There was concern, however, about the general direction of safer sex information (e.g. 'Who Said Gay Sex Needs "Cleaning Up"', CG, 8 March 1985). In particular, the idea of simply giving up certain forms of sex and sexuality deemed more 'risky' (such as 'promiscuous' sex and fucking), which some saw as an integral part of sexual liberation, was questioned. In a letter to Capital Gay, headlined 'We Must Question Safer Sex' the author raised points which were to re-emerge later in the context of behavioural research and intervention strategies.

> The other 'lie' that we are fooling ourselves with is that by changing our sexual practices we are not denying our sexuality but perhaps giving ourselves the opportunity to become fuller more sensual beings. The freedom of gay men to fuck and be fucked by each other is not something to be dismissed by equating it with an absence of sensuality ... In a situation where it should be all too easy to see that our sexuality is being socially reconstructed we should be asking a lot more questions about the long term effects of the way we are dealing with the crisis'. (CG, 13 December 1985)

Consequently, as the details of what 'safer sex' meant were argued out, the transition to safer sexual practices in this early period was far from smooth. Despite this, the eventual influence of the gay community in disseminating ideas about the possibility of safer sex became increasingly evident over the coming years (Fitzpatrick *et al.*, 1992). Yet this was only belatedly and reluctantly acknowledged by government institutions. Instead, in the moral hysteria that was to follow, attempts were made to link AIDS with gay sexuality in itself, and to subsequently define it out of existence (Watney, 1993).

GAY MEN'S RESISTANCE TO HETEROSEXIST AND HOMOPHOBIC DISCOURSES ON AIDS

That AIDS in the UK appeared to be confined to 'politically and morally embarassing' communities was absolutely central in the period of moral hysteria that occurred in the mid-1980s (Weeks, 1989). The identification of AIDS as a 'gay plague' escalated throughout the media, and the result was the kind of 'rituals of decontamination' where gay men and lesbians were refused services and sacked from jobs (Weeks, 1989: 5).

Nonetheless, the mid-1980s represented a turning point in the management of the AIDS crisis. It was the point at which the government began to respond on a scale which approximated more to the magnitude of the problem. Consequent on a generalization of risk, policy was organized around a public health campaign aimed at preventing the spread of AIDS. With an increased 'professionalization' of the AIDS organizations, and a general broadening of the understanding of the nature of AIDS and its modes of transmission, by the early 1990's safer sex and sex education had moved to centre stage in the strategic struggles of morality and politics.

The centrality of moral concerns in terms of the advocacy of 'appropriate' forms of sexual practice and sexuality was reflected in debates over the relative influence of various 'lobbies' in their attempts to direct government policy. The two sides of the debate, with the 'moral right' on one side and the 'gay community' broadly on the other, was well represented in an article called 'Moral Campaigners Demand – "Cut Funding For AIDS Info"' (CG, 10 May 1991):

> The Department of Health decided to work with homosexual organisations which had previous experience of AIDS. However this soon led to a distortion of the campaign to reflect the concerns of homosexual activists.
>
> [Family and Youth Concern]

> Their whole platform is that people should have one sexual partner for life – celibacy before marriage and monogamy after, so while those aims may be applicable to some, for many of us they are a complete irrelevance.
>
> [Terrence Higgins Trust]

On the one hand there was an emphasis on 'risk groups', forms of sexuality that put individuals more at risk, and a return to 'traditional' values around monogamy, marriage and the family. While, on the other, the emphasis was on 'risky sexual practices', and the advocacy of 'sexual safety'. Such arguments seemed to come to a head around August 1991 with the launch by a consortium of AIDS organizations of the 'Declaration of Human Rights for People With AIDS and HIV'. In direct opposition the Conservative Family Campaign launched its 'HIV Infected Citizens Charter of Human Responsibility' in which it urged those 'whose debauched lifestyles led them to contracting HIV [to] take up the mantle of moral integrity' ('Tory Call For HIV Clampdown: Charter Splits Family Campaign', CG,

30 August 1991). The influence of such messages in the construction of Conservative policy on sex education after 1992 was evident. In the *Health of the Nation* it was clear that overall change in 'lifestyle' was to be emphasized over and above 'risk activities'. In education about HIV and AIDS there was to be emphasis on:

> the health risk of casual and promiscuous sexual behaviour and to encourage pupils to have due regard to moral considerations, the value of family life and the responsibilities of parenthood. ('White Paper Looks to Changes in Sexual Practices', CG, 10 July 1992).

Not only was the influence of moral campaigners evident in public policy on sex education, but it often impacted on HIV and AIDS education within the gay community itself (e.g. 'Insight: Countless Storms in a Teacup of Public Decency', CG, 29 May 1992). In February 1992 the Gay Men's Advisory Group to the Health Education Authority resigned en masse as a protest at the lack of funding and ineffectiveness of the campaigns being proposed ('Gays Quit Top Health Authority: Mass Resignation' CG 21 February 1992), and this later led to the setting up of the organization Gay Men Fighting AIDS. Despite these problems, community-based initiatives founded on an 'erotics of safer sex' and a 'respect for diversity and choice' did challenge the continual definition of gay sexuality as either 'immoral' or 'obscene' (Watney, 1990: 31), and continued to promote 'safer sex' in explicit and sexy ways. In general, however, because government officials could not face the reality that gay sex was practised far more widely than was visible from just the 'out' gay community, the kind of general information produced was largely irrelevant to the specific needs of gay men (Field, 1992: 2; Watney, 1990: 26). The result was that the failure of government-funded campaigns to address the different sexual experiences and needs of gay men was largely swept aside, while epidemiological and behavioural research into the adoption of safer sex tended to rely on highly problematic conceptions of 'unsafe sex' (Hart *et al.*, 1992: 221; Davies and Project SIGMA, 1992: 137; Donovan *et al.*, 1994: 611).

'RELAPSE' AND HETEROCENTRIC CONCEPTUALIZATIONS OF SAFER SEX

By the end of the 1980s and early 1990s, a great deal of sociological and psychological evidence had been produced to show a major move towards the adoption of 'safer sex' behaviours among gay and bisexual men (Hart *et al.*, 1992: 217; Fitzpatrick *et al.*, 1992: 121; Fitzpatrick *et al.*, 1989: 127–8). In the early 1990s, however, concerns were expressed by a number of researchers in the field that many men were failing to sustain such behaviours (Donovan *et al.*, 1994: 606–11). Quantitative behavioural research indicated an increase in the number of men reporting unprotected anal sex (Davies and Project SIGMA, 1992: 138), and this led to the idea that there was a significant 'relapse' to 'unsafe' sexual behaviour (Hart *et al.*, 1992: 217–21; Donovan *et al.*, 1994: 611).

There were, however, many problems with this 'relapse' model, especially in that it was unclear exactly what *standard* of sexual behaviour the men concerned were 'relapsing' from. It appeared that because anal intercourse is most 'risky', gay men were being criticized for not giving it up regardless of the context in which it occurred (Donovan *et al.*, 1994: 611–12, 614; Kippax, 1996: 96–7). Straight away this commits an 'individualistic fallacy' in that it takes a definition of 'safety' outside of any emotionally significant or meaningful social context (Davies and Project SIGMA, 1992: 134–5). What was ignored was the significance of 'partner formation' (Fitzpatrick *et al.*, 1992: 131), and the fact that many of the men engaging in unprotected anal sex were more likely to be in long-term, primary relationships, where serostatus and degree of exclusivity were known (Hart *et al.*, 1992: 222; Davies and Project SIGMA, 1992: 138–9; Ames *et al.*, 1995: 68–71). Consequently, all unprotected sex was defined as 'unsafe' and, by implication, 'wrong' in advance. By using methodologically restrictive definitions of 'safe' sex, the 'probability that the same response to a particular [question about sexual practice] may be produced for a variety of different reasons' is overlooked in favour of absolute categories of behaviour (Ingham *et al.*, 1992: 221-2). It is assumed that given the correct information on HIV and AIDS no one could possibly 'make a conscious and reasoned decision to fuck' (Davies and Project SIGMA, 1992: 135-7). At the same time, insofar as 'relapse' implied a 'falling back into illness or wrongdoing', the use of the concept demonstrated a 'barely disguised homophobia' (Dowsett *et al.*, 1992: 6).

Yet a transition in regulative and normative discourses disciplining gay men's sexuality was taking place here. While it is unlikely that very much of the research into gay men's sexual practices was motivated by the kind of heterosexist, 'moral right' agenda described above, in that the implications of the interventions required to restore people to 'safe' behaviour would have meant giving up 'risky' forms of sex *entirely*, the research revealed a kind of heterocentric naivety about the 'disposability' of many forms of gay sexuality (Donovan *et al.*, 1994: 607; Parnell, 1996: 104). It seems extremely unlikely that hetero-sexual people would be asked to give up unprotected penetrative sexual intercourse in *all* circumstances simply because it is most 'risky'.

Behavioural research, and the intervention strategies linked to it, were clearly based at this stage on the 'rationalistic' idea that informa-tion-giving about 'risks' would be straightforwardly translated into people's sexual behaviour and repertoires. A new 'rationalistic' dis-course was beginning to replace the 'repressive' one that had existed prior to it. As more research was conducted, however, it became clearer that there needed to be a more sophisticated qualitative assessment of how knowledge of risk is 'incorporated into people's understanding of their own situation [as an] active process of reflection' (Holland *et al.*, 1992: 142). Such an elucidation of meaning also needed to go beyond traditional dichotomies of *rational* and reflective mind versus irrational and *emotional* body in order to examine the deep sexual and emotional dilemmas that gay men face in the age of AIDS (Prieur, 1990; Dowsett *et al.*, 1992; Ames *et al.*, 1995; Boulton *et al.*, 1995).

THE DIFFICULTIES OF RATIONALISTIC APPROACHES TO THE SUBJECT OF 'SAFER SEX', AND THE DISEMBODIED BODY

There can be little doubt that a great deal of the 'invasion' of bodily intimacy among gay men (represented by a 'rationalistic' discourse) is motivated by a genuine concern by the researchers concerned to 'foster life' and to protect public health. Yet persistent advocacy of behavioural change can be intrusive where there is a failure critically to reflect on the political and moral nature of the kind of interventions being made, or on the disciplinary, regulative and normative aspects of what is being said (Kippax, 1996: 97). There is a danger that, in reconstructing gay sexuality, few questions are asked about what the exact *objectives* of HIV prevention are to be (Donovan *et al.*, 1994: 612). It appears that there is now a move to go beyond the simple cor-relations of behavioural change, and reflect a greater consideration of the physical and emotional needs of gay men in their sexual lives (Dowsett *et al.*, 1992; Davies and Project SIGMA, 1992; Ames *et al.*,

1995; Boulton *et al.*, 1995). Yet, even here, the identification of the continued need for intervention can often resort to a *rationalistic* approach to the assessment of 'risk' in terms of the strategies and solutions put forward.

While 'moral right' discourses may have subsided considerably in terms of their effects on public perceptions of AIDS, and the sexual practices and subjectivities of gay men, even the more sensitive prevention campaigns devised by AIDS organizations and health authorities can have subtle *disciplinary* and *regulative* effects. Part of the problem is that, despite attempts to take into account the sexual and emotional needs of gay men, because of a Western tradition that has tended to 'divorce body from mind [and] reason from emotion', the physical and emotional aspects of life have been dismissed as 'irrational' and in need of being 'tamed', 'harnessed', or 'driven out' by the hand of reason (Williams and Bendelow, 1996: 125). Clearly, in the context of HIV, AIDS and safer sex, there is a great deal of room for a mindful reflectiveness and rationalistic reason. However, the continued 'risk taking' of some gay men, and their resistance to narrowly defined definitions of sexual 'safety', could be better understood if we try to examine the relationship between discourses and subjectivity in terms of how 'people's experiences of, and responses to, social structures are shaped by their *sensory* and *sensual* selves' (Shilling and Mellor, 1996: 2). As Shilling and Mellor continue:

> These variables are important as they can exert an important impact on whether people feel at ease with, and tend to reproduce, the 'rules' and 'resources' most readily accessible to them, or sensorily experience these 'structures' as unpleasant, undesirable and worthy of transformation. (Shilling and Mellor 1996: 2)

My argument is not that people should put themselves unconditionally at risk in the pursuit of sexual pleasure, but rather that safer sex strategies based solely on interventions of rationalistic reflexivity fail to understand the difficulties of giving up completely sexual practices which people find *physically* and *sensually* pleasurable (Parnell, 1996: 104). The danger is that people become seen as *disembodied* beings whose sexual desires count for nothing, just as the 'relapse' model so uncritically considered many forms of gay male sexuality 'disposable' in the context of rational assessments of 'risk'. In a context where the physical, emotional and sensate aspects of sexuality clearly still do make a difference to people's practice of 'safer sex', it would seem to make more sense to empower people to make decisions about *how to get the sex they want 'safely'* (Billington *et al.*, 1997) within an *ethical context of mutual care* (Watney, 1990: 31), rather than simply continue to pump out information about 'risks' (Parnell, 1996; Kippax, 1996; Ridge, 1996).

SAFER SEX 'STRATEGIES' AND THE PHYSICAL-EMOTIONAL SIGNIFICANCE OF SEXUAL PRACTICES

It is now well established that there is a high degree of knowledge about the transmission of HIV and safer sex guidelines among gay men (Fitzpatrick, 1989; Ames, 1995; Gold, 1996). While it is true that some gay men are continuing to take chances with their sexual health when assessed by any definition of 'safer sex' (Ames *et al.*, 1995: 63, 65–66), a substantial number appear to have developed elaborate 'strategies' or 'protocols' for ensuring sexual safety or maximum risk reduction (Hart *et al.*, 1992; Mitchell, 1992; Kippax *et al.*, 1993; Ames *et al.*, 1995). While the importance of sex, and particularly anal sex, varies in gay men's lives, many have tried to develop safer sex strategies which allow them to strike a balance between minimizing the risk of HIV infection and leading a full and happy sex and love life (Ames, 1995; Billington *et al.*, 1997). For many men access to the 'riskier' forms of sexual practice is reserved for a monogamous relationship or a primary partner of the same, 'concordant' HIV status. It is still controversial whether such strategies are 'safe' or not (see below), and this was reflected in how the more restrictive definitions of 'safety' were contradictorily incorporated into the sexual practice of respondents included in my own research:

> I am aware of differing approaches to being HIV positive ... some HIV positive people do not practise safer sex with other HIV positive people.
>
> [Chris, 35]

> I have practised safer sex with a couple of exceptions. My partner and I fuck without rubbers, call it love, but we both have the same HIV status'.
>
> [Gary, 30]

While none of these strategies might be considered entirely 'fool proof', they do demonstrate that choices about sexual practice need to be contextualized in terms of individuals' needs for love, intimacy and the expression of sexual desire (Boulton *et al.*, 1995). When raising the issue of why it is that gay men continue to have 'risky' sex, the uncomfortable answer that is often avoided is that they actually *enjoy* the sex in which they are engaging. As Ames *et al.* (1995) found from their respondents, emotional needs, sexual desire, and sexual pleasure are integral parts of sexual decision making. When asking their respondents why they still engaged in receptive anal intercourse (which although protected was still potentially most risky) they received some very revealing replies (Ames *et al.*, 1995: 64): 'It's the best way of getting close to another person'; 'It's the most intimate act'; 'I don't give up anal sex because I like it'; 'Having my lover inside me is emotionally satisfying'.

It would seem, therefore, that in respect of the desire for sex and bodily intimacy in general, and anal sex in particular, definitions of 'safer sex' that imply (intentionally or otherwise) that *abstinence* or *avoidance* are the best strategies under all circumstances will be inappropriate and ineffective. Arguably, simple abstinence does not work because when people abstain from sex they fail to learn about the safer sexual strategies they will need when they do have sex (Watney, 1990: 24). Sustaining safer sex becomes progressively more difficult as overly restrictive sexual repertoires can translate into sexual and emotional unhappiness (Dowsett *et al.*, 1992: 5–6). Even further, over-zealous messages may create resistance to any kind of safer sex as they appear to deny any existence to 'gay' sexuality at all (Treichler, 1987: 286–7).

Significantly, though, these arguments are not just about the physical and emotional significance of sexual practices to gay men, but also take us back to the relationship between discourses, subjectivity and the body. Clearly, gay men's resistance to the more restrictive definitions of safer sex are not just about the creation of alternative discourses, but are also about flesh and blood, sensual responses to rules and structures in embodied terms (Burkitt, 1997: 53; Shilling and Mellor, 1996: 4). In this sense, people are not just the subjects of discourse, but through their embodied experience of them also respond to them as 'objects', either individually or as part of a social group. People's sensual responses to the disciplinary rules and interventions within discourses will often lead them to reproduce them, but in some cases to *reject* them because they 'contradict' their bodily needs. As Shilling and Mellor (1996) put it, in some cases, actors:

> take up a certain distance from the rules in order to view them as social objects requiring strategic intervention ... people, as active

and often collective subjects, are often involved in a strategic monitoring of structures, as objects, which they perceive as requiring transformation. (Shilling and Mellor, 1996: 4)

If the 'rules' here are messages about the meaning of 'safer sex' (power over gay men's bodies – a form of anatamo-politics), then it seems that the relationship between society and the body, structure and agency, are clearly demonstrated in the gay community's 'strategic intervention' and 'strategic monitoring' of those rules as described above through the gay press. What also becomes possible is the development of a critical gay 'standpoint' along the same lines described by Hartsock (1983), where the *embodied* experience of discourse allows gay men to see the specific issue of HIV prevention in more *appropriate* and *effective* ways (Mitchell, 1992: 9).

'CONTEXTUAL' APPROACHES TO 'SAFER SEX' AND THE ISSUE OF 'NEGOTIATED SAFETY'

Since the early 1990s there has been a move towards greater discussion and acceptance of a 'contextual' approach to the meaning of 'safer sex'. This involves a closer examination of the '*details* and *context* of sexual decision making' (Ames *et al.*, 1995: 54; Kippax, 1996: 96), whilst also understanding that the development of safer sex messages requires recognition that gay men employ different sexual strategies in order to enjoy good sexual health (Hart *et al.*, 1992: 222). The implication, therefore, would appear to be that there is the possibility of developing more complex and less normative definitions of safer sex that allow people to make more choices for themselves.

During 1996 the main discussion in the gay press around the meaning of 'safer sex' focused on the concept of 'negotiated safety' – a term first developed by Kippax *et al.* (1993). The discussion in the gay press was stimulated initially by Camden and Islington Health Services NHS Trust's decision to publish a leaflet, and later a booklet, that suggested, given the right circumstances, gay men who are HIV-negative need not always use condoms for riskier forms of sex such as anal intercourse (Billington *et al.*, 1997). The booklet, called 'Thinking It Through', examined the different strategies that some men had devised so that they could enjoy the sex they wanted without necessarily using condoms, and used 'real-life accounts' of men who had faced such choices to help people 'think through the possible outcomes'

(Billington *et al.*, 1997: 4). These ideas were presented in the *Pink Paper* by Edward King who outlined the basic parameters of this new concept.

> Most safer sex messages insist all gay men should always use condoms. But uninfected men are only at risk during unprotected sex if their partner is HIV positive or doesn't know his HIV status ... Negotiated safety offers a way of minimising risk of infection for men who choose not to use condoms. The key is to find out your own – and your partner's – HIV status and implement a set of rules about sex outside the relationship' ('Edward King Discusses 'Negotiated Safety', PP, 5 April 1996).

Similar discussions were also put forward in relation to men who are HIV positive, and who may want to give up the use of condoms with another HIV positive partner (Billington *et al.*, 1997: 24–28). As Edward King put it in an article called 'Edward King on Thinking Positive':

> Safer sex is usually seen only as a way of preventing new infections, but condoms may play an important part in the sex lives of partners who know that they're both already HIV positive ... There's plenty of theory about but little hard evidence to suggest that positive men are more likely to become ill if they have unprotected sex (PP 3, May 1996).

The response to these articles, and to the concept of 'negotiated safety', varied from mixed to hostile. Some commentators reiterated the message that 'being in a relationship is no protection against HIV' (PP, 12 April 1996: 10), while others questioned the idea that negotiated safety was 'safe' at all. The most damning criticism came in a letter where the commentator stated:

> Of course we should talk about the fact that some gay couples do choose not to use condoms when fucking, but why call it negotiated safety when it is transparently unsafe? ... Such couples are negotiating risk taking: they are not ensuring their safety, whether they believe themselves to be positive or negative ... The term 'safety' legitimizes this choice which, particularly for HIV negative men, should still be considered as too dangerous. (PP, 19 April 1996: 10)

Clearly the meaning of 'safer sex' is still highly controversial, among AIDS professionals and researchers (Ridge, 1996; Gold, 1996; Pinkerton and Abramson, 1992), as well as within the gay community. What the discussions reveal, however, is the re-emergence of *'embodied'* and *'rationalistic'* discourses on sexual practice, with different regulative and normative impacts on the 'anatamo-politics' of gay men's sexual lives. While 'negotiated safety' recognizes the desire for uninterrupted sexuality, the idea of 'negotiated risk taking', or 'negotiated danger' (Ekstrand *et al.*, 1993: 281), re-emphasizes the control of the body by the rational mind. What the debate also demonstrates is the dominance of the 'rationalistic' discourse as the 'orthodox' view. Edward King made this clear in his reply to the responses made to his original articles. As he put it:

> the episode does illustrate the power of an orthodox view when it comes to HIV prevention. It strikes me that many lesbians and gay men tend to follow a perceived party-line on the epidemic, one which has been defined by AIDS organisations over the years. After more than a decade of campaigns with slogans such as 'A condom everytime', 'safer sex for all', and 'Rubber up or leave it out', the conditioned response is to denounce a new initiative that dares to suggest that fucking without condoms can be OK' (PP, 10 May 1996: 22).

This 'orthodox' view, however, does not always emphasize condom use. In many cases, it is simply the *negative consequences* of 'risk taking' that are emphasized. For example, one of the series of the Terrence Higgins Trust's 'Reality Campaign' (which featured pictures of HIV positive men in their everyday lives), a picture of a couple shopping is headed with the caption: 'You might feel safe together. Like many gay men I got HIV from sex with my long term partner' (PP, 12 July 1996: 9). While this advertisement importantly makes people think about their sexual practice, it is in many ways a condemnation of the 'negotiated safety' strategy by default. By concentrating only on such *negative* messages, there can be a danger of inducing a kind of AIDS paranoia while failing to give out any *positive* or *supportive* messages that would empower others not to end up in the same situation. It needs to be considered how such 'negative' and 'rationalistic' messages will be received by men who have already *decided* that sexual desire, physical intimacy, and love are more central to their decision making about sexual practice (Parnell, 1996: 104). It is possible that the message will simply be rejected out of hand as such men resist messages which appear to give little room to sexual desire or sensuality at all.

THE IMPORTANCE OF CONTINUED COMMUNITY INVOLVEMENT IN THE DEFINITION OF 'SAFER SEX'

While it may be the case that there can never be one single message about safer sex that is appropriate or effective for everyone, it is important that the gay community continues to involve itself in relevant discussions and debates. In this respect, it is somewhat ironic that debate about the meaning of safer sex seems, increasingly, to be left to AIDS professionals and academics (Parnell, 1996: 104), while discussion appears to have decreased in the gay press. During 1996/97 there were 25 'substantial' (more than two paragraphs) articles in the *Pink Paper* relating to 'safer sex' and HIV/AIDS 'prevention' in the six months between January and June, 15 between July and December, and only 9 in the first six months of 1997. The equivalent number of articles relating to issues to do with 'treatments' and 'care' for the same periods were 27 (Jan–June 1996), 52 (July–Dec 1996), and 49 (Jan–June 1997). Obviously the emphasis of the gay press (at least in terms of the *Pink Paper*) has shifted significantly to the discussion of treatment and care of people who are already HIV positive. While no one would want to see this discussion diminish, it is clear that, at the time of writing, there are beginning to be concerns that such a focus could obscure the issue of prevention (e.g. 'Editorial: A Matter of Life and Death' PP, 29 November 1996: 8). Even more recently this has become not only a matter of emphasis but a case of competing for limited funds as preventive work is set off against the expense of providing combination therapies (PP, 8 August 1997: 9). Some commentators have argued that there is a 'lull period for health education for gay men', and linked this to the 11 percent rise in new HIV infections between 1995 and 1996 ('New Infection Rate Hits Peak Among Gay Men' PP, 31 January 1997). Since prevention requires continual re-messaging, not only will the growing absence of discussion about safer sex in the gay press need to be addressed, but the issue of the funding of prevention programmes will also continue to re-emerge in the years to come.

No doubt discussion of the meaning of safer sex will continue. The debate now appears to have moved out of the highly controversial arena set by the 'moral right' during the 1980s into the more subtle arena of 'sexual safety' and sexual strategies in the 1990s. While preserving a certain degree of sceptical caution given a Conservative determination to roll back the state (Russell *et al.*, 1996: 2), there does appear to be an increased recognition that community-based initiatives can be more appropriate and effective than broad based government campaigns in certain situations. This was partly evident in the decision by the last government to transfer safer sex initiatives from the Health Education Authority to the Terrence Higgins Trust's CHAPS (Community Based HIV and AIDS Prevention Strategy) project (PP, 28 June 1996). While there may no longer be one universally agreed 'gay' approach to safer sex, initiatives such as those by Rubberstuffers (PP, 5 January 1996), and various outreach projects that provide free condoms in the places where they are needed, allow gay men to continue to get on with the pragmatics of safer sex whatever their individual strategies. Nonetheless, it will be interesting to evaluate the relationship between what I have called 'embodied' and 'rationalistic' discourses, and the relative 'quality' of their disciplinary impact on gay men's sexual subjectivities in the years to come.

CONCLUSIONS

By examining the discursive construction of 'safer sex' it has been possible to explore the nature of disciplinary interventions and resistances as a form of 'anatamo-politics of the human body' (Foucault, 1981: 139). What this analysis has revealed is that, not only have discourses around HIV prevention changed quite substantially in a short period of time, but also the relationship between changing discourses and changing subjectivities is by no means as straightforward as the creators of intervention policies and social theorists initially suspected. In particular, the importance of the body as a site of resistance, or change, may have been seriously underestimated by the more moralizing and 'rationalistic' safer sex discourses. In this respect, *'embodied'* discourses, which do not make the mistake of separating body and mind when examining the nature of subjectivity, may offer more appropriate and effective ways of promoting safer sexual behaviour. From the point of view of sociological analysis, the study of safer sexual strategies among gay men reveals the extent of the relationship between social discourses and their disciplinary power over our bodies. While from the health promotion and AIDS prevention point of view, they allow us the chance to examine the 'implications for interventions aimed at changing behaviour and sustaining change over time' (Ames *et al.*, 1995: 55). In terms of implementation, effectiveness, and evaluation of social policies more broadly, issues raised here demonstrate that normative and regulative interventions in people's lives may meet with continued resistance where their needs and desires are systematically denied, or fail to be sensitively understood. The matter is clearly not as simple as changing social discourses to create new forms of sexuality.

Sexual behaviour must be set in a context where people can be empowered to make decisions about their sexual lives as 'responsible actors' rather than as 'manipulable objects of interventions' to be unconditionally controlled and regulated (Reid, 1994: 551). Yet, while it may be the case that 'embodied' discourses on safer sex offer a better way forward, it is important that such strategies have continued and sustained funding in order to create the degree of personal, mutual and community empowerment necessary for them to be effective. Both the gay community and the gay press will continue to have a role to play alongside the AIDS organizations and health professionals in the continuing construction and re-construction of the meaning of 'safer sex'.

9 The Equality of Bodies: Animal Exploitation and Human Welfare

José Parry and Noel Parry

HUMANITARIANISM: ANTI-CRUELTY AND THE INSTITUTIONALIZATION OF COMPASSION

Starting in the eighteenth century, the humanitarian movement had as its objectives the reduction of suffering, the abolition of cruelty and the institutionalization of compassion through legislation. 'Organized moral indignation' became the principal driving force of the movement and its method was the mobilization of public opinion (Kitson Clark, 1962: 38).

Although primarily a pragmatic movement, humanitarianism had its intellectuals, not least of whom was Jeremy Bentham. He might arguably be regarded as one of the seldom acknowledged grandfathers of what, in the age of William Beveridge and Richard Titmuss, became known as the modern academic discipline of social policy and administration (though, for a rather different perspective on Bentham, see Dean, Chapter 5 in this volume). Bentham saw himself as a critic of existing institutions, a legal reformer and a promoter of legislation. His utilitarianism was a philosophy which assumed that social progress was possible and desirable. Rational analysis, the scrutiny of existing institutions and the development of practical policies could lead to reforms. Ultimately, by small steps, progress could be made towards a better society (Baumgardt, 1952; Campos Boralevi, 1984). This thought was adopted more than fifty years after Bentham's death by the Fabian Society, which coined the term 'the inevitability of gradualism'. Even today, elements of social policy arguably continue to be fuelled by the force of moral indignation, plus rational analysis and the setting of policy objectives.

Bentham espoused a sensationalist, psychological doctrine which asserted that the behaviour of bodies was governed by the twin masters of pleasure and pain. Morality and social policy, he believed, could best be judged in terms of the maximization of pleasure (utility) and the minimization of pain. This doctrine was a way of intellectualizing/theorizing the profound belief of the humanitarians that suffering and cruelty should at the very least be diminished and where possible abolished. As a non-believer, Bentham rejected the Christian idea of the immortal soul and of eternal life. For him, the mind and body were one and could best be understood in materialistic terms. Perfection must be sought in this world rather than in a non-existent next world. Since animals have bodies and are as capable of suffering as we humans, the idea of human uniqueness and the notion of the *insuperable line* separating man from 'beast' is undermined. A body is a body and because every body is capable of suffering, all bodies – whether animal or human – are equal. Bentham's views are admirably expressed in the following:

> The day *may* come, when the rest of the animal creation may acquire those rights which never could have been withholden from them but by the hand of tyranny. The French have already discovered that the blackness of the skin is no reason why a human being should be abandoned without redress to the caprice of a tormentor. It may come one day to be recognized, that the number of the legs, the villosity of the skin, or the termination of the *os sacrum*, are reasons equally insufficient for abandoning a sensitive being to the same fate. What else is it that should trace the *insuperable line* (our italics)? Is it the faculty of reason, or, perhaps, the faculty of discourse? But a full-grown horse or dog is beyond comparison a more rational, as well as a more conversable animal, than an infant of a day, or a week, or even a month, old. But suppose the case were otherwise, what would it avail ? The question is not, Can they *reason* ? nor, Can they *talk* ? but, Can they *suffer* ? (Bentham 1960: 412).

The anti-slavery movement was the first and certainly the most momentous of the movements which emerged under the umbrella of humanitarianism (Klingberg, 1926). It argued that institutionalized cruelty, namely, the enslavement of people's bodies should be abolished. This necessarily involved a process of rolling back and setting strict limits to commodification and the operation of market forces. The supporters of anti-slavery, however, were in disagreement about the best methods of achieving their objective. There were those who argued for the abolition of the slave trade and the institution of slavery at one stroke. Others, like Bentham, thought that practical politics would suggest an incremental approach; first abolish the trade and later the institution. The British Parliament abolished the slave trade in 1807 and the institution of slavery (freeing those born into slavery) in 1833. The enormous success of the anti-slavery movement led to other agitations being consciously planned on the same model. This included the anti-cruelty to animals movement.

Not only were there similarities in the motivation and methods of anti-slavery and the anti-cruelty to animals movements, but there were important differences. Practically, theoretically and historically the issues are complex and cannot be fully treated here. For heuristic purposes only we may distinguish between humanism and humanitarianism as distinct perspectives. Ted Benton (1988: 4–18) says that 'humanism=anthropocentrism' – that is, giving exclusive place and primary moral value to humans. The term 'anthropocentrism' only appeared in *The Oxford English Dictionary* in 1863 – though the underlying distinction was age-old. Anthropocentrism was coined during the period of fierce debate, including the clash between T. H. Huxley and Bishop Samuel Wilberforce (1805–73), following the publication of Darwin's *On the Origin of Species*, 1859.

Darwin may be best understood as the greatest, if not one of the last, representatives of a long tradition of British humanitarian liberal professionals – including priests and ministers, lawyers and many doctors – who played an influential role in the leadership of British science and society (Rupke, 1987: 11). The doctrines of common origins, natural selection and evolution undermined God's special act of creation and brought into being that simplified cartoon character – the ape as ancestor. Darwin assaulted the *insuperable line* by showing that we are all animals now. This was unacceptable and insulting to traditional Christianity. Paradoxically, Darwin's humanitarian inclusiveness of the animals was rejected unwittingly by T. H. Huxley, who was his greatest champion. Although Huxley admired Darwin to the point of hero-worship and adopted him as his mentor, as we shall see later, his own career marked a sharp break with humanitarianism in general, and humanitarian science in particular, in favour of humanist anthropocentric science and vivisection.

The new humanists, following the French model, accepted the doctrine of human uniqueness, and sustained a belief in the *insuperable line* drawn between humans and animals. They rested their case on the arguments of classical Aristotelianism. Humanists disaggregated the Christian/Aristotelian amalgam woven together as Catholic orthodoxy by St. Thomas Aquinas (1226–74). They rejected the Christian belief that God had made man/woman in his own image, with an immortal soul. Aristotelianism states that man is rational but animals are not. René Descartes carried this view to the extreme *reductio ad absurdum*. Humans are rational and can therefore experience pain; animals are not rational and are unable to experience pain. For Descartes, animals are *like* machines and feel no pain. Of course it is logically inadmissible to go from the assertion that animals are *like* machines to say that animals *are* machines. Descartes is willing to gloss over this problem. He claims that if animals feel no pain then there is no moral or political reason why we should object to slaughtering them, eating them, or vivisecting them. Animals exist for our use. Descartes himself practised vivisection and his doctrine became the standard justification for the rapid and uninhibited development of animal-vivisecting physiology in France.

Since Bentham's focus was on the body, and not the soul, we shall now examine briefly two cases: one of the animal body (the Act to Prevent Cruel and Improper Treatment of Cattle 1822) and the other of the human body (the Anatomy Act 1832). These were the objects in their different ways of anti-suffering/anti-cruelty reform movements.

THE ANIMAL BODY

There were many agitations in the late eighteenth century about public scenes of cruelty to animals. Take the following scene as an example.

> Fights were arranged between dogs and cats, or dogs and monkeys, and a delighted audience roared its approval as the stronger of the two animals tore his adversary to pieces and stood triumphant over a mangled heap of blood and fur (quoted by Sweeney, 1990: 8 from Moss).

Among the leading campaigners against animal cruelty was Lord Erskine who unsuccessfully attempted to introduce legislation in the House of Lords in 1809. Richard Martin (1754–1834) was more successful. He was responsible for the 1822 Act, which was the first piece of national animal legislation in the world (Brooman and Legge, 1997: 41). It established the principle of using the law to protect animals against cruelty. Thereafter, the Act was popularly known as Martin's Act and he was nicknamed 'Humanity Dick'.

Key personalities who campaigned for the Act subsequently founded, in 1824, the Society for the Prevention of Cruelty to Animals (SPCA). The society eventually became wealthy and successful. Many notable figures donated or subscribed to the RSPCA and Queen Victoria conferred the prefix 'Royal' in 1840. Bentham himself is recorded as having made a donation to the SPCA in 1831, and Mr and Mrs John Stuart Mill donated money in 1856. Edwin Chadwick, who was a key exponent of Victorian social policy, took out a lifelong membership subscription (Harrison 1973: 815).

Harrison has studied the previously neglected historical role of the RSPCA and its relationship to the state in Victorian society. He pointed out that:

> historians pursuing 'the origins of the welfare state' have studied legislation on public health, factory hours and education – but have ignored legislation on animal cruelty. The latter is peculiarly interesting because it never curtailed the work of voluntary bodies (Harrison, 1973: 787).

This suggests that scholarship itself – whether in history or social policy – has been divided by the *insuperable anthropocentric line*. Yet a comparison of the development of policy towards humans on the one hand, and towards animals on the other, across the line, is highly illuminating. Campaigns against cruelty to animals were successful precisely because they adopted the same approach as the anti-slavery movement. Harrison clearly admired the RSPCA because he thought that it was, and is, pragmatic and willing to compromise. It has, therefore, in his opinion, been more effective than radical abolitionist organizations.

The RSPCA is a registered charity. English charity law was reformed by the Charitable Trusts Act 1853. The Charity Commissioners were appointed to administer the legislation. Its aims were broadly drafted. They included trusts for the relief of poverty, for education, for the advancement of religion and other purposes beneficial to the community. Anti-vivisection societies, along with other animal charities, enjoyed full charitable status until 1947 when, as a result of a campaign by the Research Defence Society, the anti-vivisection societies were declassified on appeal to the House of Lords. The position was clarified by the Commissioners in 1969; they reaffirmed the established principle that organizations which seek legislative reform are ineligible for charitable status (Hollands, 1980: 21–4).

The RSPCA needs the status and funding conferred by charitable status to support its corps of inspectors. Since the early days the RSPCA has employed its own inspectors, as a sort of private police force, to ensure that regulations flowing from anti-cruelty legislation will be enforced. It also encouraged 'active subscribers' who either would enforce regulations themselves, or call for trained inspectors to carry out these duties (Harrison, 1973: 793). The inspectors were employed to police cruelty to animals and emerged at the same time as the new model police force for humans, set up by Sir Robert Peel under the Metropolitan Police Act 1829. Later the National Society for the Prevention of Cruelty to Children (NSPCC) was established on a model consciously similar to that of the RSPCA. Likewise the Charity Organization Society (founded in 1869) began the systematic training of social workers to inspect, police and regulate the 'deserving poor', the undeserving poor being left to the state-funded Poor Law system (Parry and Parry, 1979: 26).

THE ANATOMY ACT AND THE REGULATION OF HUMAN DISSECTION

We noted earlier that a central theme of Bentham's work was the rational reform of English law and the legal system. As a law reformer Bentham was one of the leading figures in the movement which led to the Anatomy Act of 1832 (Richardson, 1987). In Britain, in his day, there was increasing public agitation about the trade in stolen corpses. This trade was principally associated with the acquisition of bodies for dissection in anatomy schools and art schools. Due to the shortage of bodies an illicit trade grew up. The body snatchers, or 'resurrection men' as they were called, stole newly-buried bodies from the grave for sale to the anatomists. As Ruth Richardson shows, there was a profound conflict between popular culture and the new scientific medical culture over the treatment of corpses. Ordinary people, however poor, refused to sell the bodies of their dead relatives to the anatomists. Christian beliefs about the resurrection of the body were carried into popular culture. It was thought necessary to keep the bones and dust of the individual together lest resurrection be prevented at the last trump.

Surgeons argued that, if medicine were to progress, it would be necessary to find a balance between adverse popular sentiment, clinical detachment and commercialism (Richardson, 1987). Bentham, as a non-believer and a rationalist, advocated a voluntaristic approach to the acquisition of bodies for dissection. He thought that intellectuals, professionals and enlightened members of the upper classes ought to take a lead by offering their own mortal remains for dissection. He requested in his will that a public dissection of his own body should be carried out by his personal doctor and close friend, Southwood Smith, who would also give a public lecture. By this action, Bentham saw himself as taking a lead in the voluntary supply of bodies for medical education.

Southwood Smith was a Christian whose thoughts on dissection had been published nearly a decade earlier. As Richardson and Hurwitz explain, Southwood Smith was a persuasive advocate of the 'immeasurable utility of anatomical knowledge' to scientific medicine and society. But if pain were to be minimized and utility maximized, dissection should be practised on the insensible dead and never on the living.

> Who, then, would provide subjects for anatomical inquiry: the living or the dead, the rich or the poor [and one might add the sick or the healthy]? A public choice must be made: *allow the dissection of the dead or accept that surgeons would otherwise be driven to obtain knowledge by practising on the bodies of the living* [our italics]. The social implications of adopting the latter course were stark. The rich, Southwood Smith pointed out, would always have it in their power to select experienced surgeons. Such a choice was not available to the poor. Public hospitals and poorhouses would therefore be converted 'into so many schools where the surgeon by practising on the poor would learn to operate on the rich with safety and dexterity'. In 1824 the resolution to this problem was clear to Southwood Smith: the unclaimed dead from poorhouses and hospitals must be requisitioned for dissection. 'If the dead bodies of the poor are not appropriated to this use, their living bodies will and must be' (Richardson and Hurwitz, 1987: 2).

Southwood Smith's ideas about requisitioning the dead bodies of the poor fitted well with the Poor Law Amendment Act of 1834 (in which Chadwick also played a leading role).

Contrary to Bentham's hope, members of the professional classes did not rush forward to donate their bodies. As far as is known, none of those present at the famous lecture donated their bodies for dissection. Most of them undoubtedly held the popular view that dissection was a 'fate worse than death'. The phrase derived from the fact that hanged criminals could be condemned to the extra and exemplary punishment of dissection – the so-called double indemnity. Reform of the Poor Law provided exactly the opportunity to requisition the corpses of the destitute from the workhouses by compulsion for dissection, where permission would never have been voluntarily given.

> The 1832 Anatomy Act permitted those having lawful custody of dead bodies to donate them for dissection. The masters of poorhouses and hospitals could cut expenditure on pauper funerals by donating the bodies of patients too poor to provide for their own burial. By creating a cheap, legal, and institutionalized source of bodies, the Act led to the collapse of the body snatching trade. The Anatomy Act and the inspectorate it established are still in effect (*ibid.*: 3).

It is worth noting that the introduction of a sufficient system of voluntary donation of dead bodies, which Bentham had hoped for, was delayed for more than a hundred years. Voluntary donation of cadavers and voluntary donation of living blood both increased between the two world wars and at the time of the emergence of the NHS following World War II.

THE DISCOURSES OF DISSECTION AND VIVISECTION

Samuel Johnson wrote in 1758:

> Among the inferior professors of medical knowledge is a race of wretches, whose lives are only varied by varieties of cruelty ... . I know not that by living *dissections* [our italics] any discovery has been made by which a single malady is more easily cured ... . he surely buys knowledge dear, who learns the use of the lacteals at the expense of his humanity. It is time that universal resentment should arise against these horrid operations, which tend to harden the heart, extinguish those sensations which give man confidence in man, and make physicians more dreadful than gout or stone (quoted in French, 1975: 17).

Nowadays a clear distinction is made between dissection and vivisection, but this has not always been so. At one time these terms were interchangeable; "'vivisect" comes from two Latin words, *vivus* (alive) and *secare* (to cut); just as the word "dissect" means to cut apart or to take to pieces' (Westacott, 1949: 5). Westacott pointed out that the word 'vivisection' takes its modern meaning in terms of the legal definition adopted in the world's first ever piece of legislation governing vivisection – namely, the UK Cruelty to Animals Act of 1876. (The latter was eventually superseded by the Animals [Scientific Procedures] Act 1986).

The Act to Prevent the Cruel and Improper Treatment of Cattle was several times extended so that its scope was thought eventually to be very wide. The 'Norwich case' in 1874 proved that it was not wide enough. It brought many people to the conclusion that fresh legislation directed specifically at vivisection was needed. A well-known French physiologist, Magnan, visiting England, gave a lecture and demonstration in Norwich, but some of the witnesses were so horrified by the cruelty involved that the occasion broke up in disarray. The RSPCA took out proceedings against Magnan and others under the 1876 Act. When the case came before the magistrates Magnan had returned to France. In his absence the Bench decided that the prosecution had failed to demonstrate the involvement of the remaining defendants in the vivisection. There was a public furore and the RSPCA emerged the moral victor. This, together with many frightful incidents of cruel vivisection in France and Italy, which had been exposed by British residents, students and visitors, led to strong anti-vivisection campaigning abroad. Frances Power Cobbe (1822–1904) – a journalist and feminist – organized a campaign which ultimately led to the introduction of new specific anti-vivisection legislation (French, 1975: 36–111). The Cruelty to Animals Act 1876, which she helped to promote and which was intended to abolish the practice of vivisection, eventually turned out very differently from what she wanted.

Although the intention of the anti-vivisectionists was to abolish or severely restrict vivisection, Brooman and Legge demonstrate that the Act actually decriminalized animal experimentation. Following pressure from the General Medical Council and scientific lobby, the Act permitted experiments under licence, provided they demonstrably resulted in knowledge useful for saving or prolonging human life, or alleviating suffering. The influence the scientific lobby was subsequently able to exert over the granting of licences resulted in a rapid growth in the use of animals in research (1997: 126).

The discovery of anaesthesia crystallized the debate between vivisectionists and anti-vivisectionists. The men who made the discovery were opposed to vivisection, whether upon animals or upon other people. The very term 'anaesthesia' was coined by a medical antivivisectionist, Oliver Wendell Holmes in 1846 (Beddow Bayly, 1961: 12). Experiments in anaesthesia were carried out not on animals or other people, but first upon the doctors themselves (Sharpe, 1993). But anaesthesia was Janus-faced. On the one side, it seemed to offer everything that humanitarianism could desire by eliminating pain; on the dark side, operations could be conducted on living human and animal bodies, not just for immediate therapeutic purposes to help the suffering individual, but also for experimentation. It seemed now that experimentation could be publicly justified (Rupke, 1987). The 'dark face of science' was shortly to be revealed (Vyvyan, 1971).

THE RISE OF THE ANTHROPOCENTRIC STATE

The Cruelty to Animals Act (1876) played a key role in the transition to a formalized anthropocentric state. Animal experiments and animal tests were for the first time institutionalized under statute. Likewise systems for managing animal health in agriculture were also being set up under the supervision of the emerging veterinary profession. Animal health was not the prime objective. In moral and political terms these services were secondary and instrumental, and were directed to the satisfaction of human requirements for meat, milk, hides, wool and other animal products. Under pressure of total war, as we shall see, state subsidization of animal production, on the one hand, and the regulation of animal health, on the other, became key state activities. During the Second World War the supply and distribution of food was regulated by a Ministry of Food under a national system of food rationing.

The process of anthropocentrizing the state is demonstrated at the level of practical politics by the career of T. H. Huxley (mentioned earlier), who was dubbed the high priest of science. He believed in the active state and was an important member of the (first) Royal Commission on Vivisection in 1875 (Westacott, 1949: 427). In addition, he was a leading figure in the formation of the science lobby in opposition to the anti-vivisection movement. Unlike the new laboratory scientists, the medical profession was divided both about what should be its future relationship to the state (Parry and Parry, 1976) and to vivisection (French, 1975). Some medical men, such as the surgeon Lawson Tate, were entirely opposed to vivisection and animal experimentation (Sharpe, 1988: 78–81). The introduction of state regulation under the 1876 Act started the process of institutionalizing cruelty towards animals. The products of the laboratory were judged to be of increasing utility to the state and society. These 'benefits' ensured that the advancement of science, including the professionalization and protection of vivisection, were seen as one of the state's vital interests.

The 'birth of the laboratory' – particularly the experimental animal laboratory – brought into the world a new transforming institution, but one tainted by cruelty. The forward march of humanitarian compassion was slowed. The lab became exceedingly influential as a new model of science during the mid- and late nineteenth century. This may be compared and contrasted to Michel Foucault's thoughts about the 'birth of the clinic and the 'medical gaze', as seminal processes occurring in the late eighteenth and early nineteenth centuries. There were important leads and lags in the timing of the development of laboratory science as between Britain, the USA and continental countries. France and Germany, especially, were well ahead in the development of laboratory science in general, and vivisection in particular. This was in part because of the dominance of anthropocentric humanist rather than humanitarian stances. In the 1870s, we may chart the growth of laboratory science in Britain by reference to the rise of state funding (Desmond, 1997). Small at first, state funding for science was to grow massively under the threat of war and during war itself.

Huxley represented the attitude to policy of a new generation of scientists. Take for example the address called the 'Duties of the State' he delivered in 1871, in Birmingham.

> [He] appeared as the well-fledged State interventionist [and] challenged Herbert Spencer's hands-off, do-nothing demand of government. [Huxley] praised the Education Act – something Chamberlain's Radical and Nonconformist National Education League had pressured for. He had no qualms about government running the Post Office or telegraph services, and he saw the State's vaccination, sanitation and road-building programmes (like Birmingham's) lessen the misery which had fuelled the revolutionary movements across Europe (Desmond, 1997: 61).

We have already identified the Cruelty to Animals Act, with its focus on regulating laboratory work, as pivotal in the formation of modern links between science and the state. The new alliance between laboratory science and the state centred on the use of animals. From 1876 onwards, the balance of power shifted decisively. Prior to this, the state seemed relatively indifferent as between humanitarian anti-vivisectionists' interests, on the one hand, and those of animal experimenters, on the other. Thereafter, the state saw its interests best served by an alliance with science. Science, including vivisection, was increasingly believed to affect the state's vital interests. Traditional, yet latent, anthropocentric values inevitably became manifested and institutionalized in the workings of the state. Science became – and remained – the powerful insider, while the humanitarian anti-vivisection movement emerged from the struggles of the 1870s as the outsider. In consequence, the conflict between the two protagonists was greatly intensified. There seemed little likelihood of the issue being resolved to the satisfaction of the anti-vivisectionists.

However, the anti-vivisectionists were not prepared to give up the cause but, on the contrary, became more radical. The RSPCA, with its meliorist approach, was rejected by many who sought refuge in the formation of new, specifically anti-vivisectionist, societies totally committed to abolition. These included the Victoria Street Society – founded in 1875, which changed its name to the National Anti-Vivisection Society in 1897 – and the British Union for the Abolition of Vivisection. There was also the Humanitarian League, set up by Henry Salt and others in 1891, which took a radical stance based on animal rights. Among the cruelties in the countryside which it wished to see abolished was the shooting of birds (Itzkowitz, 1977). The new, radical anti-vivisectionists joined forces with other anti-establishment interests.

This phase in the conflict may be illustrated by the arousal of public feeling in the Brown Dog affair, starting in 1902. Two female Swedish medical students witnessed a lecture/demonstration undertaken by a physiologist, Dr. Bayliss, in which a brown dog was vivisected at University College, London. The women kept a systematic record of their medical studies in the form of a diary (Lind-af-Hageby and Schartau, 1903). Notes were kept on what they had seen at the lecture/demonstration. They showed the material to the secretary of the National Anti-Vivisection Society, the Honourable Stephen Coleridge. On reading the diary, his eye was caught by the painful details of the vivisection on the brown dog and he was convinced that there had been a serious infringement of the 1876 Act.

Coleridge publicly accused Bayliss of breaking the law (Vyvyan 1971). The vivisector had no other recourse but to sue Coleridge for libel in order to protect his reputation and that of University College. Publicity about the libel action in the new mass circulation newspapers generated fierce debate up and down the country. Coleridge lost the libel case yet, in the public eye, he emerged as the moral victor. Such was the public mood that money was subscribed to defray the costs and damages of the trial to the NAVS. In addition, a separate fund was raised by public subscription devoted to erecting a memorial to the Brown Dog in the then radical borough of Battersea, London.

For a coalition of anti-vivisectionists, suffragettes and trade unionists the statue of the dog became an anti-establishment emblem, and sparked off the 'brown dog riots' of 1907. Medical students seeking to destroy the statue were confronted by local working class youths who defended it (Lansbury, 1985; Parry, 1985: 92–3; Mason, 1997). The brown dog affair triggered the second Royal Commission on Vivisection in 1906 which recommended a refinement – but no fundamental change – to the rules governing scientific experimentation on animals. In June 1914, just prior to the outbreak of World War I, an Abolition of Vivisection Bill was brought before Parliament, but failed to achieve a Second Reading (Westacott, 1949: 633–35). War entrenched vivisection because it was deemed to be vital to national survival and it re-affirmed more deeply the anthropocentrism of the state.

WAR AND SOCIAL POLICY

Richard Titmuss, the official historian of social policy in the Second World War, set out in an essay the manifold ways in which war had affected the formation of social policy from Florence Nightingale's work in the Crimean War (1854–56) up to the 1950s.

> Among these, perhaps the dominating one has been the increasing concern of the State in time of war with the biological characteristics of its people [it depended on these for its war-fighting capacity]. The growing scale and intensity of war has stimulated ... . concern about the quantity and quality of the population (Titmuss, 1963: 78).

Titmuss showed how, in Britain, modern wars stimulated the development of the state. He focused particularly on how war had an impact on the shaping of health policy, culminating in the implementation of the National Health Service in 1948. War has paradoxical effects. On the one hand, the horror, the frightful casualties, and the use of new weapons such as poison gas tended to destroy the belief in progress and the advance of civilization (Harris and Paxman, 1982). On the other hand, Titmuss noted that war could forge a sense of community, for example, during the blitz in Britain in the Second World War. He believed, as did many others, that the shared experience of men in the trenches in World War I fostered a sense of brotherhood in the face of sudden death, mutilation and the guilt of survival. Titmuss thought that success in modern industrial warfare required the state to reduce inequalities of wealth, class and gender if it were to mobilize and motivate the population to commit itself to the goal of collective national survival. A welfare policy would be essential in achieving victory and necessary after the war in securing peace.

THE WELFARE STATE

To British people in the second half of the twentieth century, the dual phrase 'welfare state' is so familiar that it is taken for granted. To academics, it opens the door to the whole discourse of social policy. Yet José Harris notes that 'welfare' was originally used as a stand-alone concept and was imported from the United States at the beginning of the twentieth century. In American discourse, 'welfare' has only been weakly linked with the 'state', and then in reverse order; state welfare is hardly the same thing as welfare state. Even in Britain, the concept of 'welfare' only gradually replaced earlier terms such as the 'social question'.

The phrase 'animal welfare' was introduced in Britain at about the same time as welfare was applied to humans (Westacott, 1949: 512). Elizabeth Douglas Hume's *The Mind Changers* (1939) indicates that new animal welfare bodies began to be named as such as early as the 1920s. For example, the National Council for Animal Welfare and the University of London Animal Welfare Society (now known as the Universities Federation of Animal Welfare) were started in the mid-1920s. Hume's book, published at the outset of the Second World War, is still written in the earlier discourse of the humanitarian movement and yet, in her text, she makes a number of references to animal welfare. Historically, the discourse of humanitarianism is giving way to the new discourse of welfare, both in relation to animals and humans. Humanitarian discourse has continued to dominate to the present day in the sphere of international relations. In the domestic sphere, it has continued to flourish to a far greater extent in the USA than in Britain. This is exemplified by the name of the Humane Society of the United States (1997), which is devoted to animal causes.

Michael Bruce points out that the idea of welfare probably emerged from the Elizabethan notion of the common weal or the common-wealth. This suggests that there has long been a connection with government. Writing in 1961, Bruce says:

> ... the 'Welfare Services ', in all their modern variety, are essentially those which exist for the care of people unable to care for them-selves or needing personal help of a special kind; old people, mothers and babies, children at school and others who are now the particular concern of the local authorities (Bruce, 1961: ix).

Bruce anticipated what was later to become a key debate in the 1970s and 80s raised by the late Sir Keith Joseph. Bruce says: 'In this sense "welfare" suggests dependence, and is not therefore an acceptable description of the relationship between government and people in a free society (*ibid*: ix). 'Welfare' and 'dependency' are more acceptable – at least to some – in relation to animals. But a powerful moral theme in the animal rights movement has been a rejection of the idea that animals should be placed in a state of dependency on humans. This view asserts that animals should be left in the wild and even pet-keeping is rejected as morally unacceptable. Beveridge preferred the term 'social service state' rather than 'welfare state' and this probably best described the British system 'based partly on insurance, partly on a mutual pooling of resources, and supplemented by welfare services for special needs' (*ibid.*: ix). 'Nevertheless, in the sense of the common weal, welfare may ... . be used, and ... . has the advantage of euphony' (*ibid.*: ix).

The first use of 'welfare state' is attributed to Alfred Zimmern in the 1930s. It was a translation of the German *der Wohlfahrtsstaat*, a term dating back to Bismarck's creation of the original German welfare system in the 1880s. During the 1920s, *der Wohlfahrtsstaat* was used by German Conservatives as a term of abuse to characterize the social welfare provisions of the Weimar Republic. Zimmern – with his German family connections – brought the term 'welfare state' into English usage in a favourable sense. He posed it as an ideal for demo-cratic societies in opposition to the anti-democratic, militaristic dicta-torships – the war states – of Fascist Italy and Nazi Germany. Zimmern, Temple, Beveridge and others moved in a close social circle: they had all been contemporaries at Balliol, and shared the same discourse. Archbishop Temple – a supporter of the Workers' Education Association and the Labour Party, and a Christian socialist – contrasted the 'Power-State' and the 'Welfare-State' (Temple, 1941:

35). Paradoxically, as we have noted, although Beveridge personally preferred the description 'social service state', it was his wartime report (Beveridge 1942) which led to the term 'welfare state' being adopted by the media and by his crusaders for reform. But, as Harris points out, it did not fully enter popular usage until it was revived in the election campaign of 1950 when Conservatives deployed 'welfare state' as a term of abuse. Despite this, it became fixed in popular discourse as a positive label synoymous with the policies put foward in the Beveridge plan and implemented in Labour's post-war reforms (Harris, 1997: 452).

Several commentators have thought that, in many ways, Beveridge's notion of the social service state was more apt in the description of the evolutionary hotch-potch of institutions and policies which made up the British system. Others believed that the welfare state fitted in much better with Beveridge's claim that his proposed reforms would amount to a 'British revolution'. There is no doubt, however, that 'welfare state' evoked a grander, more ideal notion of a coherent system constructed from first principles and applied in a uniform and systematic manner. This, the British welfare state, has never been. However, idealized notions of the welfare state, whether latent or explicit, have inspired generations of people and policy makers.

BLOOD, ETHICS AND ANTHROPOCENTRISM

Two related versions of the welfare state appear in the work of Beveridge and Titmuss respectively. In the case of Beveridge the overall vision of the welfare state is harder to extract, whereas Titmuss explicitly sets out his ideal in *The Gift Relationship. From Human Blood to Social Policy* (1973); Beveridge never really did so. Only in the conclusion of the second edition of her biography of Beveridge was Harris finally able to come close to distilling the essence of his beliefs.

In terms of *political* thought he [Beveridge] probably owed most to the long tradition of low-key classical republicanism [civic idealism] that had informed liberal dissent and anti-plutocracy in Britain over several centuries, and that had received a new lease of life from the turn-of-the-century revival of 'public service'-oriented philosophical Idealism (Harris, 1997: 488).

Titmuss made his ideal much more explicit. As we have seen, he was concerned with two major issues: the quality of population (health policy) and the ever-closer engagement of science with state policy. Here again we find him addressing a central moral and political paradox: science in peacetime produces human benefit; in times of war it generates and multiplies human suffering. And, yet, out of this suffering there come rapid advances in medicine and in the organization and delivery of state medical and social services. 'Scientific advances have profoundly influenced the social and administrative organization of medical care' (Titmuss, 1963: 183). It was from his exploration of the relationship between these two concerns that Titmuss went on to crystallize his humanist and altruistic philosophy. Titmuss showed how altruism can arise from the circumstances of war to shape social policy.

Blood transfusion is based on a form of vivisection which is not very painful, namely venesection. After Harvey demonstrated the circulation of the blood in 1628, numerous experiments on blood transfusion had been made. Some were between animal and animal and some between human and human, but significantly animal to human transfusion proved to be fatal. In 1824 Blundell demonstrated that it was absolutely necessary, if transfusion were to be effective, to use blood of the same species; cross-species transfusion is always fatal (Sharpe, 1988: 158). Even between humans, blood transfusion was unpredictable until the work of Karl Landsteiner (1900) on the classification of blood groups A, B, O, positive and negative (Gunson and Dodsworth 1996). It was his research which led to the possibility of safe and routine use of inter-human transfusion.

In the 1914–18 war, the enormous casualties on the Western Front led to the use of blood transfusion for wounded soldiers on a substantial scale. In the face of death and injury, few soldiers would refuse to donate blood freely to save their comrades. Under the pressure of war, transfusion technology developed rapidly and saved many lives, and the first, limited blood banks were set up. Just before and during the Second World War, in Britain, blood donation and transfusion were organized by the government nationally, among civilians as well as the military. Between the wars, such limited services as were available were organized on a voluntary basis. Post war, in 1946, a permanent National Blood Transfusion Service was established, based on the principle of altruism. The donor gave a gift of blood which went to a stranger. Later the original donor expected to draw from the blood bank free of charge when he or she was in need. Titmuss thought that this system represented quintessentially the altruism underlying the National Health Service. He contrasted Britain with the United

States, where blood was bought and sold in the marketplace, as was medical care itself. Titmuss's moral and political ideas resonated with the long humanitarian tradition which, as we have seen goes back as far as anti-slavery in the eighteenth century.

From the point of view of anti-vivisectionists, however, the altruism of the gift relationship was tarnished because blood transfusion depended upon animal experimentation and animal testing. Embedded in the discourse of blood transfusion is the term 'rhesus factor', which is a testament both to the use of the rhesus monkey in animal experiments and – whether consciously or not – an indicator of anthropocentric values in medical science and social policy. Titmuss himself was a Bedfordshire farmer's son who, according to the testimony of his daughter, Ann Oakley, shared the anthropocentric attitudes of his day (personal communication, March 1998). Titmuss's altruistic principle, so far as anti-vivisectionists were concerned, was flawed because its 'universalism' was not universal enough; it did not extend to animals. The anthropocentrism of the blood transfusion service rested on the fact that the blood gift was only between humans (Reisman, 1997). Humanist values (humans only) appeared to science to conform strictly to the 'facts' of nature. It seemed evident that the species barrier was just such a 'fact'; it was permanent, irremediable and this was proved by the impossibility of transfusing blood from one species to another. Titmuss shared this widely-held assumption about the *insuperable line*.

Anti-vivisectionists stood on stronger ground when they objected to the use of animals who were 'conscripted' to serve in laboratory experiments because, without *compulsory* testing on animals, human blood transfusion would have been impossible. Blood transfusion is but one example of the instrumental ways in which the use of animals in the laboratory for experimentation and routine pharmaceutical testing underpin contemporary scientific medical practice. These animal techniques were approved both by the state and by the commercial pharmaceutical industry, not least in the development of military advantage. For example, the government laboratories and testing facilities at Porton Down started from scratch during World War I, in 1915, to counter German poison gas attacks on the Western Front. Porton Down's influence grew rapidly. Chemical research and animal experimentation emerged as the basis for major industrial mass production. Indeed after the war, ICI was created by deliberate state policy out of these wartime efforts to bring the British chemical industry up to the technical and commercial standards which the German industry had already reached. Huge numbers of animals were bred for use in gruesome experiments. Many soldiers participating in the chemical warfare programme complained vociferously about the gross cruelty to animals involved, and they were themselves often experimental subjects (report of J. B. S. Haldane quoted in Harris and Paxman, 1982: 40). From 1911 the Official Secrets Act placed a cloak around the government's own expansion of animal testing for the purposes of warfare. It likewise covered civilian commercial practices, which were brought within the protection of the secret state.

SUMMARY

The eighteenth century witnessed the rise of the humanitarian movement which aimed to diminish or abolish cruelty and foster compassion. Anti-slavery was the great model for all modern social movements, both in the style of its aims and its methods. Humanists, like certain Christians, defended the doctrine of human uniqueness and human superiority. Humanitarians – and some Protestant sects – had an inclusive attitude towards animals and argued that they should be treated equally with humans (Thomas, 1983).

The movement against cruelty to animals was based on the principle of breaking what Bentham called the *insuperable line* between animals and people, which he hoped one day would be abolished. Bentham thought that since human bodies and animal bodies both suffer pain, this suffering is the basis of their equality. The Anatomy Act, which Bentham's circle supported, set up regulations to control the supply of human bodies for dissection but these did not prevent living bodies being used or abused for vivisection. Bentham personally was opposed to compulsion but the Anatomy Act and the reformed Poor Law gave minimal choice. It licensed the conscripting of cadavers from among the destitute poor.

The Act to Prevent the Cruel and Improper Treatment of Cattle 1822 led to the formation of the RSPCA, which instituted a private force of inspectors to enforce the Act, funded via voluntary charitable donations. Dissection was the first activity ever to be regulated by state inspectors and allowed medical training and research without cruelty to the living; but it was soon realized that vivisection on humans and animals was an entrenched practice. In any case, the Anatomy Act excluded animals, which were butchered every day for human use. With the coming of anaesthesia and the development of large-scale animal vivisecting physiology, a crisis was reached. The 1876 Cruelty to Animals Act was promoted specifically to abolish vivisection, but was turned round by the new science lobby and ended up institutionalizing cruelty. Science and the state came to have a mutual vested interest in the products of the laboratory rooted in systematic vivisection.

The modern state is an anthropocentric state. War and preparations for war, as Richard Titmuss pointed out, fostered the growth of the state. War brought suffering but also, paradoxically, a powerful sense of bonding and community. State welfare policy was necessary to motivate and sustain the population to carry the burdens of war through to victory and the hoped-for better world. But war also promoted the more intensive use of animals for food production and industrialized the scale of animal experimentation. From the 1920s onwards, the discourse of welfare came to displace that of humanitarianism, both for humans and animals. It was in the 1930s that the terms 'welfare' and 'state' were linked as a way of promoting the democracies over the fascist dictatorships, particularly Germany, which since the time of Bismarck had had *der Wohlfahrtsstaat*.

William Beveridge still preferred the term 'social service state'. Titmuss in *The Gift Relationship* saw blood and blood transfusion on a non-commercial basis as representing the ideal of equality underlying the National Health Service. Supporters of human/animal equality might have seen Titmuss's vision as tainted because it still supported the *insuperable line* and the anthropocentric state. Science, too, it seemed supported anthropocentrism because blood could not be transfused from animals to humans; the species barrier was sustained.

Bentham's hope that one day the *insuperable line* would be overcome seemed far from realization. The struggle of the anti-cruelty to animals campaigners would have to wait until the 1960s for a new revival, and another attack upon the *insuperable line* – but that is the subject of another paper.

References

Advisory Group on the Ethics of Xenotransplantation (1997) *Animal tissue into humans* (London: Department of Health).

Aggleton, P., Davies, P. and Hart, G. (eds) (1990) *AIDS: Individual, Cultural and Policy Dimensions* (Brighton: Falmer Press).

Aggleton, P., Davies, P. and Hart, G. (eds) (1992) *AIDS: Rights, Risk and Reason* (London: Falmer Press).

Aggleton, P., Hart, G. and Davies, P. (eds) (1989) *AIDS: Social Representations, Social Practices* (Brighton: Falmer Press).

Aldridge, M. (1996) 'Dragged to Market: Being a Profession in the Postmodern World', *British Journal of Social Work*, vol. 26, pp. 177–194.

Alexander, F. (1923) *Constructive Conscious Control of the Individual* (London: Methuen).

American Council on Transplantation (1985) *The US public's attitudes toward organ transplants* (Princeton NJ: American Council on Transplantation).

Ames, L., Atchinson, A. and Thomas Rose, D. (1995) 'Love, lust, fear: safer sex decision making among gay men', *Journal of Homosexuality*, vol. 30, no. 1.

Andrews, I. and McIntosh, V. (1992) *Patient's Charter Standard: Respect for religious and cultural beliefs* (London: Mount Vernon Hospital).

Annandale, E. and Clarke, J. (1996) 'What is Gender? Feminist theory and the sociology of human reproduction', *Sociology of Health and Illness*, vol. 18, no. 1.

Archer, M. (1995) *Realist Social Theory: The Morphogenetic Approach* (Cambridge: Cambridge University Press).

Armstrong, D. (1983) *Political anatomy of the body. Medical knowledge in Britain in the twentieth century* (Cambridge: Cambridge University Press).

Arney, W. (1982) *Power and the Profession of Obstetrics* (Chicago: The University of Chicago Press).

Arney, W. and Neill, J. (1990) 'The Location of Pain in Childbirth: Natural childbirth and the transformation of obstetrics', *Sociology of Health and Illness*, vol. 4, no. 1.

Assiter, A. (1996) *Enlightened Women: Modernist Feminism in a Post-modern Age* (Routledge: London).

Audit Commission (1985) *Managing Social Services for the Elderly More Effectively* (London: HMSO).

Audit Commission (1986) *Making a Reality of Community Care* (London: HMSO).

Audit Commission (1992) *The Community Revolution: The Personal Social Services and Community Care* (London: HMSO).

Audit Commission (1993) *Taking Care: Progress with Care in the Community* (London: HMSO).

Baines, C., Evans, P. and Neysmith, S. (eds) (1991) *Women's Caring: Feminist Perspectives on Social Welfare* (Toronto: McClelland and Stewart).

Baker, C., Wuest, J. and Stern, P. (1992) 'Method slurring: the grounded theory/phenomenology example', *Journal of Advanced Nursing*, vol. 17, pp. 1355–1360.

Balaskas, J. (1989) *New Active Birth: A Concise Guide to Natural Childbirth* (London: Thorsons).

Baldock, J. (1994) 'The personal social services: The politics of care' in V. George and S. Miller (eds) *Social Policy Towards 2000: Squaring the Welfare Circle* (London: Routledge).

Baldwin, S. and Twigg, J. (1991) 'Women and Community Care, reflections on a debate', in M. Mclean and D. Groves (eds), *Women's Issues in Social Policy*, (London: Routledge).

Bamford, T. (1990) *The Future of Social Work* (Basingstoke: Macmillan).

Bar On, Bat-Ami (1993) 'Marginality and Epistemic Privilege', in L. Alcoff and E. Potter (eds) *Feminist Epistemologies*, (London: Routledge).

Barclay, P. (1982) *Social Workers: Their Role and Tasks: Report of a Working Party* (London: Bedford Square Press).

Barlow, W. (1973) *The Alexander Principle* (London: Victor Gollancz).

Barnes, C. (1991) *Disabled People in Britain and Discrimination. A Case for Anti-Discrimination Legislation* (London: Hurst Calgary).

Barrett, M. and Roberts, H. (1978) 'Doctors and their Patients: The social control of women in General Practice', in C. and B. Smart (eds) *Women, Sexuality and Social Control* (London: Routledge & Kegan Paul).

Baumgardt, D. (1952) *Bentham and the Ethics of Today* (Princeton: Princeton University Press).

Beck, U. (1992) *Risk Society: Towards a new modernity* (London: Sage).

Beddow Bayly, M. (1961) *Clinical Medical Discoveries* (London: National Anti-Vivisection Society).

Bell, D. (1990) *Husserl* (London: Routledge).

Bendelow, G. and Williams, S. (1995) 'Pain and the Mind-Body Dualism: A sociological approach', *Body and Society*, vol. 1, no. 2.

Benner, P. (1984) *From Novice to Expert: Excellence and Power in Clinical Nursing Practice* (Menlo Park, California: Addison-Wesley).

Benner, P. and Wrubel, J. (1989) *The Primacy of Caring: Stress and Coping in Health and Illness* (Menlo Park, California: Addison-Wesley).

Benner, P., Janson-Bjerklie, S., Ferketich, S. and Becker, G. (1994) 'Moral dimensions of living with a chronic illness: autonomy, responsibility and the limits of control' in P. Benner (ed.) *Interpretive Phenomenology: Embodiment, Caring, and Ethics in Health and Illness.* (London: Sage).

Bentham, J. (1789) 'An introduction to the principles of morals and legislation', in M. Warnock (ed.) (1962) *Utilitarianism* (Glasgow: Collins).

Bentham, J. (1823) 'An introduction to the principles of morals and legislation', edited with an introduction by W. Harrison (1960) *A Fragment on Government and An Introduction to the Principles of Morals and Legislation* (Oxford: Basil Blackwell).

Benton, T. (1988) Humanism=Speciesism: Marx on Humans and Animals, *Radical Philosophy*, vol. 50, pp. 4–18.

Berger P. and Luckmann T. (1967) *The Social Construction of Reality: A Treatise in the Sociology of Knowledge* (Harmondsworth, Penguin).

Bermúdez, J., Marcel, A. and Eilan, N. (eds) (1995) *The Body and the Self* (Cambridge, Massachusetts: MIT Press).

Beveridge, W. (1942) *Social Insurance and Allied Services*, Cmd. 6404 (London: HMSO).

Bhaskar R. (1986) *Scientific Realism and Human Emancipation* (London: Verso).

Billington, A., Hickson, F., Maguire, M., Calleja, M. and Taylor, J. (1997) *Thinking It Through, A New Approach to Sex, Relationships and HIV for Gay Men* (London: Camden and Islington Health Services NHS Trust).

Blair, T. (1996) 'Ideological Blurrings', *Prospect*, June, pp. 10–11.

Blaxter, M. (1976) *The Meaning of Disability* (London: Heinemann).

Bleier, R. (1984) *Science and Gender* (Oxford: Pergamon Press).

Bleier R. (1986) 'Lab Coat: Robe of Innocence or Kansman's sheet', in T. de Lauretis, (ed.) *Feminist Studies* (Bloomington: Indiana University Press).

Blumer, H. (1969) *Symbolic Interactionism* (Englewood Cliffs: Prentice Hall).

Bordo, S. (1993) *Unbearable Weight: Feminism, Western Culture and the Body* (Berkeley: University of California Press).

Boulding, K. (1967) 'The boundaries of social policy', *Social Work*, vol. 12, no. 1.

Boulton, M., McLean, J., Fitzpatrick, R., and Hart, G. (1995) 'Gay men's accounts of unsafe sex', *AIDS Care*, vol. 7, no. 5.

Bounds, J. and Hepburn, H. (1994) 'Up the Standards', *Community Care*, June 23.

Bourdieu, P. (1984) *Distinction; A Social Critique of the Judgement of Taste* (London: Routledge & Kegan Paul).

Bourdieu P. (1990) *In Other Words: Essays Towards a Reflexive Sociology* (Cambridge: Polity Press).

Bowden, P. (1997) *Caring: Gender-Sensitive Ethics* (London: Routledge).

Bowes, A. and Domokos, T. (1996) 'Pakistani Women and Maternity Care: Raising muted voices, *Sociology of Health and Illness*, vol. 18, no. 1.

Brah, A. (1997) *Cartographies of Diaspora* (London: Routledge).

Branson, J. and Miller, D. (1989) 'Beyond Integration Policy – The Deconstruction of Disability' in L. Barton (ed.) *Integration: Myth or Reality* (Brighton: Falmer Press).

Braude, S. (1991) *First Person Plural: Multiple Personality and the Philosophy of Mind* (London: Routledge).

Brooks, F. (1991) *Alternatives to the Medical Model of Childbirth: A Qualitative Study of User Centred Maternity Care*, Unpublished PhD Thesis, University of Sheffield.

Brooman, S. and Legge, D. (1997) *Law Relating to Animals* (London: Cavendish).

Brown, H. and Smith, H. (1993) 'Women Caring for People: the Mismatch between rhetoric and reality', *Policy and Politics*, vol. 21, no. 3.

Browne, M. (1996) 'Needs Assessment and Community Care' in J. Piercy-Smith (ed.) *Needs Assessments in Public Policy* (Buckingham: Open University Press).

Bruce, M. (1961) *The Coming of the Welfare State* (London: Batsford).

Bryan, B., Dadzie, S. and Scafe, S. (1985) *The Heart of the Race. Black Women's Lives in Britain* (London: Virago).

Bunton, R. and Macdonald, G. (1992) *Health Promotion: Disciplines and Diversity* (London: Routledge).

Burkitt, I. (1997) 'Social relationships and emotions', *Sociology*, vol. 31, no. 1.

Butler, J. (1993) *Bodies that Matter: On the discursive limits of sex* (London: Routledge).

Callender, C. (1989) 'The results of transplantation in Blacks: Just the tip of the iceberg', *Transplantation Proceedings*, vol. 21, pp. 3407–3410.

Callinicos, A. (1989) *Against Postmodernism: A Marxist Critique* (Cambridge: Polity Press).

Campbell, B. (1996) 'Old Fogeys and Angry Young Men: A critique of communitarianism', *Soundings*, Issue 1.

Campbell, J. and Oliver, M. (1996) *Disability Politics. Understanding our past, changing our future* (London: Routledge).

Campbell, R. and Porter, S. (1997) 'Feminist theory and the sociology of childbirth. A response to Ellen Annandale and Judith Clark', *Sociology of Health and Illness* vol. 19, no. 3, pp. 348–358.

Campos Boralevi, L. (1984) *Bentham and the Oppressed* (Berlin: Walter de Gruyter).

Carlisle, D. (1995) 'Life-giving fatwa – Editorial' *Nursing Times*, vol. 91, no. 29–30.

Carter. J. and Rayner, M. (1996) 'The Curious Case of Post-Fordism and Welfare', *Journal of Social Policy*, vol. 25, no. 3.

Cartwright, A. (1979) *The Dignity of Labour? A Study of Childbearing and Induction* (London: Tavistock).

Castel, R. (1991) 'From dangerousness to risk', in G. Burchell, C. Gordon and P. Miller (eds) *The Foucault Effect: Studies in Governmentality* (Brighton: Harvester Wheatsheaf).

Challis, D. (1992) 'Providing alternatives to long stay hospital care for frail elderly patients: Is it cost effective?', *International Journal of Geriatric Psychiatry*, vol. 7, pp. 773–81.

Chalmers, I. and Richards, M. (1977) 'Intervention and Causal Inference in Obstetric Practice', in T. Shard and M. Richards (eds) *Benefits and Hazards of the New Obstetrics* (London: Heinneman).

Cheetham, J. (1993) 'Social work and community care in the 1990s: Pitfalls and potential', in R. Page and J. Baldock (eds) *Social Policy Review 5* (Canterbury: Social Policy Association).

Chodorow, N. (1978) *The Reproduction of Mothering: Psychoanalysis and the Sociology of Gender* (Berkeley: University of California Press).

Clark, C. and Whitfield, G. (1981) 'Deaths from chronic renal failure', *British Medical Journal*, vol. 283, pp. 283–287.

Clarke, J. and Newman, J. (1997) *The Managerial State* (London: Sage).

Clarke, M. and Stewart, J. (1990) *General Management in Local Government: Getting the Balance Right* (Harlow: Longman).

Code, L. (1991) *What can she know? Feminist Theory and the Construction of Knowledge* (New York: Cornell University Press).

Commission of the European Communities (1993) *Green Paper: European Social Policy: Options for the Union* (Luxembourg: Office for Official Publications of the European Communities).

184 *References*

Commission on Social Justice (CSJ) (1994) *Social Justice: Strategies for National Renewal* (London: Vintage/IPPR).

Conference of European Health Ministers (1987) *Ethical and socio-cultural problems raised by organ transplantation* (Paris: Council of Europe).

Coward, R. (1989) *The Whole Truth: the Myth of Alternative Health* (London: Faber and Faber).

Craib, I. (1995) 'Some comments on the sociology of emotions', *Sociology*, vol. 29, no. 1.

Critical Social Policy editorial (1982) 'Birth Rights: Radical consumerism in health care', *Critical Social Policy*, Issue 2, pp. 62–65.

Croft, S. (1986) 'Women, caring and the recasting of need – a feminist appraisal', *Critical Social Policy*, vol. 6. no. 1.

Crossley, N. (1996) 'Body-subject/body-power: Agency, inscription and control in M. Foucault and M. Merleau-Ponty, *Body and Society*, vol. 2, no. 2.

Crow, L. (1996) 'Including All Our Lives: Renewing the social model of disability', in J. Morris (ed.) *Encounters with Strangers. Feminism and Disability* (London: The Women's Press).

Dalley, G. (1993) 'Caring: a legitimate interest of older women', in M. Bernard and K. Meade (eds) *Women Come of Age* (London: Edward Arnold)

Daly, M. (1979) *Gyn/Ecology: The Metaethics of Radical Feminism* (London: The Women's Press).

Davidson, A. (1986) 'Archaeology, geneaology, ethics', in D. Hoy (ed.) *Foucault: A Critical Reader* (London: Blackwell).

Davies, P. and Project SIGMA (1992) 'On relapse: recidivism or rational response', in P. Aggleton *et al.* (eds) *AIDS: Rights, Risk, Reason* (Brighton: Falmer Press).

Davis, A., Ellis, K. and Rummery, K. (1997) *Access to Assessment: Perspectives of practitioners, disabled people and carers* (Bristol: The Policy Press).

Davis, K. (1997) 'Embody-ing Theory: Beyond modernist and post-modernist readings of the body' in K. Davis (ed.) *Embodied Practices: Feminist Perspectives on the Body* (London: Sage).

Davis, L. (1995) *Enforcing Normalcy: Disability, Deafness and the Body* (New York: Verso).

de Beauvoir, S. (1975) *The Second Sex* (Harmondsworth: Penguin).

de Certeau, M. (1984) *The Practice of Everyday Life* (Berkeley: University of California Press).

Dean, H. (1991) *Social Security and Social Control* (London: Routledge).

Dean, H. (1995) 'Paying for children: Procreation and financial liability' in H. Dean (ed.) *Parents' Duties, Children's Debts: The limits of policy intervention* (Aldershot: Arena).

Dean, H. and Khan, Z. (1997) 'Muslim perspectives on welfare', *Journal of Social Policy*, vol. 26, no. 2.

Dean, H. and Melrose, M. (1997) 'Manageable Discord: Fraud and resistance in the social security system', *Social Policy and Administration*, vol. 31, no. 2.

Dean, H. and Thompson, D. (1996) 'Fetishizing the family: The construction of the informal carer', in H. Jones and J. Millar (eds) *The Politics of the Family* (Aldershot: Avebury).

Dean, H. with Melrose, M. (1998) *Poverty, Riches and Social Citizenship* (Basingstoke: Macmillan).

Dean, M. and Bolton, G. (1980) 'The administration of poverty and the development of nursing practice in nineteenth century England', in C. Davies (ed.) *Rewriting Nursing History.* Totowa, NJ: Croom Helm).

Department of Health (DH) (1989) *Caring for People*, Cmd. 849 (London: HMSO).

Department of Health (DH) (1991) *Assessment Systems and Community Care* (London: HMSO).

Department of Health (DH) (1992a) *The Health of the Nation*, Cmd. 1986 (London: HMSO).

Department of Health (DH) (1992b) Letter from Herbert Laming, Chief Social Services Inspector on Assessment, CI (92) 34, December 14 (London: Department of Health).

Department of Health (DH) (1993) *Implementing Community Care: Population Needs Assessment Good Practice Guidance* (London: Department of Health).

Department of Health and Social Security (DHSS) (1981) *Growing Older*, Cmnd. 8173 (London: HMSO).

Department of Health and Social Security (DHSS) (1988) *Community Care: An Agenda for Action* (London: HMSO).

Descartes, R. (1985) 'The Discourses and Meditations', in *The Philosophical Writings of Descartes*, trns. J. Cottingham, R. Stoothoff, and D. Murdoch, 2 vols. (Cambridge: Cambridge University Press).

Desmond, A. (1997) Huxley: *Evolution's High Priest* (London: Michael Joseph).

Dominelli, L. (1996) 'Deprofessionalising Social Work: Anti-oppressive practice, competencies and postmodernism', *British Journal of Social Work*, vol. 26, pp. 153–175.

Dominelli, L and Hoogvelt, A. (1996) 'Globalisation and the technocratization of social work', *Critical Social Policy*, vol. 47, no. 16.

Donovan, C., Mearns, C., McEwan, R. and Sugden, N. (1994) 'A review of the HIV-related sexual behaviour of gay men and men who have sex with men', *AIDS Care*, vol. 6, no. 5.

Donzelot, J. (1980) *The Policing of Families: Welfare versus the state* (London: Hutchinson).

Douglas, M. (1978) *Natural Symbols*, (Harmondsworth: Penguin).

Douglas Hume, E. (1939) *The Mind-Changers* (Letchworth: Hume Books Trust).

Dowsett, G., Davies, M. and Connell, B. (1992) 'Gay men, HIV/AIDS and social research: an Antipodean perspective', in P. Aggleton *et al.* (eds) *AIDS: Rights, Risk, Reason* (Brighton: Falmer Press).

Doyal, L. and Gough, I. (1991) *A Theory of Human Needs* (Basingstoke: Macmillan).

Dreyfus H. (1994) *Being-in-the-World: A Commentary on Heidegger's Being and Time, Division I*, (Cambridge, Mass.: MIT).

Dunlop, M. (1994) 'Is a science of caring possible?', in P. Benner (ed.) *Interpretive Phenomenology: Embodiment, caring, and ethics in health and illness* (London, Sage).

Ehrenreich, B. (1990) *The Fear of Falling: The inner life of the middle class* (New York: Harper).

Ehrenreich, B. and English, D. (1978) *For her Own Good: 150 years of the experts' advice to women* (London: Pluto Press).

Ekstrand, M., Stall, R., Kegeles, S. and others (1993) 'Safer sex among gay men: What is the ultimate goal?', *AIDS*, vol. 7, pp. 281–82.

Ellis, K. (1993) *Squaring the Circle: User and carer participation in needs assessment* (York: Joseph Rowntree Foundation/Community Care).

Ellis, W. (1993) 'Hanging on for dear little life', *Sunday Times*, 22 August.

Englehardt, H. (1986) *The Foundations of Bioethics* (Oxford: Oxford University Press).

Esping-Andersen, G. (1990) *The Three Worlds of Welfare Capitalism* (Cambridge: Polity Press).

Esping-Andersen, G. (ed.) (1996) *Welfare States in Transition* (London: Sage).

Etzioni, A. (1994) *The Spirit of Community* (New York: Touchstone).

Evandrou, M., Falkingham, J. and Glennerster, H. (1991) 'The personal social services: everyone's poor relation but nobody's baby', in J. Hills (ed.) *The State of Welfare* (Oxford: Clarendon Press).

Evans, R. and Manninen, D. (1988) 'US public opinion concerning the procurement and distribution of donor organs', *Transplantation Proceedings*, vol. 20, pp. 781–785.

Evidence-Based Medicine Working Group (1992) 'Evidence-based medicine: a new approach to teaching the practice of medicine' *Journal of the American Medical Association*, vol. 268, pp. 2420–2425.

Expert Maternity Group (1993) *Changing Childbirth* (London: HMSO).

Falk, P. (1994) *The Consuming Body* (London: Sage).

Featherstone, M. (1991) 'The Body in Consumer Culture' in M. Featherstone, M. Hepworth and B. Turner (eds) *The Body, Social Process and Cultural Theory* (London: Sage).

Ferguson, A. (1979) 'Women as a New Revolutionary Class', in P. Walker (ed.) *Between Labour and Capital* (Boston: South End Press).

Field, N. (1992) 'Take over bids and monopolies: HIV and the gay community', *Mainliners Newsletter*, Issue 25/26, pp. 1–3.

Finch, J. (1989) *Family Obligations and Social Change* (Cambridge: Polity Press).

Finch, J. (1990) 'The Politics of Community Care in Britain', in C. Ungerson (ed.) *Gender and Caring* (Brighton: Harvester).

Finch J. and Groves, D. (1980) 'Community Care and the Family: A case for equal opportunities', *Journal of Social Policy*, vol. 9, no. 4.

Finch J. and Groves, D. (eds) (1983) *A Labour of Love: Women, work and caring* (London: Routledge).

Firestone, S. (1971) *The Dialectic of Sex: The case for feminine revolution* (New York: Bantam).

Fitzpatrick, R., Boulton, M. and Hart, G. (1989) 'Gay men's sexual behaviour in response to AIDS – insights and problems', in P. Aggleton *et al. (eds) AIDS: Social Representations, Social Practices* (Brighton: Falmer Press).

Fitzpatrick, R., Boulton, M., McLean, J., Hart, G. and Dawson, J. (1992) 'Variation in sexual behaviour in gay men' in P. Aggleton *et al.* (eds) *AIDS: Rights, Risk and Reason* (Brighton: Falmer Press).

Flint, C. (1982) 'Where Have We Gone Wrong?' *Nursing Mirror*, 24 November, pp. 26–29.

Forster, W. (1870) 'Speech introducing Elementary Education Bill, House of Commons' in S. Maclure (ed.) (1986) *Educational Documents* (London: Methuen).

Foucault, M. (1973) *The Birth of the Clinic: An Archaeology of Medical Perception* (London: Tavistock).

Foucault, M. (1977) *Discipline and Punish: The birth of the prison* (Harmondsworth: Penguin).

Foucault, M. (1978) 'Politics and the study of discourse', *Ideology and Consciousness*, vol. 3, pp. 7–26.

Foucault, M. (1980) *Power/Knowledge* (New York: Pantheon).

Foucault, M. (1981) *The History of Sexuality: An introduction* (Harmondsworth: Penguin).

Fox, N. (1994) *Postmodernism, Sociology and Health* (Toronto: University of Toronto Press).

Frank, A. (1991) 'For a sociology of the body: An analytical review', in M. Featherstone, M. Hepworth and B. Turner (eds) *The Body: Social process and cultural theory* (London: Sage).

French, R. (1975) *Antivivisection and Medical Science in Victorian Society* (Princeton: Princeton University Press).

Freud, S. (1932) 'New Introductory Lectures on Psychoanalysis, Lecture XXXIII, Femininity', standard edition of *The Complete Psychological Works of Sigmund Freud*, Vol. 12, trns. and edited by J. Strachey and A. Freud (London: The Hogarth Press and the Institute of Psychoanalysis).

Gaarder, J. (1996) *Sophie's World* (London: Phoenix).

Gamble, A. (1988) *The Free Economy and the Strong State* (Basingstoke: Macmillan).

Garcia, J. (1984) 'Womens' Views of Antenatel Care', in M. Enkin and I. Chalmers (eds) *Effectiveness and satisfaction in Maternity Care* (London: Heinemann).

Garcia, J., Kilpatrick, R. and Richards, M. (1990) *The Politics of Maternity Care: Services for childbearing women in twentieth century Britain* (Oxford: Clarendon Press).

Garfinkel, H. (1967) *Studies in Ethnomethodology* (Englewood Cliffs: Prentice Hall).

Gaukroger, S. (1995) *Descartes: An Intellectual Biography* (Oxford: Clarendon Press).

Giddens, A. (1984) *The Constitution of Society* (Cambridge: Polity Press).

Giddens, A. (1990) *The Consequences of Modernity* (Cambridge: Polity Press).

Giddens, A. (1991) *Modernity and Self-Identity: Self and society in the late modern age* (Cambridge: Polity Press).

Giddens, A. (1992) *The Transformation of Intimacy: Sexuality, love and eroticism in modern societies* (Cambridge: Polity Press).

Giddens, A. (1994) *Beyond Left and Right: The future of radical politics* (Cambridge: Polity Press).

Gilligan, C. (1982) *In a Different Voice: Psychological Theory and Women's Development* (Cambridge, Mass.: MIT Press).

Gladstone, D. (1995) 'Individual welfare: locating care in the mixed economy', in D. Gladstone (ed.) *British Social Welfare: Past, present and future* (London: UCL Press).

Glaser, B. and Strauss, A. (1967) *The Discovery of Grounded Theory* (Chicago: Aldine).

Goffman, E. (1968) *Asylums* (Harmondsworth: Penguin).

Gold, R. (1996) 'Dangerous liasons: negotiated safety, the safe sex culture and AIDS education', *Venerology*, vol. 9, no. 2.

Gore, S., Cable, D. and Holland, A. (1992) 'Organ donation from intensive care units in England and Wales: Two year confidential audit of deaths in intensive care', *British Medical Journal*, vol. 304, pp. 349–355.

Gough, I. (1979) *The Political Economy of the Welfare State* (Basingstoke: Macmillan).

Graham, H. (1983) 'Caring: a Labour of Love', in J. Finch and D. Groves (eds) *A Labour of Love: Women, work and caring* (London: Routledge).

Graham, H. and Oakley, A. (1981) 'Competing Ideologies of Reproduction: Medical and maternal perspectives on pregnancy', in H. Roberts (ed.) *Women, Health and Reproduction* (London: Routledge & Kegan Paul).

Grant, J. (1993) *Fundamental Feminism: Contesting the core concepts of feminist theory* (London: Routledge).

Griffiths, M. (1995) *Feminisms and the Self: The web of identity* (London: Routledge).

Grimshaw, J. (1986) *Feminist Philosophers: Women's perspectives on philosophical traditions* (Brighton: Harvester).

Gunson, H. and Dodsworth, H. (1996) 'Fifty Years of Blood Transfusion,' *Transfusion Medicine* vol. 6, supplement 1.

Habermas, J. (1987) *Theory of Communicative Action*, vol. 2 (Cambridge: Polity Press).

Hacking, I. (1990) *The Taming of Chance* (Cambridge: Cambridge University Press).

Hadley, R. and Clough, R. (1996) *Care in Chaos: Frustration and challenge in community care* (London: Cassell).

Hadley, R. and Hatch, S. (1981) *Social Welfare and the Failure of the State* (London: Allen and Unwin).

Hägerstrand T. (1973) 'The domain of human geography' in R. Chorley (ed.) *Directions in Geography* (Andover: Methuen).

Haire, D. (1972) 'The Cultural Warping of Childbirth', in J. Erenrich (ed.) *The Cultural Crisis of Modern Medicine* (London: The Monthly Review Press).

Haraway, D. (1991) *Simians, Cyborgs, and Women: The reinvention of nature* (London, Free Association Books).

Harding, S. (1987) *The Science Question in Feminism* (Milton Keynes: Open University Press).

Harris, J. (1993) *Wonderwoman and Superman – The ethics of human biotechnology* (Oxford: Oxford University Press).

Harris, J. (1997) *William Beveridge. A Biography* Revised paperback edition (Oxford: Clarendon Press).

Harris, R. and Paxman, J. (1982) *A Higher Form of Killing. The secret story of gas and germ warfare* (London: Chatto & Windus).

Harrison, B. (1973) 'Animals and the State in nineteenth-century England', *English Historical Review*, vol. 88, pp. 786–820.

Hart, G., Boulton, M., Fitzpatrick, R., McLean, J. and Dawson, J. (1992) 'Relapse' to unsafe sexual behaviour among gay men: a critique of recent behavioural HIV/AIDS research', *Sociology of Health and Illness*, vol. 14, no. 2.

Hartsock, N. (1983) 'The feminist standpoint: Developing the ground for a specifically feminist historical materialism', in S. Harding and M. Hintikka (eds) *Discovering Reality: Feminist Perspectives on Epistemology, Metaphysics, Methodology and the Philosophy of Science* (Dordrecht: D. Reidel).

Hazell, L. (1975) 'A Study of 300 Elective Home Births', *Birth and the Family Journal*, vol. 2, no. 1.

Hegel, G. (1973) *Philosophy of Right*, trns. and edited T. Knox (Oxford: Oxford University Press).

Hegel, G. (1977) *Phenomenology of Spirit*, trns. A. Miller (Oxford: Oxford University Press).

Heidegger M. (1962) *Being and Time*, trns. J. Macquarrie and E. Robinson (London: SCM Press).

Hekma, G., Oosterhuis, H. and Steakley, J. (1995) 'Sexual politics and homosexuality: An historical overview', *Journal of Homosexuality*, vol. 29, no. 2/3.

Held, D. (1987) *Models of Democracy* (Cambridge: Polity Press).

Henman. P. (1997) 'Computer Technology – a Political Player in Social Policy Processes', *Journal of Social Policy*, vol. 26, no. 3.

Henwood, M. (1992) *Through a Glass Darkly. Community Care and Elderly People*, Research Report 14 (London: King's Fund Institute).

Hewitt, M. (1991) 'Bio-Politics and Social Policy: Foucault's account of Welfare', in M. Featherstone, M. Hepworth and B. Turner (eds) *The Body, Social Process and Cultural Theory* (London: Sage).

Higgins, J. (1989) 'Defining community care', *Social Policy and Administration*, vol. 23, no. 1.

Hill, M. and Bramley, G. (1986) *Analysing Social Policy* (Oxford: Martin Robertson).

Hirst, P. (1994) *Associative Democracy* (Cambridge: Polity Press).

Hobbes, T. (1651) *Leviathan*, 1968 edition, edited by C. Macpherson (Harmondsworth: Penguin).

Holland, J., Ramazanoglu, C., Scott, S., Sharpe, S. and Thompson, R. (1992) 'Pressure, resistance, empowerment: Young women and the negotiation of safer sex' in P. Aggleton *et al.* (eds) *AIDS: Rights, Risk, Reason* (Brighton: Falmer Press).

Hollands, C. (1980) *Compassion is the Bugler. The struggle for animal rights* (Edinburgh: Macdonald).

Hollway, W. (1989) *Subjectivity and Method in Psychology: Gender and science* (London: Sage).

Hooker, A. (1994a) *Organ donation in the West Midlands and the Asian community* (Harrogate: Paper presented at the Fifth British Renal Symposium).

Hooker, A. (1994b) *Organ donors and the Asian community* (Birmingham: West Midlands Health Review).

Horn, S. and Munafò, M. (1997) *Pain: Theory, Research and Intervention* (Buckingham: Open University Press).

Hughes, B. (1995) *Older People and Community Care: Critical theory and practice* (Buckingham: Open University Press).

Hughes, B. and Mtezuka, E. M. (1992) 'Social work and older women' in M. Langan and L. Day (eds) *Women, oppression and social work* (London: Routledge and Kegan Paul).

Hugman, R. (1994) 'Social Work and Case Management in the UK: Models of Professionalism and Elderly People', *Ageing and Society*, vol. 14, pp. 237–253.

Humane Society of the United States (1997) *HSUS News*, vol. 42, no. 3.

Hunsicker, L. (1991) 'Medical considerations of procurement', in C. Keyes and W. Wiest (eds) *New Harvest – Transplanting body parts and reaping the benefits* (New Jersey: Humana Press).

Hussain, M. (1947) *Islam and Socialism* (Lahore: Ashraf).

Ignatieff, M. (1994), *The Needs of Strangers* (London: Vintage).

Ingham, R., Woodcock, A. and Stenner, K. (1992) 'The limitations of rational decision-making models as applied to young people's sexual behaviour' in P. Aggleton *et al.* (eds) *AIDS; Rights, Risk, Reason* (Brighton: Falmer Press).

Irigarary, L. (1974) *Speculum of the other woman*, trns. G. Gill (New York: Cornell University Press).

Irigarary, L. (1977) *This sex which is not one*, trns. C. Porter (New York: Cornell University Press).

Itzkowitz, D. (1977) *Peculiar Privilege. A Social History of English Foxhunting 1753–1885* (Brighton: Harvester Press).

Jackson, K. (1996) 'The final lever?', *British Journal of Midwifery*, vol. 4, no. 9.

Jackson, S. (1993) 'Even sociologists fall in love: An exploration of the sociology of emotions', *Sociology*, vol. 27, pp. 218–220.

James, J. (1993) *One Particular Harbour* (Chicago: The Noble Press).

Jasper M. (1994) 'Issues in phenomenology for researchers of nursing', *Journal of Advanced Nursing*, vol. 19, pp. 309–314.

Jennett, B. and Hessett, C. (1981) 'Brain deaths in Britain as reflected in renal donors', *British Medical Journal*, vol. 283, pp. 359–362.

Jessop, B. (1994) 'The transition to post-Fordism and the Schumpterian work-fare state', in R. Burrows and B. Loader (eds) *Towards a PostFordist Welfare State* (London: Routledge).

Jordan, B. (1998) *Social Justice and the New Politics of Welfare* (London: Sage).

Jordanova, L. (1989) *Sexual visions: Images of gender in science and medicine between the eighteenth and twentieth centuries* (Hemel Hempstead: Harvester Wheatsheaf).

Judge, K. (1978) *Rationing Social Services* (London: Heinemann).

Kant, I. (1959) *Foundations of the Metaphysics of Morals*, trns. L. Beck (New York: Liberal Arts Press).

Keller, E. (1986) *Science and Gender* (New York; Yale University Press).

Keller, E. (1995) *Reflections on Gender and Science* (New Haven: Yale University Press).

Kilbrandon, Lord (1968) in G. Wolstenholme and M. O'Connor (eds) *Law and ethics of transplantation* (London, Ciba Foundation).

Kingdom, J. (1991) *Government and Politics in Britain: An introduction*, (Cambridge: Polity Press).

Kippax, S. (1996) 'A commentary on negotiated safety', *Venerology*, vol. 9, no. 2.

Kippax, S., Crawford, J., Davis, M. and others (1993) 'Sustaining safe sex: a longitudinal study of a sample of homosexual men', *AIDS*, vol. 7, pp. 257–263.

Kirkham, M. (1987) *Care in Labour*, Unpublished PhD thesis, University of Manchester.

Kitson Clark, G. (1962) *The Making of Victorian England* (London: Methuen).

Kitzinger, S. (1978) *Women and Mothers* (Glasgow: Fontana).

Klingberg, F. J. (1926) *The Anti-Slavery Movement in England. A Study in English Humanitarianism* (New Haven: Yale University Press).

Koechlin, F. (1996) 'The Animal Heart of the Matter: Xenotransplantation and the threat of new diseases', *The Ecologist*, vol. 26, no. 93–97.

Kuhn, T. (1977) *The Essential Tension* (Chicago: University of Chicago Press).

Kyle, T. (1995) The concept of caring: A review of the literature. *Journal of Advanced Nursing*, vol. 21, pp. 506–514.

Kyriakides, G., Hadjigavriel, P., Hadjicostas, A. and others (1993) 'Public awareness and attitudes toward transplantation in Cyprus', *Transplantation Proceedings*, vol. 25, p. 2279.

Lamaze, F. (1958) *Painless Childbirth* (London: Burke).

Lamb, D. (1990) *Organ transplants and ethics* (London, Routledge).

Land, H. (1991) 'Time to care' in M. McLean and D. Groves (eds) *Women's Issues in Social Policy* (London: Routledge).

Langan, M. (1993) 'The rise and fall of social work' in J. Clarke (ed.) *A Crisis in Care? Challenges to Social Work* (Buckingham: Open University Press).

Langan, M. and Clarke. J. (1994) 'Managing in the Mixed Economy of Care' in J. Clarke, A. Cochrane and E. McLaughlin (eds) *Managing Social Policy* (London: Sage).

Langan, M. and Ostner, I. (1991) 'Gender and welfare: Towards a comparative framework' in G. Room (ed.) *Towards a European Welfare State?* (Bristol: SAUS).

Lansbury, C. (1985) *The Old Brown Dog. Women, Workers and Vivisection in Edwardian England* (Wisconsin: University of Wisconsin Press).

Lasch, C. (1980) *The Culture of Narcissism: American Life in an Age of Diminishing Expectations* (New York: Abacus).

Lash, S. and Urry, J. (1987) *The End of Organised Capitalism* (Cambridge: Polity Press).

Latour, B. (1993) *We Have Never Been Modern*, trns. C. Porter (Hemel Hempstead: Harvester Wheatsheaf).

Laurence, J-R. and Perry, C. (1988) *Hypnosis, Will and Memory: A Psycho-Legal History* (London: Guildford Press).

Lawson, R. (1993) 'The new technology of management in the personal social services' in P. Taylor-Gooby and R. Lawson (eds) *Markets and Managers. New Issues in the Delivery of Welfare* (Buckingham: Open University).

Leboyer, F. (1977) *Birth Without Violence.* (London: Burke).

LeGrand, J. (1997) 'Knights, knaves or pawns? Human behaviour and social policy', *Journal of Social Policy*, vol. 26, no. 2.

Leibfried, S. (1993) 'Towards a European welfare state? On integrating poverty regimes into the European Community', in C. Jones (ed.) *New Perspectives on the Welfare State in Europe* (London: Routledge).

Leininger, M. (1984) *Care: The Essence of Nursing and Health* (Detroit: Wayne State University Press).

Leonard, P. (1997) *Postmodern Welfare: Reconstructing an emancipatory project* (London: Sage).

Leplin, J. (ed.) (1984) *Scientific Realism* (Berkeley: University of California Press).

Levick, P. (1992) 'The janus face of community care legislation: An opportunity for radical possibilities?', *Critical Social Policy*, vol. 12, no. 1.

Levitas, R. (1996) 'The concept of social exclusion and the new Durkheimian hegemony', *Critical Social Policy*, vol. 16, no. 2.

Lewis, A. and Snell, M. (1986) 'Increasing kidney transplantation in Britain: the importance of donor cards, public opinion and medical practice', *Social Science and Medicine*, vol. 22, pp. 1075–1080.

Lewis, J. (1992a) *Women in Britain since 1945. Women, Family, Work and the State in the Post-War Years* (Oxford: Blackwell).

Lewis, J. (1992b) 'Gender and the development of welfare regimes', *Journal of European Social Policy* vol. 44, no. 2.

Lewis. J. and Glennerster, H. (1996) *Implementing the new community care* (Buckingham: Open University Press).

Lind-af-Hageby, L. and Schartau, L. (1903) *The Shambles of Science: Extracts from the diary of two students of physiology* (London: Ernest Bell).

Locke, J. (1924) *Of Civil Government: Two treatises*, Every man edition, (London: Dent and Sons).

Lomax, H. (1995) '"What's Your Loss Like Love?": An analysis of midwife-client interaction during the postnatal examination', invited symposium at British Psychological Society Annual Conference, *The Psychology of the Postpartum*, University of Warwick, 31 March–3 April.

Lupton, D. (1994) *Medicine as Culture. Illness, disease and the body in Western societies* (London: Sage).

Macdonald, C. (1989) *Mind-Body Identity Theories* (London: Routledge).

MacIntyre, S. (1982) 'Communications: Pregnant women and their medical and midwifery attendents', *Midwives Chronicle and Nursing Notes*, November, pp. 387–394.

Macpherson, C. (1962) *The Political Theory of Possessive Individualism* (Oxford: Oxford University Press).

Mann, M. (1987) 'Ruling class strategies and citizenship', *Sociology*, vol. 21, no. 3.

Marquand, D. (1996) 'Moralists and Hedonists' in D. Marquand and A. Seldon, *The Ideas That Shaped Post-War Britain* (London: Harper Collins).

Martin, E. (1987) *The Woman in the Body: A Cultural Analysis of Reproduction* (Milton Keynes: Open University Press).

Marx, K. (1845) 'Theses on Feuerbach' in *Marx-Engels Gesamtausgabe*, Volume 1, Section 5 [translated extract in T. Bottomore, and M. Rubel, (1963) *Karl Marx. Selected writings in sociology and social philosophy* (Harmondsworth: Penguin).

Marx, K. (1887) *Capital*, Vol. 1, 1970 edition, Lawrence and Wishart, London.

Mason, P. (1997) The *Brown Dog Affair* (London: Two Sevens Publishing).

Maternity Advisory Committee (1970) *Domiciliary and Maternity Bed Needs*, (The Peel Report), HMSO.

Maternity Services Advisory Committee (1984) *Care During Childbirth* (London: HMSO).

Mayo, M. and Weir, A. (1993) 'The future for feminist social policy', in R. Page and J. Baldock (eds) *Social Policy Review 5*, Canterbury: Social Policy Association.

McCulloch, G. (1995) *The Mind and its World* (London: Routledge).

McDonald, F. (1990) 'Organ donation, new issues, new controversies', *Dialysis and Transplantation*, vol. 19, pp. 238–239.

McIntosh, M. (1996) 'Feminism and Social Policy', in D. Taylor (ed.) *Critical Social Policy: A Reader* (London: Sage).

Mckie, R., Jones, J., Bewins, A., Durham, M. and Harrison, D. (1996) 'A conspiracy to drive us all mad', *The Observer*, 24 March.

McLaughlin, E. and Glendinning, C. (1994) 'Paying for care in Europe: Is there a feminist approach?', in L. Hantrais and S. Mangen (eds) *Concepts and Contexts in International Comparisons: Family policy and the welfare of women, Cross-National Research Papers*, Series 3, No. 3, (Loughborough: Centre for European Studies).

Mead, M. (1949) *Male and Female* (New York: Morrow).

Means, R. (1995) 'Older people and the personal social services', in D. Gladstone (ed.) *British Social Welfare: Past, present and future* (London: UCL Press).

Meek, C. (1992) 'Organ Crisis', *BMA News Review*, November, pp. 16–17.

Mehl, L. (1977) Research and Childbirth Alternatives: What can it tell us about hospital practices', in A. Stewert, and B. Stewert (eds) *21st Century Obstetrics Now.* (London: The National Association of Parents and Professionals for Safer Alternatives in Childbirth/Chapel Hill).

Miller, E. and Gwynne, G. (1972) *A life apart* (London: Tavistock).

Mishra, R. (1977) *Society and Social Policy* (Basingstoke: Macmillan).

Mishra, R. (1990) *The Welfare State in Capitalist Society* (Hemel Hempstead: Harvester Wheatsheaf).

Mitchell, M. (1992) *A Critical Gay Perspective on HIV/AIDS Discourses: The construction and experience of safer sex discourses in relation to the lives of gay and bisexual men in London, 1981–1992*, unpublished Master's dissertation (London: Goldsmiths' College).

Morgan, D. and Scott, S. (1993) 'Bodies in a Social Landscape', in S. Scott and D. Morgan (eds) *Body Matters: Essays on the Sociology of the Body* (Brighton: Falmer Press).

Morgan, R. (1970) 'Goodbye to all that', in L. Tanner (ed.) *Voices from Women's Liberation* (New York: New American Library).

Morris, J. (1991) *Pride Against Prejudice: Transforming attitudes to disability* (London: The Women's Press).

Moulton, J. (1983) 'A Paradigm of Philosophy: The adversary method', in S. Harding and M. Hintikka (eds) *Discovering Reality* (Dortrecht: Reidel).

Muir, K. (1993) 'Can saving the life of little Laura be worth £1 million?' *Times*, 22 September.

Munhall P. (1994) *Revisioning Phenomenology: Nursing and Health Science Research* (New York: National League for Nursing Press).

Munro, A. (1985) Maternity Care: A Challenge to Health Authorities. *NAHA News*, no. 83.

Nandan, G. (1994) 'India outlaws trade in human organs – Editorial', *British Medical Journal*, vol. 308, pp. 1657.

New, B., Solomon, M., Dingwall, R. and McHale, J. (1994) *A question of give and take: Improving the supply of donor organs for transplantation* (London: King's Fund Institute).

Newman, J. and Clarke, J. (1994) 'Going about our business? The managerialisation of public services', in J. Clarke, A. Cochrane and E. McLaughlin (eds) *Managing Social Policy* (London: Sage).

Noddings, M. (1984) *Caring: A Feminine Approach to Ethics and Moral Education* (Berkeley: University of California Press).

O'Connell, K. and Duffy, M. (1978) 'Research in nursing practice: Its present scope', in N. Chaska (ed.) *The Nursing Profession: Views Through the Mist* (New York: McGraw-Hill).

O'Neill, J. (1985) *Five Bodies. The human shape of modern society* (New York: Cornell University Press).

Oakley, A. (1980) *Women Confined: Towards a Sociology of Childbirth* (Oxford: Martin Robertson).

Oakley, A. (1981) 'From Patient to Participant – The role of the consumer in government reports on the maternity services since 1917', a paper given at a study day at the National Childbirth Trust, London, 26 February.

Oakley, A. (1982) Review Article on S. Romalis (1981) 'Alternatives to Medical Control', *Times Higher Educational Supplement*, 8 August.

Oakley, A. (1984) *The Captured Womb: A History of the Medical Care of Pregnant Women*, Oxford: Basil Blackwell.

Oakley, A. (1987) 'Home Birth: A class privilege', *New Society*, 6 November.

Odent, M. (1984) 'How to help women in labour', in L. Zander and G. Chamberlain (eds) *Pregnancy care for the 1980s* (London: The Royal Society of Medicine and Macmillan Press).

Offe, C. (1984) *Contradictions of the Welfare State* (Cambridge, Mass.: MIT Press).

Offe, C. (1993) 'Interdependence, difference and limited state capacity', in G. Drover and P. Kerans (eds) *New Approaches to Welfare Theory* (Aldershot: Edward Elgar).

Oliver, M. (1990) *The Politics of Disablement* (Basingstoke: Macmillan).

Oliver, M. (1996) *Understanding Disability. From Theory to Practice* (Basingstoke: Macmillan).

Oppenheim, C. and Harker, L. (1996) *Poverty: The facts*, third edition (London: Child Poverty Action Group).

Oxman, A., Sackett, D. and Guyatt, G. (1995) 'Users' guide to the medical literature: How to get started', *Journal of the American Medical Association*, vol. 270, pp. 2093–2095.

Page, R. (1997) 'Caring for strangers: Can the altruisitic welfare state survive?, paper given at a conference, *Citizenship and the Welfare State: Fifty years of progress?*, Ruskin College, Oxford, 18–19 December.

Paley, J. (1997) 'Husserl, phenomenology and nursing', *Journal of Advanced Nursing*, vol. 26, pp. 187–193.

Paley, J. (1998) 'Misinterpretive phenomenology: Heidegger, ontology and nursing', *Journal of Advanced Nursing* vol. 27, no. 4.

Parker, G. (1985) *With Due Care and Attention: A review of research on informal care* (London: Family Policy Studies Centre).

Parnell, B. (1996) 'Unprotected sexual intercourse in "safe" contexts: deciding what matters most', *Venerology*, vol. 9, no. 2.

Parry, J. (1985) 'Brown Dog Lies Doggo No More', *Animals' Defender* (Journal of the National Anti-Vivisection Society), Nov/Dec pp. 92–3.

Parry, N. and Parry, J. (1976) *The Rise of the Medical Profession* (London: Croom Helm).

Parry, N. and Parry, J. (1979) 'Social work, professionalism and the state', in N. Parry, M. Rustin and C. Satyamurti (eds) *Social Work, Welfare and the State* (London: EdwardArnold).

Pascall, G. (1997) *Social Policy: A New Feminist Analysis* (London: Routledge).

Pashukanis, E. (1978) *General Theory of Law and Marxism* (London: Ink Links).

Pateman, C. (1989) *The Disorder of Women* (Cambridge: Polity Press).

Pawson, R. and Tilley, N. (1997) *Realistic Evaluation* (London: Sage).

Perkin, H. (1996) *The Third Revolution. Professional Elites in the Modern World* (London: Routledge).

Perls, F., Hefferline, R. and Goodman, P. (1973) *Gestalt Therapy: Excitement and Growth in the Human Personality* (Harmondsworth, Penguin).

Perry, R. (ed.) (1964) *Sources of Our Liberties* (New York: New York University Press).

Petersen, A. and Lupton, D. (1996) *The New Public Health: Health and self in the age of risk* (London: Sage).

Pinkerton, S. and Abramson, P. (1992) 'Is risky sex rational', *Journal of Sex Research*, vol. 29, no. 4.

Piore, M. and Sabel, C. (1984) *The Second Industrial Divide* (New York: Basic Books).

Pitts, M. (1996) *The Psychology of Preventive Health* (London: Routledge).

Plato (1948) 'Phaedo', in S. Buchanan (ed.) *The Portable Plato* (Harmondsworth, Penguin).

Plato (1965) *Timaeus and Critias*, edited by D. Lee (Harmondsworth: Penguin).

Plato (1974) *The Republic* (Harmondsworth: Penguin).

Polanyi, K. (1944) *The Great Transformation* (New York: Rinehart).

Pollitt, C. (1990) *Managerialism and the Public Services* (Oxford: Blackwell).

Prieur, A. (1990) 'Gay men: Reasons for continued practice of unsafe sex', *AIDS Education and Prevention*, vol. 2, pp. 110–117.

Prottas, J. and Batten, H. (1989) 'The willingness to give: the public and the supply of transplantable organs', *Journal of Health Politics, Policy and Law*, vol. 16, no. 121–134.

Randhawa, G. (1995) 'Improving the supply of organ donors in the UK: a review of public policies', *Health Education Journal*, vol. 54, pp. 241–250.

Randhawa, G. (1996) 'The prospect of xenotransplantation in India', *Indian Journal of Asian Affairs*, vol. 9, pp. 114–120.

Randhawa, G. (1997) 'Enhancing the health professional's role in requesting transplant organs', *British Journal of Nursing*, vol. 6, pp. 429–434.

Randhawa, G. (1998) 'Identifying religious beliefs towards organ donation among the UK's Asian population', *Trends and Topics in Transplantation*, vol. 2.

Randhawa, G. and Darr, A. (1997) 'The introduction of the NHS Organ Donor Register and its impact in the UK', *TransplantationsMedizin*, vol. 9, pp. 10–16.

Reed, J. and Ground, I. (1997) *Philosophy for Nursing* (London: Arnold).

Reeder F. (1985) 'Hermeneutics', in B. Sarter (ed.) *Paths to Knowledge: Innovative Research Methods for Nursing* (New York: National League for Nursing Press).

Rees, D. (1990) 'Terminal care and bereavement', in B. McAvoy and L. Donaldson (eds) *Health Care for Asians* (Oxford: Oxford University Press).

Reid, E. (1994) 'Approaching the HIV epidemic: the community response', *AIDS Care*, vol. 6, pp. 551–57.

Reisman, D. (1977) *Richard Titmuss: Welfare and Society* (London: Heinemann).

Richardson, R. (1987) *Death, Dissection and the Destitute* (London: Routledge & Kegan Paul).

Richardson, R. and Hurwitz, B. (1987) 'Jeremy Bentham's Self-Image: An Exemplary Bequest for Dissection', *British Medical Journal*, vol. 357, pp. 1–10.

Ridge, D. (1996) 'Negotiated safety: Not negotiable or safe', *Venerology*, vol. 9, no. 2.

Ritzer, G. (1993) *The McDonaldization of Society* (London: Sage).

Roberts, H. (ed.) (1981) *Women, Health and Reproduction* (London: Routledge & Kegan Paul).

Roche, M. (1992) *Rethinking Citizenship: Welfare ideology and change in modern society* (Cambridge: Polity Press).

Rogers, L. (1996) 'A heartbeat for history', *Sunday Times*, 29 September.

Romalis, S. (1981) *Childbirth Alternatives to Medical Control* (Austin: University of Texas Press).

Rose, P., Beeby, J. and Parker, D. (1995) 'Academic rigour in the lived experience of researchers using phenomenological methods in nursing' *Journal of Advanced Nursing*, vol. 21, pp. 1123–1129.

Rothman, B. (1982) *In Labour: Women and Power in the Birth Place* (New York: Norton).

Rothman, B. (1987) 'Reproduction', in M. Feree and B. Hess (eds) *Analysing Gender: A Handbook of Social Science Research*, (London: Sage).

Rupke, N. (ed.) (1987) *Vivisection in Historical Perspective* (Beckenham: Croom Helm).

Russell, L., Scott, D. and Wilding, P. (1996) 'The future of the voluntary sector: Deepening dependence on the state?', *Crucible*, July–September, pp. 114–24.

Ruth, S. (1979) 'Methodocracy, Misogyny, and Bad Faith: Sexism in the philosophical establishment', *Metaphilosophy*, vol. 101, pp. 44–61.

Ryle, G. (1949) *The Concept of Mind* (London: Hutchinson).

Sackett, D., Rosenberg, W., Gray, J., Haynes, R. and Richardson, W. (1996) 'Evidence-based medicine: What it is and what it isn't', *British Medical Journal*, vol. 312, pp. 71–2.

Sainsbury, S. (1995) 'Disabled people and the personal social services' in D. Gladstone (ed.) *British Social Welfare: Past, present and future* (London: UCL Press).

Saks, M. (ed.) (1992) *Alternative Medicine in Britain* (Oxford: Clarendon Press).

Salter, B. (1994) 'The Politics of Community Care: Social rights and welfare limits', *Policy and Politics* vol. 22, no. 2.

Sanderson, I. (1996) 'Needs and Public Services' in J. Piercy-Smith (ed.) *Needs Assessments in Public Policy* (Buckingham: Open University Press).

Sayer, A. and Walker, D. (1992) *The New Social Economy: Reworking the Division of Labour* (Oxford: Blackwell).

Sbisa, M. (1996) 'The feminine subject and female body in discourse about childbirth', *The European Journal of Women's Studies*, vol. 3, pp. 363–376.

Schutz A. (1972) *The Phenomenology of the Social World*, trns. G. Walsh and F. Lehnert (London: Heinemann).

Schwartz, H. (1985) 'Bioethical and legal considerations in increasing the supply of transplantable organs: From UAGA to baby Fae', *American Journal of Law and Medicine*, vol. 10, pp. 397–438.

Scorsone, S. (1990) 'Christianity and the significance of the human body', *Transplantation proceedings*, vol. 22, pp. 943–944.

Scruton, R. (1995) *A Short History of Modern Philosophy: From Descartes to Wittgenstein*, second edition (London: Routledge).

Scull, A. (1977) *Decarceration* (Englewood Cliffs: Prentice Hall).

Seebohm, F. (1968) *Report of the Committee on Local Authority and Allied Personal Social Services*, Cmnd. 3703 (London: HMSO).

Sells, R. (1990) 'Organ commerce: Ethics and expediency', *Transplantation Proceedings*, vol. 22, pp. 931–932.

Sharpe, R. (1988) *The Cruel Deception: The Use of Animals in Medical Research* (Wellingborough: Thorsons).

Sharpe, R. (1993) *Consenting Guinea Pigs. In Focus Scientific* (Washington, DC: American Anti-Vivisection Society).

Sherwin, S. (1992) *No Longer Patient: Feminist Ethics and Health Care* (Philadelphia: Temple University Press).

Shilling, C. (1991) 'Educating the Body: physical capital and the production of social inequalities', *Sociology*, vol. 25, no. 4.

Shilling, C. (1993) *The Body and Social Theory* (London: Sage).

Shilling, C. and Mellor, P. (1996) 'Embodiment, structuration theory and modernity: Mind/body dualism and the repression of sensuality', *Body and Society*, vol. 2, no. 4.

Short Report (1980) *Second report from the social services maternity committee: Perinatal and neonatal mortality* (London: HMSO).

Silburn, R. (1995) 'Beveridge' in V. George and R. Page (eds) *Modern Thinkers on Welfare* (Hemel Hempstead: Prentice Hall/Harvester Wheatsheaf).

Smith, D. (1988) *The Everyday World as Problematic* (Toronto: University of Toronto Press).

Smith, G. (1980) *Social need. Policy, practice and research* (London: Routledge and Kegan Paul).

Social Services Inspectorate (SSI) (1991a) *Care Management and Assessment, Managers' Guide* (London: HMSO).

Social Services Inspectorate (SSI) (1991b) *Care Management and Assessment, Practitioners' Guide* (London: HMSO).

Soh, P. and Lim, T. (1991) 'Organ procurement in Singapore', *Annals of the Academy of Medicine*, vol. 20, pp. 439–442.

Spender, D. (1980) *Man Made Language* (London: Routledge).

Spicker, P. (1991) 'Solidarity' in G. Room (ed.) *Towards a European Welfare State?* (Bristol: SAUS).

Spicker, P. (1995) *Social Policy: Themes and approaches* (Hemel Hempstead: Prentice Hall / Harvester Wheatsheaf).

Spina, F., Sedda, L., Pizzi, R. and others (1993) 'Donor families' attitudes toward organ donation', *Transplantation Proceedings*, vol. 25, pp. 1699–1701.

Squires, P. (1990) *Anti-Social Policy: Welfare, Ideology and the Disciplinary State* (Hemel Hempstead: Harvester Wheatsheaf).

Stacey, M. (1988) *The Sociology of Health and Healing: A Textbook* (London: Unwin Hyman).

Standing Maternity and Midwifery Advisory Committee (The Peel Report) (1970) *Domiciliary Midwifery and Maternity Bed Needs: Report of the Sub-Committee* (London: HMSO).

Stoller, R. (1984) 'Sex and Gender: Vol. 1 The development of masculinity and femininity' (New York: Jason Aronson).

Strawson, P. F. (1964) *Individuals: An Essay in Descriptive Metaphysics* (London: Methuen).

Summers A., McKeown, K. and Lord, J. (1997) 'Different Women, Different Views', *British Journal of Midwifery*, vol. 5, no. 1.

Sweeney, N. (1990) *Animals and Cruelty and Law* (Bristol: Alibi).

Synnott, A. (1992) 'Tomb, temple, machine and self: The social construction of the body', *British Journal of Sociology*, vol. 43, no. 1.

Tawney, R. (1926) *Religion and the Rise of Capitalism* (New York: Harcourt Brace).

Taylor, B. (1994) *Being Human: Ordinariness in Nursing* (Melbourne: Churchill Livingstone).

Taylor, C. (1985) 'Interpretation and the sciences of man', in *Philosophical Papers*, vol. 2 (Cambridge: Cambridge University Press).

Taylor, C. (1986) 'Foucault on freedom and truth', in D. Hoy (ed.) *Foucault: A Critical Reader* (London: Basil Blackwell).

Taylor-Gooby, P. and Lawson, R. (eds) (1993) *Markets and Managers: New issues in the delivery of welfare* (Buckingham: Open University Press).

Temple, W. (1941) *Citizen and Churchman* (London: Eyre & Spottiswood).

Tew, M. (1978) 'The Case Against Hospital Deliveries: The statistical evidence', in S. Kitzinger and J. Davies (eds) *The Place of Birth* (Oxford: Oxford University Press).

Tew, M. (1990) *Safer Childbirth? A Critical History of Maternity Care* (London: Chapman and Hall).

Thane, P. (1982) *The Foundations of the Welfare State* (Harlow: Longman).

Thatcher, M. (1988) Interview in *Sunday Times*, 9 November.

Thomas, K. (1983) *Man and the Natural World. Changing Atittudes in England 1500–1800* (London: Allen Lane).

Thrift, N. (1996) *Spatial Formations* (London: Sage).

Titmuss, R. (1963) *Essays on the Welfare State* second edition (London: Allen and Unwin).

Titmuss, R. (1973) *The Gift Relationship: From human blood to social policy* (London: Allen and Unwin).

Titmuss, R. (1974) *Social Policy. An Introduction* (London: George Allen and Unwin).

Townsend, P., Davidson, N. and Whitehead, M. (1988) *Inequalities in Health* (Harmondsworth: Penguin).

Treichler, P. (1987) 'AIDS, homophobia and biomedical discourse: an epidemic of signification', *Cultural Studies*, vol. 1, no. 3.

Trivedi, H. (1990) 'Hindu religious views in the context of transplantation of organs from cadavers', *Transplantation proceedings*, vol. 22, pp. 942.

Turner, B. (1983) *Religion and Social Theory: A materialist perspective* (London: Heinemann).

Turner, B. (1991) 'Recent Developments in the Theory of the Body', in M. Featherstone, M. Hepworth and B. Turner (eds) *The Body, Social Process and Cultural Theory* (London: Sage).

Turner, B. (1995) *Medical Power and Social Knowledge*, second edition (London: Sage).

Turner, B. (1996) *The Body and Society*, second edition (London: Sage).

Twigg, J. (1989) 'Models of Carers: How do social care agencies conceptualise their relationship with informal carers?', *Journal of Social Policy*, vol. 18, no. 1.

Twigg, J. (1997) 'Deconstructing the "Social Bath": Help with bathing for older and disabled people', *Journal of Social Policy*, vol. 26, no. 2.

Twigg, J. and Atkin, K. (1994) *Carers Perceived: Policy and practice in informal care* (Buckingham: Open University Press).

Ungerson, C. (1987) *Policy is Personal: Sex, gender and informal care* (London: Tavistock).

United Kingdom Transplant Support Service Authority (UKTSSA) (1994) *Questions and straight answers about transplants* (Bristol: UKTSSA).

United Kingdom Transplant Support Service Authority (UKTSSA) (1995) *Background to UKTSSA* (Bristol: UKTSSA).

United Kingdom Transplant Support Service Authority (UKTSSA) (1997) *Human organ information sheet* (Bristol: UKTSSA).

van Manen, M. (1990) *Researching Lived Experience: Human science for an action sensitive pedagogy* (New York: State University of New York Press).

Vyvyan, J. (1971) *The Dark Face of Science* (London: Michael Joseph).

Wakeford, R. and Stepney, R. (1989) 'Obstacles to organ donation', *British Journal of Surgery*, vol. 76, pp. 435–439.

Walby, S. (1986) *Patriarchy at Work* (Cambridge: Polity Press).

Walker, A. (1982) 'The meaning and social division of community care', in A. Walker (ed.) *Community Care: The family, the state and social policy* (London: Policy Studies Institute).

Walker, A. (1996) *The New Generational Contract: Intergenerational Relations, Old Age and Welfare* (London: UCL Press).

Walker, J. (1985) 'Meeting Midwives Midway', *Nursing Times*, 23 October, pp. 48–50.

Walton, M. and Fineman, I. (1996) 'Why can't a woman be more like a man? A Renaissance perspective on the biological basis for female inferiority', *Women and Health*, vol. 24, no. 4.

Warnes, A. (1993) 'Being Old, Old People and the Burdens of Burden', *Ageing and Society*, vol. 13, pp. 297–338.

Watney, S. (1989) 'The subject of AIDS', in P. Aggleton, G. Hart and P. Davies (eds) *AIDS: Social Representations, Social Practices* (Brighton: Falmer Press).

Watney, S. (1990) 'Safer sex an community practice', in P. Aggleton *et al.* (eds) *AIDS: Individual, Cultural and Policy Dimensions* (Brighton: Falmer Press).

Watney, S. (1993) 'The spectacle of AIDS', in H. Abelove, M. Barale and D. Halperin (eds) *The Lesbian and Gay Studies Reader* (New York: Routledge).

Watson, J. (1979) *Nursing: The Philosophy and Science of Caring* (Boston: Little, Brown).

Watson, J. (1988) *Human Science and Human Care: A Theory of Nursing* (New York: National League for Nursing).

Webb, A. and Wistow, G. (1987) *Social Work, Social Care and Social Planning: The personal social services since Seebohm* (Harlow: Longman).

Webb, B. and Webb, S. (1909) *Break up the Poor Law!*, (Part I of the Minority Report of the Royal Commission on the Poor Laws) (London: Fabian Society).

Weber, M. (1904) *The Protestant Ethic and the Spirit of Capitalism*, 1976 English edition (London: Allen and Unwin).

Weeks, J. (1989) 'AIDS: the intellectual agenda', in P. Aggleton *et al.* (eds) *AIDS: Social Representations, Social Practices* (Brighton: Falmer Press).

Weiss, D. (1988) 'Organ transplantation, medical ethics and Jewish law', *Transplantation Proceedings*, vol. 20, pp. 1071–1075.

Wendell, S. (1996) *The Rejected Body: Feminist Philosophical Reflections on Disability* (London: Routledge).

Wertz, R. and Wertz, B. (1979) 'Notes on the Decline of Midwives and the Decline of Medical Obstetricians', in P. Conrad and R. Kern (eds) *The Sociology of Mental Health and Illness* (New York: St Martins Press).

Westacott, E. (1949) *A Century of Vivisection and Anti-Vivisection* (Ashingdon, Rochford: C. W. Daniel).

Whiteside, N. (1996) 'Creating the Welfare State in Britain, 1945–1960', *Journal of Social Policy*, vol. 25, no. 1.

Williams, E. (1989) *Social Policy: A Critical Introduction* (Cambridge: Polity Press).

Williams, S. and Bendelow, G. (1996) 'The "emotional" body', *Body and Society*, vol. 2, no. 3.

Wilson, E. (1982) 'Women, the "Community" and the "Family"', in A. Walker (ed) *Community Care: the family, the state and social policy* (Oxford: Basil Blackwell).

Wilson, H. and Hutchinson, S. (1991) 'Triangulation of qualitative methods: Heideggerian hermeneutics and grounded theory', *Qualitative Health Research*, vol. 1, pp. 263–276.

Winterton, Sir N. (1992) *House of Commons Health Committee (Second Report) 'Maternity Services'* (London: HMSO).

Wistow, G., Knapp, M., Hardy, B. and Allen, C. (1994) *Social Care in a Mixed Economy* (Buckingham: Open University Press).

Yeatman, A. (1994) 'Post modern epistemological politics and social science', in K. Lennon and M. Whitford (eds) *Knowing the Difference: Feminist perspectives in epistemology* (London: Routledge).

Author Index

Subject Index